Lecture Notes in Computer Science   1096
Edited by G. Goos, J. Hartmanis and J. van Leeuwen

Advisory Board: W. Brauer   D. Gries   J. Stoer

Springer
*Berlin
Heidelberg
New York
Barcelona
Budapest
Hong Kong
London
Milan
Paris
Santa Clara
Singapore
Tokyo*

Thomas Schäl

Workflow Management Systems for Process Organisations

Series Editors

Gerhard Goos, Karlsruhe University, Germany

Juris Hartmanis, Cornell University, NY, USA

Jan van Leeuwen, Utrecht University, The Netherlands

Author

Thomas Schäl
Stallhaus 22, D-58579 Schalksmühle, Germany
and
Casetta Postale 71, I-88075 Cutro (KR)

Cataloging-in-Publication data applied for

Die Deutsche Bibliothek - CIP-Einheitsaufnahme

Schäl, Thomas:
Workflow management systems for process organisations /
Thomas Schäl. - Berlin ; Heidelberg ; New York ; Barcelona ;
Budapest ; Hong Kong ; London ; Milan ; Paris ; Santa Clara ;
Singapore ; Tokyo : Springer, 1996
  (Lecture notes in computer science ; 1096)
  ISBN 3-540-61401-X
NE: GT

D82 (Diss. RWTH Aachen)

CR Subject Classification (1991): D.2, H.5.3, J.1, J.4

ISSN 0302-9743
ISBN 3-540-61401-X Springer-Verlag Berlin Heidelberg New York

This work is subject to copyright. All rights are reserved, whether the whole or part of the material is concerned, specifically the rights of translation, reprinting, re-use of illustrations, recitation, broadcasting, reproduction on microfilms or in any other way, and storage in data banks. Duplication of this publication or parts thereof is permitted only under the provisions of the German Copyright Law of September 9, 1965, in its current version, and permission for use must always be obtained from Springer-Verlag. Violations are liable for prosecution under the German Copyright Law.

© Springer-Verlag Berlin Heidelberg 1996
Printed in Germany

Typesetting: Camera-ready by author
SPIN 10513225   06/3142 – 5 4 3 2 1 0   Printed on acid-free paper

Alla Calabria

terra aspra,
che mi ha ospitato,
mi ha affascinato;
con lo sguardo sulla Sila,
con i rumori della campagna incantata,
vivo il contrasto del mio pensiero che vola
via dalla realtà che mi circonda;
fuggo con la mente, penso al futuro:
non mi rimane altro che lasciarti,
forse per sempre,
il mio pensiero
per il tuo futuro

Foreword

As the business environment has become more and more turbulent over the past decade, information technology has begun to run into the danger of becoming an impediment rather than a motor of progress.

In order to deal with the need for rapid, continuous change, computer science is challenged to develop novel interrelated information and communication technologies, and to align them with the social needs of co-operating user groups, as well as the management requirements of formal organisations.

Workflow systems are among the most advertised technologies addressing this trend, but they mean different things to different people.

Computer scientists understand workflows as a way to extract control from application programs, thus making them more flexible. Bureaucratic organisations (and most commercial products) perceive them as supporting a linear or branching flow of documents from one workplace to another – the next try after the failure of office automation.

This book takes another perspective, that of the modern customer-driven and groupwork-oriented process organisation. Extending the language-action perspective from the CSCW field, its customer-oriented view of workflows enables novel kinds of business process analysis, and leads to interesting new combinations of information and co-operation technologies. Schäl's empirical studies show some of the pitfalls resulting from a naive use of these technologies, and exemplify ways to get around these pitfalls.

The development and evolution of such *co-operative information systems* requires not just technological innovations but also interdisciplinary co-operation and – most importantly – empirical validation in practice. The genesis of this book is an excellent example. While its empirical results stem from practical experience in the service industries, its scientific roots (represented by the undersigned as co-supervisors of the underlying doctoral thesis at Aachen University of Technology) comprise information systems in computer science, social and formal aspects of computer-supported co-operative work, and human-computer interfaces in engineering applications of informatics. Moreover, this research is a good new example of a truly European co-operation. The practical experience has been developed in Italy, while the doctoral thesis has been prepared for a German University.

All of us have learned a lot during this exercise, and we hope that the reader – scientist or practitioner – will likewise profit from it.

We are grateful to Springer-Verlag and the series editors for accepting this somewhat non-traditional volume in the LNCS series.

Aachen and Milano, March 1996

Giorgio De Michelis, Klaus Henning, Matthias Jarke

Preface

This research report is not only a scientific contribution, but reflects the last 6 years of my professional and personal life. I had the opportunity to live in different cultural settings, to work in many companies, to meet people all over the world, helping me to reflect on what I have been doing and to focus on the content of this book. While credit is due to many people, a few stand out.

First I wish to thank Dietrich Brandt, who supported from the very beginning my academic career and contributed continuously with helpful, sometimes unanticipated and also critical ideas. The close working relationship we envisaged over long distances and years was a co-operative effort in itself.

I owe a special dept to Giorgio de Michelis, who coached me in difficult private and professional situations. Giorgio forced me to write my PhD and continuously reminded myself to stay committed in finishing it. His academic and professional activities, partially done together, have significantly influenced my work.

I would like to thank for all their support and supervision of the scientific work Professor Klaus Henning (IMA – Lehrstuhl Informatik im Maschinenbau, RWTH Aachen), Professor Matthias Jarke (Lehrstuhl Informatik V, RWTH Aachen), and Professor Giorgio De Michelis (DSI – Dipartimento Science dell'Informazione, Università degli Studi di Milano).

Working with colleagues in RSO helped me to practice my ideas in organisations. I developed most work with Buni Zeller who discussed theoretical and practical issues with me over the last years. I want to thank all professionals in RSO, and especially its CEO Federico Butera. I also owe a dept of gratitude to all customers and friends who shared with me consulting and research projects, gathering case material and helping me to bring their experiences into this publication.

I discussed many ideas with several friends and colleagues in the CSCW community and the European COST Action 14 on Co-operation Technologies. The participation in conferences and in research projects, partially funded by the University of Aachen and by the Commission of the European Communities, opened my horizon and helped me to develop my research.

I would not have finished this report without the medical care received from my family doctors Heinrich Lehmkühler and Filippo Mazzotta, in addition to nursing and treatment by specialists.

Aachen, Cutro, Roma, March 1996   Thomas Schäl

Table of Contents

1.	**Introduction**	1
2.	**From Functional to Process Organisation**	7
2.1	Complex organisations in a changing environment	7
2.2	Processes between procedures and workflows	10
2.3	Models for business process re-engineering	24
3.	**Analysis and Design of Co-operative Networks**	51
3.1.	The social organisation of work	51
3.2	Computer Supported Cooperative Work	54
3.3	Co-operative networks	59
3.4	Dynamics of co-operative work	71
3.5	Computer support for co-operative work	77
4.	**Workflow Management Technology**	83
4.1	Plans and procedures in process automation	83
4.2	Workflow management technology	86
4.3	Workflow specification languages	91
4.4	Technological architecture for co-operative computing systems	96
4.5	Workflow management technology products and markets	98
4.6	The Coordinator	101
4.7	X_Workflow on Olivetti IBIsys	109
5.	**Field Study I: The Coordinator Supporting Distributed Management Processes**	113
5.1	Company profile	114
5.2	Analysis of co-operative networks in business processes	115
5.3	Analysis of communication flows	116
5.4	Introduction of The Coordinator	119
5.5	Evaluation of The Coordinator	121

5.6 Difficulties with the language/action perspective 125

6. Field Study II: X_Workflow for Overdraft Management in a Bank 129
6.1 Company Profile 129
6.2 Process analysis 131
6.3 Workflow-based reporting system for credit management 142
6.4 Results and consequences 154

7. Conclusion 161

Bibliography 163

Appendices
I   Business Process Modelling Goals 179
II   Evaluation of Co-operative Networks 181
III Functional Requirements for Workflow
     Management Technology 185

Abbreviations 191

Index 195

1. Introduction

What is the problem?

Information technology is continuing its rapid evolution. At the same time the business environment is and will remain turbulent. This turbulence in the business environment puts pressure on organisations to be sure that they can effectively meet the fundamental changes which are occurring.

In spite of the presence of information technology supporting organisations over time and space, organisations have not yet found enough coherent solutions to develop the dimensions of organisational structure, strategy, human resources, technology and business processes. Although organisations have spent tremendous amounts of money on computer hardware and software, these investments have not always raised the organisation's productivity or profitability (Strassman, 1985; Scott Morton, 1991).

There is a new wave of a promising approach to increase organisational productivity through the use of information technology; it is called *business process re-engineering* (Hammer, 1990; Hammer & Champy, 1993; Davenport, 1993; Earl, 1994; Davenport & Stoddard, 1994; White & Fischer, 1994). The general idea seems to be attractive, but again it has not always been successful in augmenting the overall productivity of organisations (Hall *et al.*, 1993; Hammer & Champy, 1993; Schwartz, 1993).

At the same time new information systems are developed to support the idea of business process re-engineering. *Workflow management technology* (Hales & Lavery, 1991; Ellis & Nutt, 1993; Abbott & Sarin, 1994; White & Fischer, 1994) is pushed by software and hardware suppliers on the market. The number of applications under development is growing (Dyson, 1990; 1990b; Hales & Lavery, 1991; White & Fischer, 1994). Users and designers express the need to understand methods, tools, benefits and implications of such applications. Moreover, first experiences with workflow management systems should allow to understand the most valuable features of existing systems and indicate guidelines for the development of future generations of this technology (Abbott & Sarin, 1994).

Scope of the research

Business seeks to become increasingly responsive to changing market conditions by *flattening out* their organisations and making use of *ad-hoc workgroups* or *project teams*. Market oriented business processes request to manage complex transaction networks in order to assure *customer satisfaction*. Responsiveness is increased by redesigning business processes and implementing process technology. The author sustains that *process management* is the way of transforming companies; it frees them from restrictions of the traditional approach by cutting across functional divisions. New information systems promise to be feasible for turning this change and organisational re-design into reality. The possible change from traditional functional organisations and centralised information systems into market-oriented service providers is an already ongoing process.

The new context of action requires a design process which can cope with the increasing complexity. One out of many new perspective for looking at complex organisations is suggested and discussed, concentrating on processes. The proposed process analysis and design methodology sees *customer satisfaction* as the key issue for information system design in the organisational context (Keen, 1991; Medina-Mora *et al.*, 1992). Customer satisfaction is achieved by designing and following a coherent *customer/supplier chain* along the working process. The single customer/supplier relation is handled following the *language/action perspective* (Winograd & Flores, 1986). The proposed model is based on the *conversational relation* of actors in the complex setting of organisations and markets, which then is a *possible space for action through language* to exploit the underlying concerns of the organisation, like product and process quality, customer satisfaction, general business objectives and social acceptance.

Many new ideas and systems to make the change happen are coming from the field of Computer Supported Cooperative Work (CSCW). The interdisciplinary CSCW field has developed models, concepts and approaches to support working processes (Suchman, 1987; Winograd & Flores, 1986; Winograd, 1986; 1987; Bannon & Schmidt, 1989; Grudin, 1988; 1994; Johansen, 1988; De Michelis, 1990; 1996; Schmidt, 1990; Ellis *et al.*, 1991; Kreifelts *et al.*, 1991; Kling, 1991; Schäl & Zeller, 1991; 1993; Schäl, 1993; 1996; Medina-Mora *et al.*, 1992; Malone *et al.*, 1993; Abbott & Sarin, 1994). Results from CSCW can be transferred to the general problems of modern organisations, but they are not a sufficient response to the encountered problems.

> *The scope of this research is to develop a framework for problem solving which allows to design and implement workflow management systems in business processes using models and approaches from the field of computer supported co-operative work. The application of the method for analysis and design of business processes as co-operative workflows in the language/action perspective improves the organisation's overall productivity and ability to survive in a turbulent environment.*

For the methodological proceeding of this thesis, the problem solving strategy developed by Harendt (1991) is used. As Schäfer (1993) sustains, the cybernetic problem solving strategy meets the requirements to support the joint design of technology and organisation. This approach is necessary to develop workflow management technology for and within process organisations.

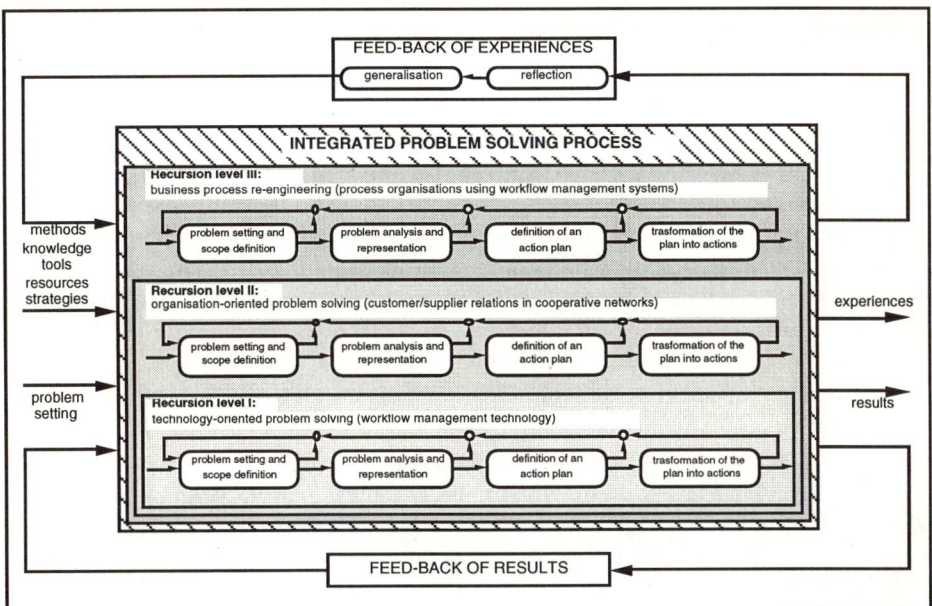

Figure 1-1: The cybernetic problem solving strategy to design workflow management systems for process organisations (adapted from Harendt, 1991: 31)

The first recursion level in Figure 1-1 concerns the *technology-oriented problem solving* strategy. Information systems have the scope to support organisations in their business. This is done, e.g., by *process automation technology* which has not always been successful. New systems, i.e., *workflow management technology*, are under development to overcome the limits of traditional information systems related to business processes. The scope is to understand potentials and limits of the new workflow management systems. Therefore two of these commercial systems (*The Coordinator* and *X_Workflow*) are studied in two different companies.

The second recursion level concerns the *organisation-oriented problem solving* strategy. The Tayloristic organisation of work has come to its limits. New organisational forms are emerging, among them the *process organisation*. Process organisations are based on *customer/supplier relations* which define *co-operative networks* working towards *customer satisfaction*. The validity of co-operative workflows following the *language/action perspective* is investigated to analyse and design business processes in two case studies.

The third recursion level combines the technical and organisational perspective in designing organisations which improve their overall productivity and ability to survive in their environment by doing *business process re-engineering*. The design of process organisations is based on the concept of business processes which serve to achieve customer satisfaction and are supported by workflow management technology.

Results and experiences from the case studies and from literature define an action plan for designing new realities as feedback of experiences.

Structure of the research report

Chapter 2 discusses the rationale around which organisations have been built and founded in the last 200 years: Adam Smith's idea to break work down into its simplest and most basic tasks which can be performed by basically skilled workers. The concept persists and also today still many companies break work down into a sequence of separate, narrowly defined tasks. The persons performing the tasks are correspondingly separated by function, such as engineering and manufacturing or machining and assembly, each function administered by a manager or foreman. Functional divisions and hierarchical structures form the basis of the way in which most work in companies is done. These arrangements have been well adapted through much of this century to support classical goals of *cost efficiency*, *growth* and *control*. Information technology has frequently been developed in accordance to these goals as centralised and rigid systems. However, there is a developing demand for change. Traditional functional management is no longer appropriate in an era when *quality*, *innovation* and *services* are of paramount importance.

In chapter 3 a methodological approach to analyse and design *co-operative networks* is introduced. The scope is to provide a response to current shortcomings of support systems and misleading understanding encountered relative to co-operative work. This is the research agenda for the field of *computer supported cooperative work* (CSCW). A distinction for *co-operative work* is proposed and a model is developed to characterise the set taxonomy of *co-ordination*, *collaboration* and *co-decision*. General functional requirements for technical systems are developed on the basis of the introduced taxonomy. There are two *design spaces* to support co-operative work: *activity synchronisation* and *information sharing*. Due to different *dynamics in co-operative work* switching from *co-operation in the small* to *co-operation in large* and vice-versa. The implications for design of computer systems for co-operative work processes in 'fairly stable' as well as 'dynamic' organisations are outlined. Co-operative networks need a mix of *domain services* and *open services* which define a *service portfolio* for co-operative networks.

In chapter 4 *workflow management technology* is proposed to support process organisations. It integrates aspects of human work traditionally separated by the way information systems have been designed, and introduces a business perspective on how processes should be supported. Different commercial workflow management systems are presented and distinguished according to their main characteristics. Two tools out of the range of products are selected for detailed case studies. These tools are *The Coordinator* and *X_Workflow*. *The Coordinator* is described as an *ad-hoc groupware tool*. Several field studies on the use of *The Coordinator* are reported. The second tool *X_Workflow* is a *business process automation system*.

Chapter 5 develops the dimension of *activity synchronisation* in *domain services* further on. A specific approach to organisational communication is discussed in a case study: the *language/action perspective* and its implementation in the software product *The Coordinator*. The model, based on the thoughtful work by Terry Winograd and Fernando Flores (1986), has some promising properties, but the software solution has a limited potential to support the proposed process working in organisations. *The Coordinator* is used in a distributed management process of a professional training company.

A second detailed case study explores in chapter 6 the application of the commercially available product *X_Workflow* in financial processes. The implementation is part of a general re-design of the information system in a bank. The project implies the use of workflow management technology to support customer-related credit processes. The application of the proposed design strategy confirms the thesis that properly designed workflow management systems and a proper approach for its introduction support the organisation in improving its performance.

2. From Functional to Process Organisation

In this chapter the developments from Tayloristic work organisations towards process-oriented structures will be shown as they are presently being demanded and tested. The scope of this chapter is to motivate the analysis and design of *business processes* as *co-operative workflows* in the *language/action perspective*, as applied subsequently in two case studies.

The required change from functional into process organisations can be achieved by applying the concept of *business process re-engineering*. For understanding the business dimension in process re-engineering, the difference between *material*, *information* and *business processes* is outlined. This distinction makes clear which kind of processes have to be considered for business process re-engineering. Business process re-engineering with a focus on customers, customer satisfaction and business processes is modelled by *workflows* in the *language/action perspective*. The difference in process modelling is shown for an example in a multinational chemical company. Data flow diagrams are compared with the representation of co-operative workflows in the language/action perspective.

This chapter prepares the basis for the discussion of different approaches to *computer supported cooperative work* (CSCW) and *workflow management technology* as discussed in the subsequent chapters 3 and 4.

2.1 Complex organisations in a changing environment

With the division of labour and industrialisation, a search began to improve efficiency by concentrating on the routine aspects of work activities. That led, in turn to Frederick Winslow Taylor's *Scientific Management* (Taylor, 1911) to the systematic investigation of work methods and the separation of *routine tasks* from *planning* and *control*, not only in the manufacturing process, but also in the office environment.

The discussion about the Tayloristic principles is an ongoing issue. The critical points related to Taylor's *Scientific Management* concentrate on several problems, like its impact on persons' *health*, the possibility of *dequalification*, the *doubtful profitability* compared to their organisational forms, the *centralised control functions* and other aspects (Braverman, 1974; Martin *et al.*, 1988; Kern & Schumann, 1984; Brödner, 1985; Fricke *et al.*, 1985; Cooley, 1987; Henning & Ochterbeck, 1988; 1988b; Bullinger & Ganz, 1990; Marks, 1991; Schäl, 1991; Henning, 1993; 1993b; Scheel, 1994).

The natural consequence of separating work activities into well-defined and formalised sub-tasks is their normalisation as functions in the organisational structure of enterprises. The functional and hierarchical organisation was reinforced by the application of rigorous planning and work studies; the purpose was to deploy scarce expertise better and to monitor and control the work executed in *bureaucracies*. The results are evident in well defined *tasks*, *roles*, *rules* and *procedures* which regulate most of the work in offices and production. Still today, one prevalent structure is the *organisational hierarchy*, also referred to as the *bureaucracy*. In this structure, there are levels of management and rules concerning what employees should do and how employees at each level should interact with the levels above and below them. For a large organisation this allows delegation of work via standard channels.

Many organisation in industrialised countries following *Taylor*'s ideas cannot cope any more with changing customer demands, innovation in production technologies, increasing requirements and capabilities of qualification, and other dynamic factors of their environment. A consequence of organising by function was a loss of flexibility. The pre-conditions for the *Scientific Management*'s validity, like a relatively stable, foreseeable and linear changing environment, are not any more valid for many organisations in Europe (AWK, 1990).

Industrialised societies find themselves in a time of pace and deep changes (Piore & Sabel, 1989). Two global developments in the political economy of industrial societies are of prime importance. Spurred by ongoing scientific research activities and the tighter coupling between research and production, the pace of technological change is accelerating in all branches of production (Albrecht, 1982). Concurrently, driven by the development of transportation and communication means and by the creation of an increasingly integrated world market, global competition is becoming increasingly fierce (Gunn, 1987). Markets become more fragmented and evolve toward a growing product differentiation, caused by customer demand for personalisation and a need for value added products and services. The increased pace of innovation and the resulting level of complexity require that organisations become more adaptable to internal and external conditions in order to survive and develop in this context of ongoing change (Hinterhuber, 1984; Beckhard & Harris, 1987). The environment does not mean only the natural environment, but includes also technological, economical, political, social, etc. aspects of the companies' environment (Rieckmann & Weissengruber, 1990; Marks, 1991; Henning, 1993). Some factors concerning the environment and their impact on the organisations are, e.g.:
- the products' lifetime is shorter than its production means,
- products have an increased number of variants or customer specific versions,
- organisations become more internationalised,
- open and common markets increase the pressure on cost reduction and lead-time reduction.

New organisational trends can be interpreted as a way to reduce the existing limitation in copying with this growing complexity of the market. Such organisational phenomena are the growing *autonomy* and *responsibility* of *professional roles*, the *flattening out* and *decentralisation of organisations*, the *emergence of adhocracies*, the *continuing education* of employees, and flexible *teams* working directly on *customer demands* (Mintzberg, 1973; 1979; Piore & Sabel, 1984; Butera, 1987; Zuboff, 1988; Brödner & Prekuhl, 1991; Warnecke, 1992; Ciborra, 1993; Grinda *et al.*, 1993; Henning *et al.*, 1994).

Today, a growing number of organisations is managing important parts of the business in a new and different way. It is called *process management*, and it differs sharply from the traditional functional approach that has been used by all but the smallest organisations. For centuries companies have been founded and built around the idea that industrial work should be broken down into its simplest and most basic tasks. In the new perspective, companies will be founded and built around the idea of reunifying those tasks into coherent *business processes*. *Process management* is the way to approach the *transformation of traditional bureaucratic organisations* into *market-oriented process organisations*. Processes have two important characteristics: they have *customers* who are internal or external recipients of the process' output, and they *cross organisational boundaries* which separate the functional units in the hierarchical organisations. Process working gives organisations the possibility to dramatically improve response times, service and quality by cutting across departmental demarcations.

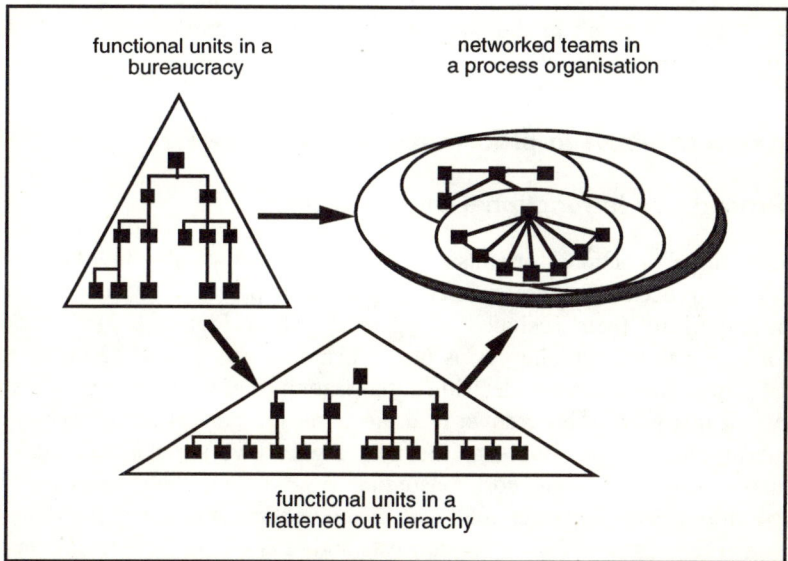

Figure 2-1: Evolving organisational models

This research is concerned with this kind of less hierarchical, more flat and networked organisation (Williamson, 1988; Belussi *et al.*, 1991; Butera, 1991; 1995) which is able to cope with changing tasks, technologies and environments. The concept of *process organisation* is used as a synonym for dynamic organisations capable to respond to the new and continually changing environments – in the literature also referred to as the *learning organisation* (Argyris & Schön, 1978; Shrivastava, 1983; Senge, 1990; Huber, 1991; Simon, 1991; Nonaka, 1993;

Isenhardt, 1994; Nonaka & Takeuchi, 1995). Figure 2-1 shows the evolution from *bureaucracy* to *networked teams* in *process organisations*, sometimes passing through the *flattened out hierarchy*.

However, organisations still have a more or less hierarchical and functional structure. The required change can rarely be seen as a radical shift from a functional to a process organisation. A crucial element in the introduction of process working is planning how it can fit into the existing management structure. There are thoughts that functional hierarchical structures will evolve into small entrepreneurial teams of knowledge workers who are tied together electronically in a network organisation. This might happen in some companies, but most of modern organisations will stay in a more or less developed hierarchy. In these settings, teams working on processes will be co-ordinated by a simplified management structure.

With this hybrid structure, organisations will aim to get the best of the two extremes. Cross functional and process-oriented teams will provide responsiveness to market changes and customer demands which large organisations are lacking at the moment. The remaining functional hierarchy will provide mechanisms for *goal setting* and *team performance measurement*, as well as setting the *strategic direction* for the entire organisation and achieving these strategic goals by *co-ordinating team activities*. This will result in the parallel existence of *functional managers*, *process managers*, and *process owners*.

2.2 Processes between procedures and workflows

2.2.1 Procedures in functional organisations

In a conventional functional organisation, a *procedure* typically involves multiple functions. The procedure progresses step by step as it passes between the *functional units* according to their assigned competencies (see Figure 2-2). Queries and exceptions are handled at higher levels in the hierarchy due to their declared level of responsibility, competence and decision authorisation (these are the typical examples of escalation in case of a breakdown in a hierarchical organisation; everybody shifts responsibility in case of trouble to the next higher level). As a consequence the procedures are highly time and cost consuming. A possible problem is the interface of the organisation; customers treat often with different persons or functional units when interacting at first instance for service requests and later on for service delivery. This is due to the fact that the organisation passes the customer's request step by step through the organisation towards delivery without closing the customer relation by the same functional unit or person. This can reduce the customer's satisfaction concerning the outcome of the procedure.

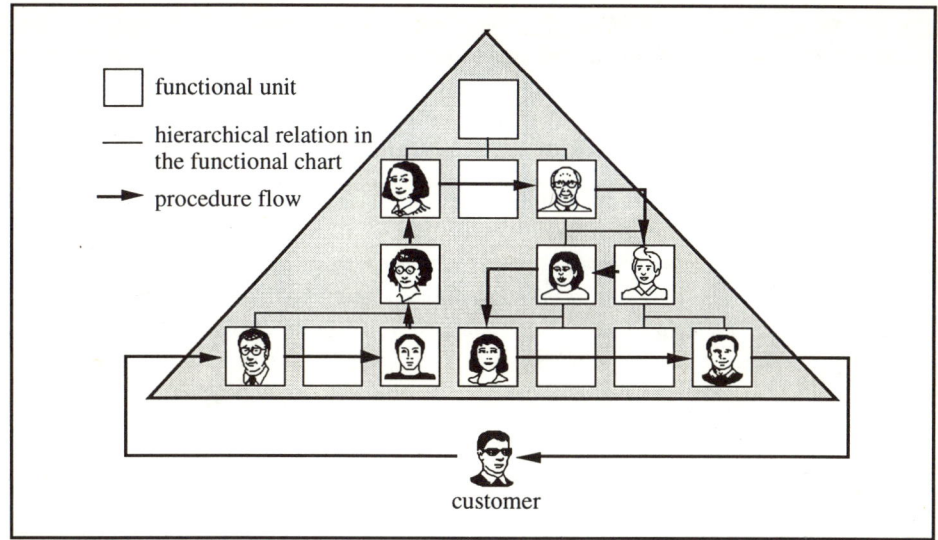

Figure 2-2: Procedure flow step by step between functional units in a hierarchical organisation

2.2.2 Products, services and customer satisfaction

Attempts are being made to augment service and quality in business organisations as well as public administration. Improving service and quality means identifying customers and designing the necessary work processes to produce the services in a more customer-oriented organisation. The problem of *customer satisfaction* is that it cannot be measured like *quality* in terms of *predefined standards*. The quality of a product or a service is defined by the correspondence of the delivery with predefined standards which can be measured. Looking at customer satisfaction in working processes implies the adoption of an appropriate quality model. A quite acknowledged definition of quality is proposed by the International Standards Organisation (ISO). According to ISO, quality is defined by the global properties and characteristics which allow a product, or a service, to satisfy explicit as well as implicit needs. It should be noted here how the notion of customer or user *satisfaction* makes evident the *intangible* aspects of quality assurance. This definition of quality should induce a focus shift from the measure of product's intrinsic quality characteristics to the measure of customer/supplier service relationships.

Sometimes the customer can be dissatisfied by high quality products, while good management of poor services is often more appreciated. Airlines report on quality (for example intended as flying on schedule and not having overbooked planes) that customer satisfaction increases when they make an error but handle it well, compared with not having made an error in the first place (Keen, 1991; Harendt, 1991).

The example shows that quality does not guarantee the perception of good service. Instead, customer satisfaction expressed by the customer has to be *the* issue for organisational re-design. Customer satisfaction is a result of a good *communicative relation which serves to manage commitments and breakdowns* within the *customer/supplier chain*. The supplier has to understand the service requested by the customer. The customer's satisfaction can only be understood after the delivery of services in gathering the customer's satisfaction through communicative interactions. Customer satisfaction cannot be measured by predefined standards, like quality.

> **Definition: Customer satisfaction**
> *Customer satisfaction is the intangible aspects of quality which the customer expresses about the global properties and characteristics which allow a product, or a service, to satisfy the customer's explicit as well as implicit needs. Customer satisfaction is a result of a good communicative relation which serves to manage commitments and breakdowns within a customer/supplier chain.*

Rethinking working processes and procedures, we need to look at every element of processes, work, and the information technologies that support or enable them in terms of customer satisfaction. But how to do this? Peter G.W. Keen (1991) states that:

> 'any methodology for analysing business processes must begin and end with the customer [...]. Too many traditional approaches to business analysis, especially in the area of information technology planning, are poorly fitted to this new thinking. Many begin with the firm and work forward to the customer, instead of starting with the customer. They look at "quality" as a dimension of a product, not as an assessment made by a customer.' (Keen, 1991: 229)

Therefore, Keen (1991) argues for powerful tools and methodologies which make customer satisfaction an integral part of the planning and design specifications of organisational design through information technology. A new process management model should be defined starting from the fundamental change of perspectives required to cope with the growing complexity of customer demand. The work process model has to change from a *production centred* (*transformation*) model to a *market centred* (*language*) model. This change shifts the focus from *quality* to *customer satisfaction*.

2.2.3 Workflows in process organisations

The argumentation has shown, that a procedural perspective does not fit in the concept of process organisations. Therefore a new concept for looking at processes is needed here. This concept is called *workflow*. A workflow, similar to activities in procedures, is a unit of work that happens repeatedly in an organisation of work. However, as a difference to procedures, and most importantly, in a workflow things get completed that are related to, or result in, producing *satisfaction for customers*. In fact, *every workflow has a customer*, who may be an external customer of the organisation, or may be another work group or an individual in the organisation (an internal customer).

> **Definition: Workflow**
> *A workflow is a unit of work generating products or services which are related*

to, or result in, customer satisfaction. Every workflow has a main customer, who is served by a supplier, or a co-operative network as being a chain of customers and suppliers, working towards the satisfaction of the main customer.

Most workflows have *sequential* and *parallel steps*. They involve the movement and tracking of people, documents, products and information. Workflows reflect the recurrent organisation of work, but their organisational and communication patterns are based on both *standard* and *ad-hoc actions* taken by specific persons in order to fulfil a particular condition of satisfaction requested by someone. Some workflows are formally defined. Others are inherited from experience, without any explicit design. Workflows can be seen as the sequence and interrelation of information, activities and communications within a process.

Differences on how persons manage the flow of work within their co-operative network form the basis for defining two types of workflows: *case-based* and *ad-hoc* workflows (Gable, 1992):

• *Case-based workflows* are central to the organisation's business. Examples are insurance claim processing, bank loan application processing, customer order production processing, etc. These workflows might occur in a specific department or cross functional boundaries. Individuals in a business team try to accomplish the process objective of satisfying the case's customer. The single instance of the customer's request can be satisfied by a more or less standardised workflow.

• A*d-hoc workflows* arise from specific, temporary needs of unique project teams. A group has a specific objective, but once the task is accomplished and the project objective is achieved, the team will disband and its members will go on to other assignments. In turn, group members often initiate other ad-hoc workflows than the initial one during the project's duration. Ad-hoc workflows are initiated when the customer's request is too specific to be worked on by more standardised case-based workflows. Instead, ad-hoc workflows are project plans aiming at the realisation of a specific output to achieve customer satisfaction.

In a *process organisation*, a workflow may involve the same set of work activities as the previously described procedure in a functional organisation (see Figure 2-2), but all these activities are managed as a single process. Everything which is necessary to assure customer satisfaction is done either by an individual or by a team. This means that the persons involved in the workflow do the same activities as in a functional organisation, but they concentrate on the process objective (to satisfy the final customer) instead of the single activities' output (to produce something). The trend toward small, dynamic, *customer-focused business teams* has been documented in the literature of management and organisational theory (Drucker, 1988; 1989; Johansen *et al.*, 1991). The procedure, that is the pre-defined set of activities, becomes part of a process which has to be managed by *teamwork* in order to achieve a specific goal, i.e., the satisfaction of the process' customer. In process organisations the work does not follow a monodirection stream. It frequently follows a *multiple circuit path*, which includes *check points* and *feed-back* to assure *customer satisfaction, quality* and *efficiency* of work.

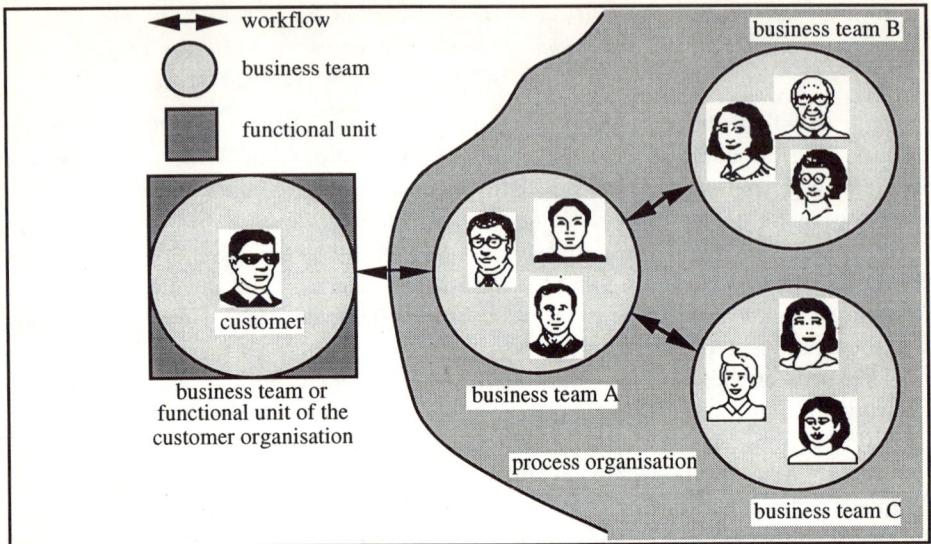

Figure 2-3: Workflow among and within business teams in a process organisation

This relation is shown in Figure 2-3 where several teams work together in order to satisfy a customer. One member of business team A has direct contact with the customers (the front-end of the organisation), while the business teams B and C interact as back-office units with somebody of the front-end team A. This configuration constitutes a relation among *internal customers* (i.e., members of team A) and *internal suppliers* (i.e., members of teams B and C). The bi-directional workflow reflects the necessity that the customer wants to be served by the person whom he asked to provide the service or product. This differs from the procedural flow in Figure 2-2 where the customer has to deal with two different persons in two functional units of the hierarchical organisation for the initial service/product request and later service/product delivery. Closing the customer/supplier relation with the same person or team with whom it is opened should assure customer satisfaction. The front-office of the customer organisation in Figure 2-3 is represented by the person who asks and receives the product or service. Not necessarily this front-office is a business team, but can also be a functional unit of a hierarchical organisation. Nobody can influence the organisational development of the customer organisation to a point where all customers follow the workflow concept of process organisations.

The main benefits which may be gained from process working in addition to customer satisfaction, are *cost reduction, flexibility* and improved *quality of working life*. The first benefit goes hand-in-hand with productivity increases. The second benefit allows to adapt to changing circumstances. This is a result of independence from hierarchical rigidities. Responsiveness and flexibility are characteristics which are often associated with small companies. Large organisation are associated as hindered by bureaucracy. Indeed, large companies adopting process working are seeking to gain small-company responsiveness, while at the same time retaining the positive attributes of size, like economy of scale, widespread recognition, etc.

Reduced costs and improved responsiveness follow from the elimination of multiple steps in the workflow in functional organisations. Instead of the work passing up and down hierarchies and across organisational demarcations, it stays with an *individual* or a *team* throughout the process. This leads to a third benefit of process working: the increased *quality of working life* (Butera, 1995). In functional organisations, people work only on pieces of a task in the whole process. In process working, by contrast, individuals are encouraged to carry out entire tasks from the beginning to the end. Moreover, the people who do the work, undertake their own monitoring and control and handle exceptions themselves, instead of making it an escalation in the hierarchy or contributing to a centralised co-ordination and control function. These middle-level functions can be overcome with process working; as a consequence a lot of overhead costs are cut.

Furthermore, process working provides a platform for continuous innovation. It promises competitive advantage which will be sustainable over time. Process improvement and innovation have been objectives for organisations for long times. However, in the present market situation, continuous process development is not always anymore sufficient to guarantee the organisation's survival. New ideas for managing the required innovation and change are emerging. One of these attempts is conducted at the MIT in the project on the *process handbook*, intending to help redesign existing organisational processes, invent new organisational processes which take advantages of information technology, and automatically generate software to support organisational processes (Malone *et al.*, 1993).

2.2.4 Business process re-engineering

Along with *process organisation* goes the concept of business *process re-engineering* (Hammer, 1990; Hammer & Champy, 1993; Davenport, 1993; Morris & Branson, 1993; Coulson-Thomas, 1994; Earl, 1994; IAO, 1995; Kutscha, 1995). The core claims of business process re-engineering (BPR) follow the idea that instead of using computers and information systems to automate the way a business has always run, the concept calls for re-thinking the operations first; one re-engineers the process in first place, before applying computing power to the newly defined process. Business process re-engineering wants to change the existing and is related in this sense to *work-analysis*, seen by Schmidt (1990) as *reverse engineering*:

> 'Since the objective of work analysis is to improve a given situation in some way – for instance, by designing and implementing information systems, by redesigning work [...], - the basic approach is reformist or therapeutical: the work analyst investigates a particular social system of work to change it for the better. Accordingly, the analysis cannot take the current behaviour of the social system of work for granted. To the contrary, the analyst must uncover the hidden rationale of current practices as well as the accidental choices of the past, the procedures turned rituals, the formalised mistakes, etc. [...] In a sense, then, work analysis can be linked with

'reverse engineering' – in the sense, namely, that the analyst approaches the given system as a product of a design effort and 'takes it apart' with the purpose of putting it together again, perhaps differently.' (Schmidt, 1990: 5)

Many efforts of the past related to organisational development and efficiency improvement are seen today in the movement of business process re-engineering. Business process re-engineering (BPR) is defined by Hammer & Champy (1993) as:

'the fundamental rethinking and radical redesign of business processes to achieve dramatic improvements in critical, contemporary measures of performance, such as cost, quality, service and speed.' (Hammer & Champy, 1993: 32)

Re-engineering for Michael Hammer does not mean to tinker with what already exists or to make incremental changes which leave basic structures intact, but to start over again. Re-engineering takes nothing for granted. It ignores what is and concentrates on what should be. Michael Hammer has a very determined way of arguing for the way of doing re-engineering and its results: *'radical change yields radical results'*.

Davenport (1993) uses the term *process innovation* instead of business process re-engineering (BPR) and defines it as:

'Stepping back from a process to inquire as to its overall business objective, and then effecting creative and radical change to realise orders-of-magnitude improvements in the way that objective is accomplished.' (Davenport, 1993: 10)

Business companies are becoming interested in BPR, because their competitiveness cannot be guaranteed any more only by cutting costs. The resulting productivity gains from BPR are the best known at the moment. According to Business Week (1991), re-engineering at its best is reducing costs by 80 per cent, improving time-to-market by 80 per cent, or doubling sales in other cases. One of the best known examples is Ford's accounts-payable procedure.

Case history 1: Ford has re-designed its accounts-payable procedure

Ford buys in about two-thirds of its car parts from outside suppliers. It changed its parts-receiving and parts-payment procedure. Previously, Ford employed about 500 people to order components, receive the parts, and pay suppliers. The Japanese car manufacturer Mazda already did the same job with fewer than 100 people. Even allowing for Ford being bigger than Mazda, the gap was considerable. Mazda did not wait for invoices from its suppliers. In contrast, when Ford's purchasing department wrote a purchase order, it first send a copy to accounts payable. Once the goods were received, goods inwards sent a copy of the receiving document to accounts payable. Meanwhile, the supplier sent an invoice to accounts payable. It was now accounts payable's job to match the purchase order against the receiving document and the invoice. Only after matching of all papers the payment was issued. In practice, the department spent most of its time investigating mis-matches.

From Functional to Process Organisation 17

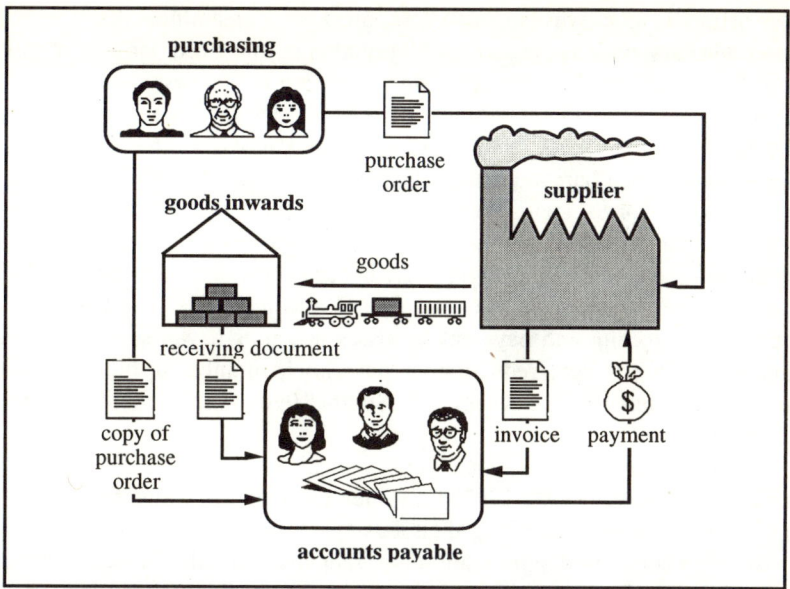

Figure 2-4: Ford's accounts payable procedure required the matching of orders, receiving documents, and invoices to issue payments (from Hammer, 1990: 106)

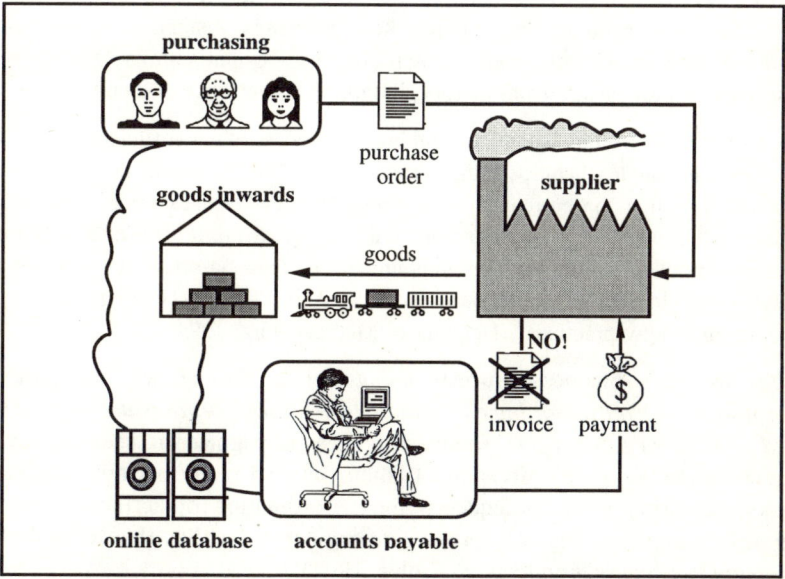

Figure 2-5: The re-engineered accounts-payable procedure eliminates invoices and issues payments by computerised matching (from Hammer, 1990: 107)

Ford's original idea was to use computers to streamline the investigation procedure. Mazda's experience, however, pointed to the need for the complete re-design of the process. Ford went ahead, implementing *invoiceless payment*.

Now, when the purchasing department places an order, the data is stored in an on-line database. When parts arrive at the goods-inwards receiving docks, a warehouseman passes a barcode reader over the goods' labels, entering details of the parts into the inventory system. Previously, Ford paid when it received the invoice. Now it pays when the goods arrive. The system sends an electronic payment to the supplier based on the bar-code reading at the inward gates. In effect, the goods-inward staff is empowered to check the incoming parts and authorise payment. The re-designed process of receipt and payment bypasses accounts payable. As a result, Ford has achieved a 75 per cent reduction in personnel, mainly in the administration department (Hammer, 1990; Davenport & Short, 1990; Hammer & Champy, 1993; Davenport, 1993).

Not everybody agrees with Hammer's radical view on business process re-engineering. Davenport (1993; 1993b) disputes the claim that companies can sweep away from current ways of running their business and start with a clean slate. He agrees with the necessity of significant improvements, but only for key processes and in terms of innovating the existing. The research program by Ernst & Young (Davenport, 1993) showed evidence that most companies, even very large and complex ones, can be broken down into fewer than 20 major processes; the larger these key processes are, the greater is the potential for radical benefit. A strong argument for innovation of the existing key processes instead of reinventing the organisation and processes from scratch is that organisations and people in organisations cannot escape from history, language, experience and culture.

> 'One of the main lessons is that redesigning the process is not sufficient to produce the change in people's habits, for the current "culture" of the organisation provides a context in which the current "way of doing business" makes sense. To effect organisational change, it is necessary not only to reveal the processes and propose redesign, but to reveal the main assumptions of the common sense, to work toward a new social contract among those involved, and to provide technology that easily supports their new practices.' (Denning & Medina-Mora, 1994: 236)

As already said, business process re-engineering can be seen as part of the *transformation of traditional bureaucratic or functional organisations into market-oriented process organisations*. Business process re-engineering seeks to overcome the fragmentation due to the division of labour into so many narrowly defined roles and tasks, requiring as a consequence the co-ordination of activities and actors. Taking this seriously, business process re-engineering shifts the focus from *task management* to *process management* (Soles, 1994).

Taking the different views on business process re-engineering as *fundamental rethinking and radical redesign*, or *innovation*, or the *transformation of organisations*, the broadest definition of business process re-engineering is given by White & Fischer (1994):

'Reengineering has to do with reviewing how a business works in order to achieve dramatic performance improvement and be more responsive to the customer. [...] BPR is the conscious reshaping of an organisation behind a new corporate vision, the marketplace and the customer. Using a holistic, innovative approach, BPR reviews all business activities across the enterprise. This may result in a redefinition of workflow processes, organisational structures and technology to allow the company to streamline, change or delete the way in which work is done. The ultimate objective is to yield sustainable improvements in profitability, productivity, customer satisfaction and quality while maximising the potential of the individual and the team.' (White & Fischer, 1994: Preface V-VI)

Although the concept of *process working* and the use of *workflow management technology* seem simple, it is not easy to introduce it in the real world. There are five main problems.

The first problem for change is the vested interests in organisations. Process working runs counter to conventional thinking; It overcomes the idea that career advancement means scrambling up the traditional hierarchical ladder in the bureaucracy. Instead, process working offers people the opportunity of carrying out challenging and broader tasks and of continually learning new skills that enable them to be empowered. Process working therefore changes totally the personnel system, and how people are motivated and encouraged in their professional career.

The second problem lies in the grouping of people in a process. Persons working in processes need a wide range of skills, covering all actual functional expertise involved in procedures and in less structured or rule-based working processes. Process working implies the coupling of multidisciplinary skilled teams.

The third problem lies in the capability of people to change their perspective concerning technology. Information system people have to develop the existing systems into workflow management technology which supports the interpersonal relations in the working processes and provides means for communication, information and data management. Otherwise they will continue to automate existing manual work processes. Studies have shown that this type of process automation can have a very slight effect on productivity (Scott Morton, 1991). Instead, if the entire process is examined, and then re-designed to take into account capabilities provided by information technologies, increases in productivity can be achieved. These increases in productivity typically arise out of reducing the number of individual steps to complete a process, beside the implementation of workflow management systems (Hales & Lavery, 1991; Abbot & Sarin, 1994; Swenson *et al.*, 1994; White & Fischer, 1994).

The fourth problem is, that in reality the problem is not technology, but the organisational model for the business which is supported by workflow management technology. Denning (1992) puts this problem as follows:

'By automating business processes that are not explicitly oriented toward customer satisfaction, organisations have accelerated the production of dissatisfied customers. It does not matter whether the organisation is a business firm or a research institute. The problem is the design of processes for conducting business.' (Denning, 1992: 314)

The fifth problem concerns the social dimension of business process re-engineering. Especially in the American BPR movement, business process re-engineering means cutting costs by heavy dismissals. The survival of re-engineered companies is a benefit for part of the original employees. Others have been laid off and might be unemployed for long periods. Although European organisations do not follow the *hire-and-fire policy* due to legal and cultural constraints, BPR can be a threat for thousands of office workers.

According to these problems, business process re-engineering is not a straight forward endeavour. The very popular re-engineering case of Ford's elimination of three-quarters of its accounts payable staff has some interesting hidden stories. It took five years from design to full implementation of the apparently adoptable process from Mazda (Davenport, 1993). However, business process re-engineering has not always been successful. The lack of complete information about re-engineering projects from the organisations which have tried BPR without breakthrough results is a major limitation. Hammer & Champy (1993) admit that:

> 'our unscientific estimate is that as many as 50 percent to 70 percent of the organisations that undertake a reengineering effort do not achieve the dramatic results they intended.' (Hammer & Champy, 1993: 200)

CSC Index corporation reported at ComputerWorld that the failure rate has been about 25 percent (Schwartz, 1993). The failure can be in a single project, but also for the entire business. McKinsey did a research into re-engineering projects in more than 100 companies with a detailed analysis of 20 of these projects (Hall *et al.*, 1993). The research reveals how difficult redesign actually is and, even more interesting, how often business process re-engineering projects with impressive results on the single process fail to achieve real and long-lasting business impact. The missing perspective in many BPR projects is the idea of continuous improvement and a general view of the business instead of concentrating on single projects which look like promising BPR winners.

However, failures are not bad in themselves, as the longitudinal research on re-engineering in CIGNA shows (Caron *et al.*, 1994). Only about 50 percent of the re-engineering efforts in the assurance company brought the type of benefits expected initially. To come to success in re-engineering, a willingness to allow for failure has been required. Learning from failures, CIGNA completed over 20 re-engineering initiatives, saving in five years more than $100 million. Anyway, CIGNA started with a small pilot project before transferring the knowledge learned into larger and more complex parts of the organisation (Caron *et al.*, 1994). The following paragraph proposes a framework for successful business process re-engineering to overcome past shortcomings.

2.2.5 Requirements for successful business process re-engineering

What is successful BPR? The objective of BPR has been defined as the organisational development of the ability to survive in the changing environment. The objective to yield sustainable improvements in profitability, productivity, customer satisfaction and quality leaves at the same time space to maximise the potential of the individual or teams. Three specific goals have been identified in relation to this definition of BPR.

Value-added services

The first relates to the driving force of the whole discourse. As organisations have to orient themselves to the market and specifically to customers, BPR has to *increase the value of services* as perceived by the customer. The idea of generating *added value* is directly linked to the concept of *customer satisfaction*. Only the customer can attribute value to the outcome of the process and the effectiveness of the relation with the supplier. In this sense value cannot be measured only in monetary terms, but includes also non economical dimensions. This is the case when the customer recognises a value in the service independently of or in addition to a monetary transaction. To its extreme, this explains the customer/supplier relation in voluntary work. Here we have services which are based only on the concept of the perceived value, because the customer does not pay for the service supplied by the voluntary. The customer/supplier relation develops value in the partnership among the actors. Therefore the value is not only generated for the customer, but also for the supplier. The generation and maintenance of value relates also to the *learning capacity* of the supplier's organisation.

Cost reduction

The second goal is to *reduce costs*. This relates directly to the dimension of profitability and productivity. The organisation has two cost types: there are direct costs for producing the product or service, and indirect costs the organisation has to sustain, but cannot be attributed directly to production. Forcing the concept of processes, all types of costs should be directly attributed to the process. This is a prerequisite to understand the process cost and to measure cost reduction due to BPR. This demands in many organisations for different cost accounting systems. Instead of attributing costs to functions and capsize indirect costs, process costs have to be defined by *activity based costing*. Understanding the cost structure of a process, cost reduction efforts can be put into place in a BPR project.

Cycle-time reduction

The third goal aims at *reducing the overall cycle-time*. The reduction of the *time-to-market* is one of the conditions to survive in the changing environment. However, the cycle-time comprises not only the production cycle, but the whole cycle from the customer's request to the conclusion of the customer/supplier relation by declaring the customer satisfaction.

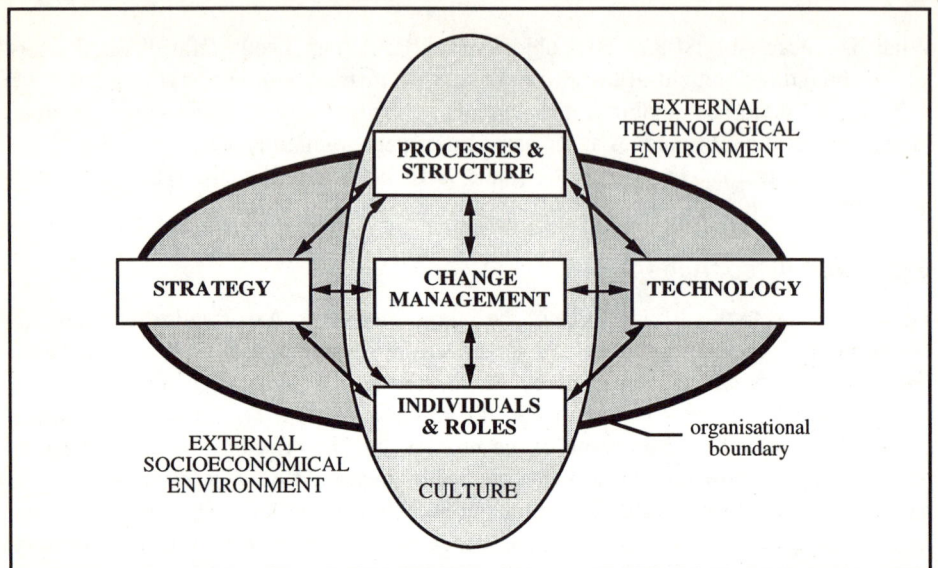

Figure 2-6: The role of change management for business process re-engineering in socio-technical systems (from Scott Morton, 1991:20)

A BPR project has to work on the principle components to achieve these goals. As already discussed, BPR optimises workflows, improves co-ordination and control mechanisms, simplifies the organisational structure, orients and defines professional roles working in processes focusing on services and customer satisfaction, makes use of workflow management technology, etc. As BPR includes organisation, people and technology, it has to be seen as the joint design of a *socio-technical system* (Emery & Trist, 1969). The relation of the components processes, organisational structure, individuals, organisational roles, strategy and technology in relation to *change management* is shown in Figure 2-6. The light grey ellipse in Figure 2-6 represents the people issues which are critical to the success of the transformation process. The point is that it is not sufficient to coherently design the single components of the socio-technical system, but to manage the change from the existing to the new by putting attention to people and cultural issues. This is also the consequence after several experiences for James Champy (1995) who sustained originally together with Michael Hammer the hard way of doing BPR (Hammer & Champy, 1993).

Only organisation which work on all dimensions of the *socio-technical system* in Figure 2-7 (business, processes, technology, people and organisation) will be able to go successfully through the transformation process. Therefore the effort of *change management* in BPR can only be successful when the required change is managed as a process in itself. BPR projects have to include different tasks of a typical organisational change management project, like goal setting, analysis, diagnosis, design, communication, training, implementation, evaluation, etc. Anyway, BPR

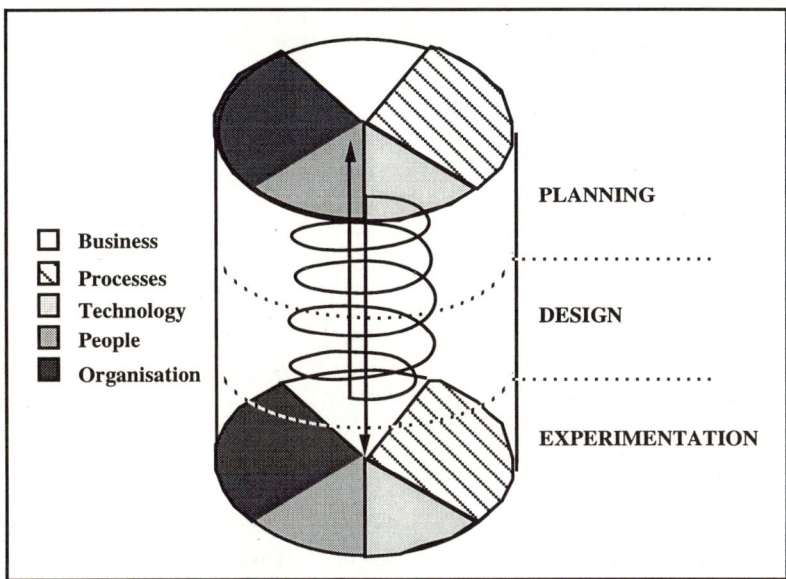

Figure 2-7: Interfunctional approaches for continuous innovation (from Butera, 1990: 90)

cannot be done by a *waterfall-model*, but has to be done as a continuous innovation, driven by the business itself.

Figure 2-7 shows a *spiral model* which allows to start the BPR initiative at any stage between planning, design and experimentation. Implicit in this model is the idea that a system is never really finished. The spiral covers simultaneously all dimensions of the socio-technical system (Butera, 1990).

The impact of BPR projects requires the involvement of different managerial roles. The managers who have to be involved vary according to the *complexity* of the project and its *depth* of organisational change. Figure 2-8 shows the main management functions for different combinations of BPR efforts. The depth of BPR projects go from the rationalisation of existing processes, to the design of components of the socio-technical system (process support technology, organisational roles, organisational structure) to a fully integrated BPR effort. The complexity of the BPR project depends on the broadness, needed qualification and impact on the organisation. Less complex BPR projects include training and acquiring the qualification to be prepared for BPR. Pilot projects and full projects on a single process imply already to handle quite complex BPR efforts. The most complex projects include a BPR-oriented business strategy and the concurrent management of several BPR projects for an overall change of the organisation. The matrix shows for the combination of depth and complexity who should be responsible for BPR projects, e.g. *management information systems* (MIS) for the design of technical support systems in pilot projects, *Personnel* or *organisation* for training on process

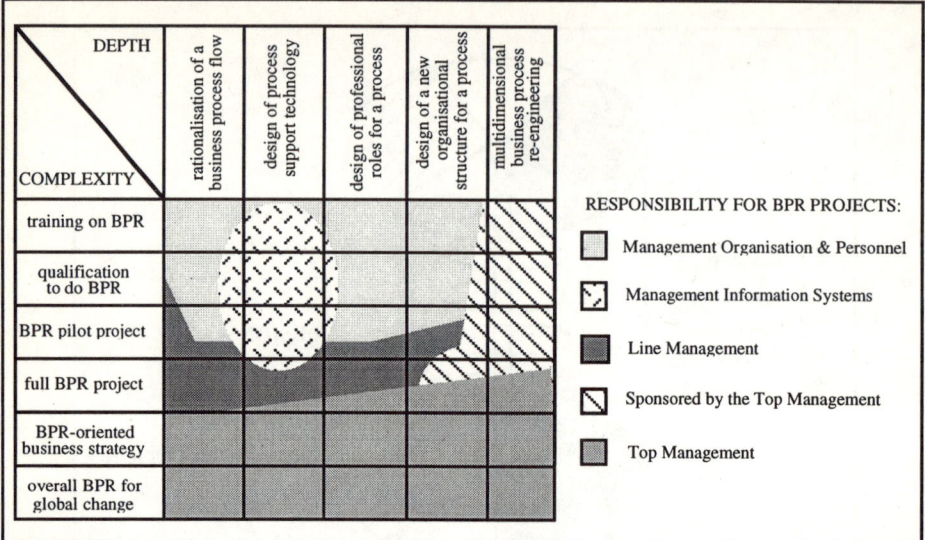

Figure 2-8: Management of complexity and depth in business process re-engineering projects

rationalisation and related design of roles and structures, *line management* for BPR projects which are relevant for their line business, *top management* for business strategy and organisation-wide BPR. The single appointed areas of responsibility for single management functions do not mean that they are not involved in the other areas of the matrix. BPR generally calls all management functions into a project. Due to possible conflicts of competence and power, it is necessary to always involve the top management for complex or deep BPR efforts (either for sponsoring the BPR project or for being directly responsible).

In the following section, different process models are analysed in terms of how they may be suited to the proposed approach. The section develops further towards the re-engineering of business processes with adequate models. The language/action perspective is proposed to be best suited for business process re-engineering.

2.3 Models for business process re-engineering

2.3.1 Material and information processes

Re-engineering efforts start with the re-modelling of all business processes. Such process models can have different goals and objectives, depending on the intended use. Many aspects of a process have to be described by its modelling, e.g., what is going to be done, who is going to do it, how and why will it be done, who is dependent on its being done, etc. To the extent that automation is involved, process representation becomes a vital issue in redesigning work and allocating responsibilities between humans and computers. Process modelling is distinguished from other types of modelling in computer science because many of the phenomena modelled must be enacted by a human rather than a machine. Newer uses of information technology extend computer use beyond transaction processing into communication and co-operation. Successfully integrating these systems into the organisation often requires modelling even the manual organisational processes into which these systems intervene. Rather than focusing solely on the user's behaviour at the interface or the flow and transformation of data within the system, process modelling also focuses on interacting behaviours among agents, regardless of whether a computer is involved in the transactions or not used at all (Henning & Ochterbeck, 1988; 1988b; Ochterbeck, 1989; Curtis *et al.*, 1992).

Medina-Mora *et al.* (1992) distinguish three different views on processes in organisations. Each of these views highlights a specific interest in understanding the nature and characteristics of a process; the different perspectives describe the same process by reducing its complexity to a specific subset of interest. The three different views concentrate on the material, informational or business perspective in processes.

Table 2-1: Three different perspectives on processes
(elaborated from Medina-Mora et al., 1992)

PERSPECTIVE	SCOPE	COMPONENTS
Material Process Perspective	assemble components to deliver products	• raw materials • devices/machines • physical layout • material flow
Information Process Perspective	process data to provide information	• data • document/record • information flow
Business Process Perspective	perform business transactions to achieve customer satisfaction	• customer/supplier relationship • condition of satisfaction • workflow • roles and responsibilities in business transactions (process owner and process manager) • total cycle-time

Material processes

Material processes relate to human activities which are rooted in the *physical world*. An observer notes the moving and changing of physical things. In this kind of process materials are transported, stored, measured, transformed and assembled. This has been the relevant domain in the tradition of factory automation. Approaches are mainly based on the disciplines of industrial and mechanical engineering. Material process re-design has been used to increase efficiency in production and industrial engineering. Examples for the optimisation of material flows are *group technology*

(Vajna, 1987), *period batch control* (Schäl, 1991) and *optimised production technology* (Goldratt & Cox, 1986; Lundrigan, 1986).

Information processes

Information processes overcome the failure of material processes to capture what is important about every-day activity in the 20th century. Theorists and information technology providers have developed sophisticated ways to analyse and facilitate the flow of information. The main approach can be described as system analysis. Traditionally, the modelling of information systems has focused on analysing data flows and transformations. This modelling accounts only for the organisation's data and that portion of its processes which interacted with data. Current techniques of data flow analysis, entity-relationship models, database storage and retrieval, transaction processing, network communication, etc. have provided a structure for effective information processing. Historically there have been three main models used for information system design:

- *Information flow models* represent office work in terms of units of information (forms, memos, etc.) and are used to define operations performed on each information unit. They describe the relation of information units in terms of source, operation, integration, destination and relation to other flows.
- *Procedural models* describe well defined and understood tasks, almost exclusively in the office environment. They are based upon the view that office work is basically procedural in nature, involving the execution by office works of pre-defined sequences of steps. They emphasise the task-oriented nature of work and operants (units of information). The models control who takes part in a task, what sequence of operations should be performed for a task to be completed, and what documents or data are needed to be exchanged. The model is prescriptive and enforces the user to do what the designer modelled of the users' working practice. Inter-procedural and inter-departmental flows are less clearly identified than in the information flow model (Ellis & Naffah, 1987). Therefore resulting *office procedure systems* are

   > 'suitable for describing office work that is structured around actions (e.g. sending a message, approving, filing) where the sequence of activities is the same except for minor variations and few exceptions. [...] These systems do not deal well with unanticipated conditions.' (Barber *et al.*, 1983: 562)

- *Activity models* expand the horizons of procedural models by presenting a more general approach to task specification. The main difference compared to procedural models is that activity models are general enough to be applicable to more than a specific task or procedure. The models concentrate on what and how information is exchanged between members of the activity and attach more significance to what these people can actually do (Trevor *et al.*, 1993). Many different systems offer these features; the COSMOS model (Bowers & Churcher, 1988; Bowers *et al.*, 1988) and the AMIGO Activity Model (Danielsen *et al.*, 1986; Danielsen & Pankoke-Babatz, 1988) are two of the most well known.

Information Systems analysis improves the availability and accuracy of information which is vital to the business. This is the main basis for applications offered by computer industries today. What is lost in the information process perspective and has to be taken up is the recognition that:

> 'information in itself is uninteresting. Information is only useful because someone can do something with it [...]' (Medina-Mora et al., 1992: 282)

This means, that information is used to make business, or in other words, useful information produces action. This is very much related to the philosophical ground of the language/action perspective which is described later in this chapter.

2.3.2 The business process perspective

Today, organisations must improve the efficiency of their working process to achieve significant gains in their overall productivity. However, applying the approaches of industrial engineering or information systems analysis, on their own, do not ensure improvements in the way people interact in the organisation. This perception leads to the domain of *business processes*. Hammer & Champy (1993) define business processes as:

> 'a collection of activities that takes one or more kinds of input and creates an output that is of value for the customer.' (Hammer & Champy, 1993: 35)

The main issue for Hammer & Champy is the *creation of value* for the customer. Davenport (1993) goes in the same direction, giving a more precise definition for business processes as being:

> 'a structured, measured set of activities designed to produce a specified output for a particular customer or market. It implies a strong emphasis on *how* work is done within an organisation, in contrast to a product focus's emphasis on *what*. A process is thus a specific ordering of work activities across time and place, with a beginning, an end, and clearly identified inputs and outputs: a structure for action.' (Davenport, 1993: 5)

Business process analysis improves the way workers interact and co-ordinate their activities to achieve a better service to their customer(s). At the same time, business processes are implemented in information processes, just as information processes are implemented in material processes. However, in moving the focus on the *business perspective* and *customer satisfaction*, rather than on material treatment, logistics, forms or database transactions, one reveals a higher level of organisation.

All tree kinds of process views are present in the organisation, and in most cases, the different perspective produces different results from an organisational analysis. Taking the wrong perspective for designing new ways of working in processes can have fatal consequences, as Redenbaugh (1994) argues for the era of the automation of the office:

'When we decided to automate the office 20 years ago, we called in the people who automated the factories of the world. As a result, we got systems for automating the paper flows in offices similar to the systems for automating materials of a factory. We looked with industrial-age eyes, and we saw what we saw in factories, which is that you need to automate the movement of components, moderate the components and sub-assemblies through inventory and flow and combine the whole thing so that at the end a car comes out.' (Redenbaugh, 1994: 15)

In order to gain a new view on business processes, it is important to distinguish the three process perspectives. Each has its own structure, components and historical evolution according to the main approaches. As a result, one has to apply the most effective method in relation to the expected type of process improvement. The material and informational perspectives conceive some elements of business processes, but not the main ones. Therefore we have to add the business perspective as complementary to the other two.

Definition: Business process
A business process creates an output which is of value for the customer. This value is expressed by the customer's satisfaction with the product/service delivered by the supplier. The business process perspective represents the scope and internal logic of the business process to achieve customer satisfaction by identifying customers (internal and external), suppliers, conditions of satisfaction, roles and responsibilities (of process owners and managers) and the total workflow cycle-time (from the customer's request until the achieved customer satisfaction).

The business process perspective is not currently covered by most process modelling approaches. Therefore we need a new way of modelling processes. Once an organisation perceives its business in terms of business processes, it can usually explore ways in which they may re-design their business to yield further improvements. Moreover, business processes can be re-designed to take advantage of the latest developments in information technology related to the field of Computer Supported Cooperative Work (CSCW). In the following paragraph the *customer/ supplier relation* is explored in the *language/action perspective* as a model to analyse and design workflows in complex organisations. Subsequently its implementation with *workflow management technology* is being discussed in chapter 4.

2.3.3 The language/action perspective

The main aspect of business processes is the existence of customer/supplier relations. The occurrence of customer satisfaction in such customer/supplier relations should be seen as a linguistic expression. Due to this communicative dimension, the *language/action perspective* is proposed to model business processes. The language/action perspective takes language as the primary dimension of human activities and, therefore, of communication and co-operation. It was developed by Fernando Flores, who served as Finance Minister of the President Allende Cabinet in Chile and is currently chairman of the board of Action Technologies Inc., one of the first software companies which developed groupware tools in the United States, and by Terry Winograd, currently with Stanford University, who owes his reputation to the work he did in research on natural language processing (e.g., Winograd, 1972). Their work takes into consideration three main concepts: *autopoiesis* (Maturana & Varela, 1980), *hermeneutics* and *phenomenology* (Gadamer, 1975; 1976; Heidegger, 1927) and *speech act theory* (Austin, 1962; Searle, 1969; 1975; 1975b; 1979; Habermas, 1973). The two authors claim, following the hermeneutics school of Western Europe philosophy, that *people act through language* (Winograd & Flores, 1986).

The language/action perspective can be described in the traditional framework of linguistic theory: *syntax*, *semantics* and *pragmatics*.
- *Syntax* is the structure of the visible (or audible) forms of language. The syntactical rules (or grammar) of a language determine the basic elements (letters, words, etc.) and the ways in which they can be combined.
- *Semantics* is the systematic relation between structures in a language and a space of potential meanings. It includes the definitions of individual elements (e.g., words) and the meaning which is generated by combining them (e.g., sentences).
- *Pragmatics* deals with issues of language use. The primary aspect of pragmatics is the role of language in evoking and interpreting actions (Winograd, 1987).

Therefore, Winograd & Flores (1986) do not look at the syntactic and semantic aspects of language, but at what people *do with language*. Language is not only a system for representing the world, or for conveying thoughts and information. Language is where we as humans live and act together. This language/action perspective is opposed to the more predominant perspective that *people process information and make decisions* (Winograd, 1987).

Speech act theory

The language/action perspective is based on *speech act theory* which was articulated by John Austin (1962) and later developed by John Searle (1969; 1975; 1975b; 1979). Austin was concerned about those utterances, as "Can you bring me a glass of water, please?" which cannot be considered true or false in any sense. He summarised his work in a general action-oriented theory of meaning in human communication: A *speech act* is composed of two elements: its *referential component* and its *illocutionary force*. The referential component is given by its semantic situation. Its force is generated in terms of pragmatic interpretation. The important aspect of a speech act is more the speaker's intention it conveys (what one wants to do with it) than its form or its meaning (Vomberg, 1989).

Searle (1975) has identified five fundamental *illocutionary categories* to which *utterances* belong:
- *assertives*: a commitment of the speaker to something true in the expressed proposition, e.g., the speaker claiming to be speaking;
- *directives* : attempt to get the hearer to do something, e.g., a request;
- *commissives*: a commitment of the speaker to some future course of action, e.g., a promise;

- *declarations*: a speech act creating a correspondence between its propositional content and reality; e.g., pronouncing a couple married;
- *expressives*: expression about the psychological state of the speaker, e.g., an apology.

Speech acts exchanged between two partners are not unrelated events, but constitute conversations (Flores, 1982; Flores & Ludlow, 1981). Four types of conversation are distinguished by Winograd (1987):
- *conversation for action*, where two partners negotiate an action which one of them will do for the other person;
- *conversation for possibility*, where two persons negotiate a modification of the setting, within which they (inter-)act (the mood is one of generating conversations for action);
- *conversation for clarification*, where the participants cope with or anticipate breakdowns concerning interpretations of the condition of satisfaction for a conversation for action;
- *conversation for orientation*, where the participants are in the mood of creating a shared background as a basis for interpreting future conversations.

Speech act theory and the resulting language/action perspective have come to be a dominant framework for the conceptualisation of communicative action within computer supported cooperative work[1]. In response to the popularity of speech act theory, a number of cogent critiques have appeared in recent years based on observations drawn from the analysis of actually occurring conversations (e.g., Bowers & Churcher, 1988; Suchman, 1993; 1994). Most work has concentrated on the first category, i.e., the conversation for action, out of the four conversation types. This is quite evident, because it is the most structured conversation, reflecting speech-act theory. Thus, this conversation is the most easy to program in software systems. This research will deal with the *conversation for action* and the *conversation for possibilities*, too. However, the *conversation for clarification* and the *conversation for orientation* are not included in the model for representing business processes. This is motivated by the fact, that customers and suppliers in business processes deal mainly with action (producing customer satisfaction through the delivery of services and products) and the definition of the setting which allows for future action. The *conversation for clarification* and the *conversation for orientation* are a context for such a business process.

---

[1] For example, ACM, 1988; Agostini et al., 1993; 1994; Bair & Gale, 1988; Bignoli et al., 1991; Bowers & Churcher, 1988; Bowers et al., 1988; Bullen & Bennett, 1990; 1990b; Carasik & Grantham, 1988; Ciborra, 1993; Colazzo et al., 1991; 1991b; De Cindio et al., 1987; 1988; De Michelis, 1995; De Michelis & Grasso, 1993; 1994; Denning, 1992; Dunham, 1991; Flores et al., 1988; Kaplan et al., 1991; Keen, 1991; Kensing & Winograd, 1991; Kreifelts et al., 1984; 1991; Malone & Crowston, 1990; 1991; Malone et al., 1992; Marca, 1989; Medina-Mora et al., 1992; Robinson, 1991; Schäl, 1988; 1991b; 1993; 1995; Schäl & Zeller, 1991; 1993; Schäl & Zenié, 1994; Shepherd et al., 1990; Suchman, 1987b; 1993; 1994; Swenson, 1993; Whiteside, 1994; Winograd, 1986; 1987; 1988; 1994; Winograd & Flores, 1986

Conversation for action

As already outlined, a *conversation for action* is used by two communication partners (here seen as customer and supplier) to negotiate an action (here seen as the delivery of a service or product) which one of them (the supplier) will do for the other person (the customer). The network of speech-acts which constitute a conversation for action, as an interplay of *requests* and *commissives*, are directed to explicit co-ordinated action (Winograd & Flores, 1986). The state-transition diagram in Figure 2-9 illustrates the possible moves in a conversation for action. It shows the case of a conversation for action initiated by a request; another possibility is to open a conversation with an offer. Each circle represents a state of the conversation; the arcs are the language acts which the participants A (as the customer) and B (as the supplier) can take.

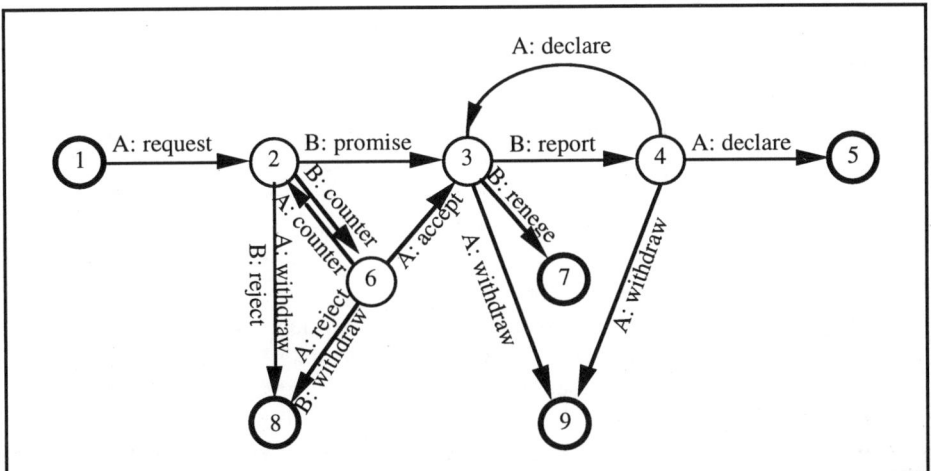

Figure 2-9: The basic conversation for action
(elaborated from Winograd & Flores, 1986: 65)

There are several points about this conversation structure represented in Figure 2-9 which should be clarified before explaining the details:
(1) At each point in the conversation for action there is a small *set of possible actions* determined by the previous *history of the relation* among A and B. Figure 2-9 shows the basic structure, not the details of content of the single speech acts.
(2) All the *relevant acts are linguistic*. The actual doing of whatever is needed to meet the customer satisfaction, e.g., to assembly a product, lies outside of the conversation.
(3) There are a few *states of completion* from where no further moves can be done. All other states represent an incomplete conversation (evidenced in bold in Figure 2-9, i.e., states 5, 7, 8 and 9).

Figure 2-9 shows the basic course of a *conversation for action* opened by a *request*. After the initial *request* by A (moving from state 1 to state 2), B has three possibilities for basic moves:

- *promising*   to do what is requested (moving from state 2 to state 3);
- *rejecting*   the request and thereby closing the conversation (moving from state 2 to state 8);
- *counteroffering*   by, e.g., suggesting an alternative (moving from state 2 to state 6).

Having, e.g., B *counteroffered*, A's next move in the conversation is changed to another three possibilities for response:

- *accepting*   what B has offered (moving from state 6 to state 3);
- *counteroffering*   something else than B's counteroffer and/or A's initial request (moving from state 6 back to state 2);
- *rejecting*   B's counteroffer (moving from state 6 to state 8).

A conversation moves this way to a state of completion where no further moves are anticipated. The sequence of moves which achieve a positive conclusion of the conversation are the straight line on the top of Figure 2-9 from state 1 through states 2, 3 and 4 into state 5. The sequence of moves in this simplest case of a conversation are:

- *requesting*   an action, i.e., a service (moving from state 1 to state 2);
- *promising*   to do what is requested (moving from state 2 to state 3);
- *reporting*   that the promised action is done (moving from state 3 to state 4);
- *declaring*   that the delivered service or product is satisfying the expectations (moving from state 4 to state 5).

Further possible moves are present in states 3 and 4. These are for state 3:

- *reneging*   what has been promised first (moving from state 3 to state 7);
- *withdrawing*   the request, although B has already promised to do what is requested (moving from state 3 to state 9).

After B reported that the promised action is done, the additional moves to the straight forward conversation are:

- *declaring*   that the delivered service or product is not satisfying the expectations and that B should rework the delivery (moving from state 4 to state 3);
- *withdrawing*   the request, although the delivered service or product is not satisfying the expectations and intending that B should not rework it (moving from state 4 to state 9).

This structure of possibilities is used in action-co-ordination systems to organise records of what has been done and present them to the conversant as possibilities for future actions (Winograd, 1988).

The illustrated network of speech-acts can be used as a basis for representing recurrent structure in conversations. This includes temporal relations among speech-acts, and the linking of moves with each other. For the implementation of the speech-act moves, the conversation for action can be represented as an automaton $<S, I, \Omega>$ where

- S is a finite set of states, representing the states of the commitment;
- I is a finite set of transitions;
- Ω is the function which receives as input the current state and a transition, calculating as an output the next state (Bignoli *et al.*, 1991; Agostini *et al.*, 1994).

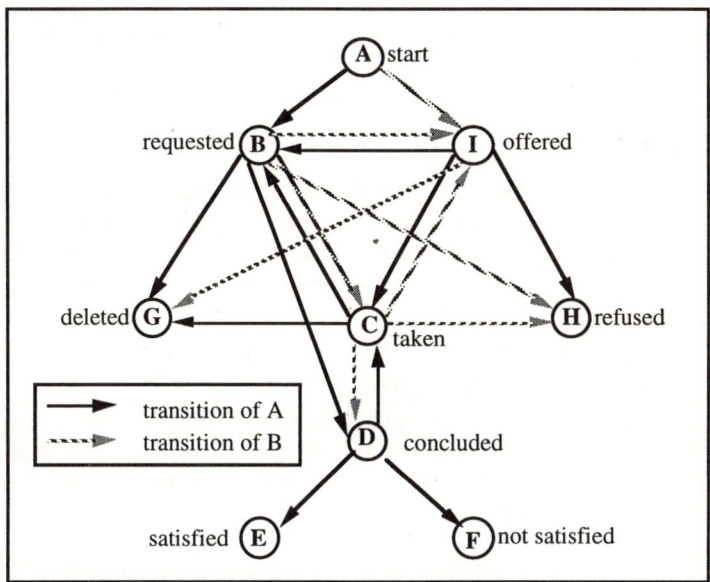

Figure 2-10: Transition diagram of a conversation for action
(elaborated from Agostini et al., 1994: 216)

The states in Figure 2-9 are not sufficiently distinct to describe such an automaton. This is for example the case for state 8, which can be reached by withdrawing A's initial request, B's counteroffer or rejecting A's request or B' counteroffer. As a consequence, state 8 has the meaning of being *deleted* or *refused*. Therefore a new set of 9 states (A to I) is defined in Figure 2-10. Table 2-2 explains the relation of states in Figure 2-10 and those in Figure 2-9.

Table 2-2: States and transitions in a conversation for action

State	Transition	Relation with Figure 2-9
A	start	this corresponds to state 1;
B	requested	this corresponds to state 2; state B can be reached because A requested a product or service(moving from state A/1 to state B/2), or because A counteroffered to a previous counteroffer by B (moving from state I/6 to state B/2);
C	taken	this corresponds to state 3; state C can be reached, because B promised to do what is requested(moving from state B/2 to state C/3), or because A declared that the delivered service or product is not satisfying the expectations and that B should rework the delivery (moving from state D/4 back to state C/3), or because A accepted B's counteroffer (moving from state I/6 to state C/3);
D	concluded	this corresponds to state 4;
E	satisfied	this corresponds to state 5;
F	not satisfied	this corresponds to state 9; state F can be reached only by withdrawing the request, although the delivered service or product is not satisfying the expectations and intending that B should not rework the delivery (moving from state D/4 to state F/9);
G	deleted	this corresponds to states 8 and 9; state G can be reached, because A withdraws the initial request before B promised to do what is requested (moving from state B/2 to state G/8), or because B withdraws a counteroffer before A accepts the new conditions (moving from state I/6 to state G/8), or because A withdraws the initial request although B promised to do what is requested (moving from state C/3 to state G/9);
H	refused	this corresponds to states 8 and 7; state H can be reached, because B rejects A's request (moving from state B/2 to state H/8), or because B reneges A's request after having promised first (moving from state C/3 to state H/7);
I	offered	this corresponds to state 6; state I can be reached, because B counteroffered to A's (moving from state B/2 to state I/6); or when a conversation for action is opened by an offer made by person B instead of a request made by A (moving from state A to state I - this alternative is not included in Figure 2-9).

Conversation for possibility

In a *conversation for possibility* (Winograd, 1986; De Cindio *et al.*, 1988; Agostini *et al.*, 1994), on the other hand, two persons explore a new *possible courses of action*, creating the adequate setting for them. The mood is one of *speculation*, anticipating the subsequent generation of conversations for action. Furthermore, the conversation for possibilities is used to solicit suggestions and opinions of other people (partners in a discussion) to define a consensus on a topic. The main steps of a conversation for possibility are the opening, the continuation and closing of a discussion. There is not such an elaborated structure as in the conversation for action. The conversation for possibilities has been formalised in the CHAOS project (De Cindio et al., 1987; 1988) and more recently in UTUCS (Agostini et al., 1994). Figure 2-11 shows the *state transition diagram* for a *conversation for possibilities* between two persons A and B.

Generally, a conversation for possibilities starts with the proposal of a topic by person A (moving from state A to state B). Person B continuous the discussion by suggesting his view on the topic (moving from state B to state C). If person B is satisfied with the discussion, B accepts A's suggestion and the conversation is closed (moving from state C to state D). Otherwise, person B can continue the discussion by re-proposing his standpoint (moving from state C to state B). At this point the conversation continuous without any heavy structure between states B and C, until one of the partners stops the conversation. This can be done by deleting the conversation by whom it was opened (moving into state E), by refusing the stand-point of the partner (moving into state F), or by accepting the result of the conversation (moving into state D).

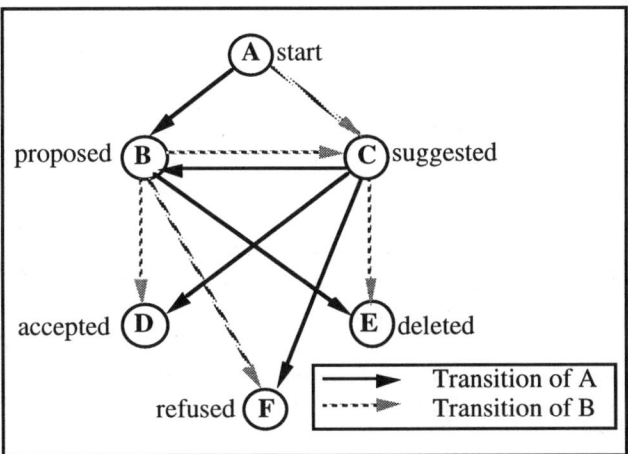

Figure 2-11: Transition diagram of a conversation for possibility (elaborated from Agostini et al., 1994: 218)

Critique on speech act theory

A criticism related to speech act theory turns on the difficulty, for the hearer/analyst, of categorising the illocutionary force of an utterance. Winograd & Flores (1986) suggest to give a response to this problem by enrolling speakers themselves in categorising their utterances with explicit illocutionary acts; Winograd & Flores are not proposing:

'that a computer can 'understand' speech acts by analysing natural language utterances. [...] What we propose is to make the user aware of this structure and to provide tools for working with it explicitly. [...] The development of a conversation requires selection among a certain finite set of possibilities that is defined by the opening directive and the subsequent responses.' (Winograd & Flores, 1986: 159)

Thus, participants may be enlisted in a coding procedure aimed at making implicit intent explicit. The premise of this procedure is that explicitly identified speech acts are clear, unambiguous and preferred (Suchman, 1993). Schrage (1990) cautions the use of language only in pragmatic terms:

'Language must be viewed as a medium to create meaning and shared understanding rather than simply to exchange information. Communication is more than to exchange contracts. There are many levels to conversations, but the best conversations are acts of collaborative creation which did not exist before.' (Schrage, 1990: 83)

In the following paragraph, an example for this approach is described and discussed for modelling workflows in the language/action perspective.

2.3.4 Workflows in the language/action perspective

Action workflow

An example to describe the workflow according to the customer/supplier model is the *Business Design Language* developed by Action Technologies (ATI, 1990; Dunham, 1991; Keen, 1991; Medina-Mora et al., 1992). This method is based on the language/action perspective as discussed before. The business design language takes the straight forward path of Figure 2-9 as its basic conversation flow (states 1, 2, 3, 4 and 5). Instead of a general interaction between A and B, the workflow describes the pragmatic linguistic moves between a customer and a supplier. The basic model describing workflows in the language/action perspective is shown in Figure 2-12.

The basic unit of processes is a four step *action workflow protocol*. In Figure 2-12, black arrows represent the requester's speech acts (A from Figure 2-9 is now the *customer*) and grey arrows the performer's speech acts (B from Figure 2-9 is now the *supplier*).

In the first phase of the loop (*request phase*), the customer asks for a service or product. This corresponds to the *request transition* from state 1 into state 2 in Figure 2-9 and from state A into state B in Figure 2-10.

In the second phase (*commitment phase*), the supplier *promises* to fulfil a specific condition. The supplier's agreement with the customers request, possibly modified during the commitment phase due to a *negotiation*, corresponds to the *promise transition* from state 2 into state 3 in Figure 2-9 and from state B into state C in Figure 2-10. Not always the second phase is straight forward. In this case, the supplier *negotiates* with the customer to meet a corresponding condition of satisfaction. The *negotiation* in the commitment phase includes the possibility to *counteroffer* (from state 2 into state 6 in Figure 2-9 and from state B into state I in Figure 2-10). In this case there are two paths for concluding the commitment phase: the customer accepts the counteroffer, or the customer makes a second counteroffer which the supplier accepts. In all other cases the commitment phase leads into states where no further moves are possible (state 8 in Figure 2-9 and states G and H in Figure 2-10).

In the third phase (*performance phase*), the supplier fulfils his work which leads to the delivery of the requested service or product. This corresponds to the *report transition* from state 3 into state 4 in Figure 2-9 and from state C into state D in Figure 2-10.

The final phase (*evaluation phase*), closes the loop and involves the customer's acknowledgement or formal declaration of satisfaction (or non-satisfaction) after the customer receives the service or product. At its simplest, this declaration is a *thank you* or the payment for the service/product. This corresponds to the *declare transition* from state 4 into the final state 5 in Figure 2-9, where no further moves are anticipated, and from state D into state E in Figure 2-10.

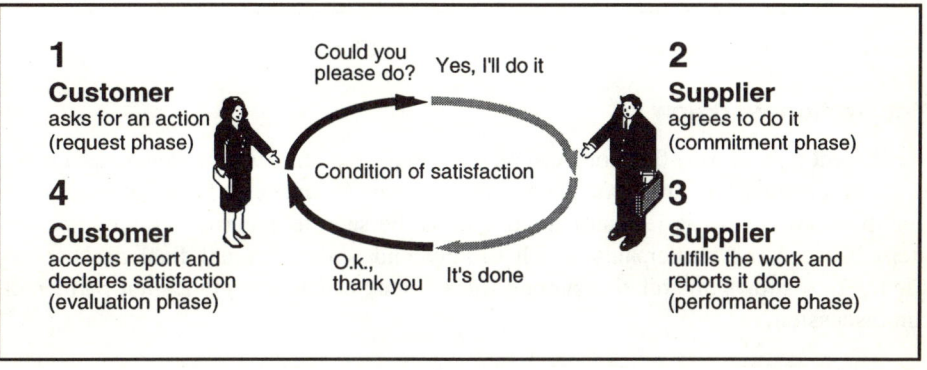

Figure 2-12: Basic workflow model describing customer/supplier relations in the language/action perspective (elaborated from Keen, 1991; Medina-Mora et al., 1992)

In the representation of Figure 2-12 the closed loop means, that the transition to link a customer and a supplier for a specific service is finished and has reached customer satisfaction. Thus, the loop represents the four transitions *request*, *promise*, *report* and *declare* from state A straight into state E according to Figure 2-10. All other transitions are not represented in the four-phase loop, but they are not neglected. They have to be seen as always implicitly present in the loop. They are omitted for not overloading the graphical representation. Otherwise, the simple loop would become for each customer/supplier relation a graph as developed in Figure 2-13. Figure 2-13 shows all transitions from Figure 2-9 and all states from Figure 2-10 mapped on the four-phase action workflow loop from Figure 2-12.

38   Chapter 2

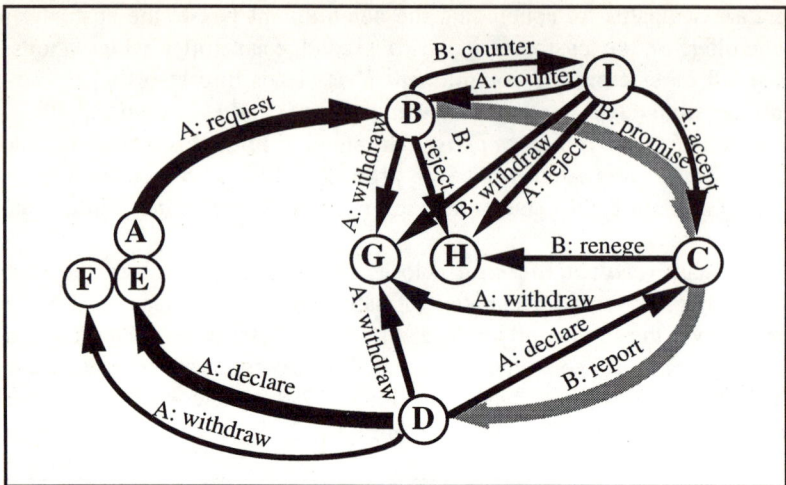

Figure 2-13: Transitions and states in the action workflow loop

Declaration workflow

A different type of workflow loop can be identified when instead of a request for an action an *exploratory or declarative conversation* is opened. In such cases the communication flow is less structured and can be seen as recurrent communication steps between the participants which usually end with a mutual final declaration. Figure 2-14 shows this relation among the initiator and a communication partner in the discussion.

Figure 2-14: Declaration workflow opened by the initiator with a partner

This declaration workflow corresponds to the *conversation for possibility* (see Figure 2-11). In the representation of Figure 2-14 the closed loop means, that the transition to link an initiator and a partner for a discussion is ongoing or finished successfully. Thus, the loop represents the two transitions *propose* and *suggest* which correspond to state B and state C in Figure 2-11. All other transitions are not represented in the two-phase loop. They have to be seen as always implicitly present in the declaration workflow loop as for action workflow loop. Figure 2-15 shows all states from Figure 2-11 mapped on the two-phase declaration workflow loop. Figure 2-15 makes clear that the discussion passes continuously from state B into state C and again into state B, until the discussion is not closed by one of the partners (moving the declaration workflow into states D, E or F).

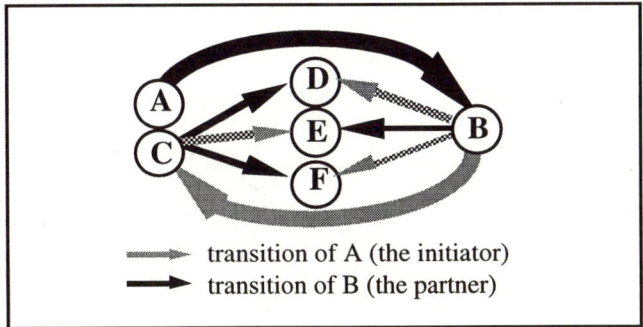

Figure 2-15: Transitions and states in the declaration workflow loop

Workflows in articulated processes

The underlying workflow model sees persons as continuously communicating individuals in the organisation who open and close conversations in their working life relations with colleagues and others. The same four-phase or two phase workflow loops describe the process at all levels of operation. At any phase there may be additional actions, such as clarifications, further negotiations about the conditions, and changes of the commitments by the participants. Complex processes are thus be broken down into *sub-workflows* according to the four-phase model. These *secondary workflows* may be modelled again according to the language/action model as developed by Winograd & Flores (1986: 65). This means that the simple structure for representation is valid for understanding and improving the fundamental interaction between the process and its customers and suppliers. In carrying out a commitment, the performer (supplier) becomes, in turn, the customer of others for pieces of work (services or products), and thus a whole network of customers, loops and performers (suppliers) comes into play for the completion of the initial request. The resulting interconnection of loops (see Figure 2-16) depicts a *co-operative network* in which a group of people, playing various roles, carry out an organisational process that renders services/products to customers.

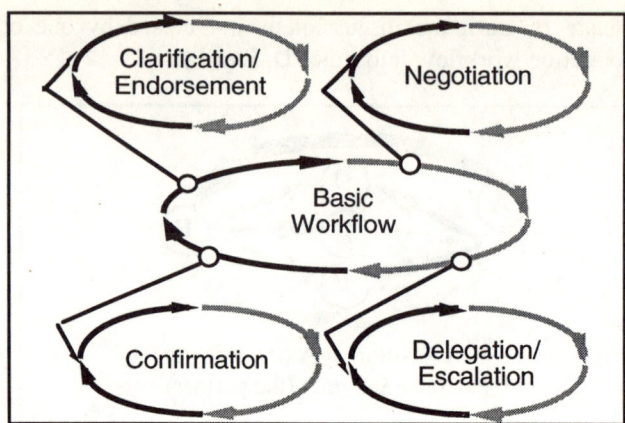

Figure 2-16: The interconnection of loops in articulated processes

The structure of the representation is defined by the language acts through which the participating persons co-ordinate their activities, but not the actions done by individuals to meet the final condition of satisfaction. The key difference is to shift from a *task structure* to a *co-ordination structure* (Medina-Mora *et al.*, 1992). This shift leads to a more potential representation of the working process than by task-analysis:

> 'The simple workflow loop structure is both general and universal. It is general in that it occurs whenever there is coordination among people, regardless of what they are doing. The word "customer" and "performer" apply to people within a single organisation as well as across boundaries. The loop structure is universal in that it is independent of any culture, language, or communication medium in which it is conducted. There are endless variations in the specifics of how the steps are taken, what other loops are triggered, and how people respond to breakdowns within them, but the basic structure is the same. The action workflow loop is like an atomic element of the chemistry of interactions. By combining these loops, all the complex phenomena of organisations are generated' (Medina-Mora *et al.*, 1992: 283).

However, the interleaving of actions and conversations cannot be modelled to its real articulation; whenever a *breakdown* occurs within a working process, a new relation (i.e., a new loop with a supplier) is opened. Due to the already discussed complexity of work, breakdowns are generally unpredictable in their total possible appearance. Therefore, if the organisational analyst tries to take into account all possible breakdowns, this would generate an exponential increase in possible combinations (i.e., the dimension of loops in the resulting model becomes confusing, loosing the sense of describing breakdowns within actions). Otherwise, the selection of only the most meaningful and recurrent breakdowns oversimplifies the resulting representation. Therefore, one has to find the balance among *detail* and *significance*.

Once a workflow is identified and modelled, two fundamental re-design interventions can be realised:
- Firstly, an analysis of critical factors can be carried out in order to recognise possible areas of optimisation. Optimisations can be realised by reducing inefficiencies and duplication of effort, and by identifying organisational and technological solutions to cope with recurrent breakdowns.
- Secondly, the design of appropriate communication and information technology can be initiated accordingly with the analysed workflow and its interactions with existing or new computer systems, such as data bases, procedures, electronic document management systems, etc.

The method for analysing workflows in the language/action perspective does not concentrate on hierarchical relations, forms and procedures, but
- who are the *customers* and *suppliers* (i.e., identifying the *organisational role* people play in the specific workflow loop as customers or suppliers);
- what are the *conditions of satisfaction* for each loop (i.e., identifying what the customer expects from the supplier);
- how and whether at all, each of the *four phases in the loop* is carried out (i.e., identifying the existence or absence of each phase in the workflow);
- how are the single loops related to each other (i.e., in which phase of the *basic workflow* are *secondary workflows* connected and where are the links to the other workflows).

These questions determine the representation of real world processes, because these processes are not always clean and complete as the model might suggest. Missing phases in a workflow loop are a recurrent phenomena. This fact has to be shown in the representation. Therefore some examples for exceptional cases from the closed loops in Figure 2-12 and 2-14 are given.

The first exception concerns the missing of one or more phases in the action workflow loop. This has not to be seen as a pathology, but should be evidenced when describing processes as an interconnection of workflows. Often the second and fourth phase of the action workflow loop are missing. Figure 2-17 represents an action workflow loop where the second phase is missing.

Figure 2-17: Representation of an action workflow loop with a missing commitment phase

This can be the case, when, e.g., the supplier starts to work on the requested service or product without explicitly promising to deliver what is requested by the customer; the supplier delivers to the customer without having committed first. The customer evaluates the supply and closes the evaluation phase being satisfied. The second phase is generally missing when bureaucratic working procedures are modelled with the action workflow loop. People pile new work on their desk without negotiating about the implicit request, start working on the relative documents at a certain point in time, and report the results to what is called here their customer. Generally, in such working culture also the fourth phase is missing. Sometimes the missing phase is planned for. This is the case when, e.g., service providers standardise their offer in a way that the customer request can be immediately processed without the negotiation phase. The ordering from a catalogue is such an example. Writing down an identification code (and maybe the price mentioned in the catalogue) on the ordering form and sending it to the supplier (request phase), the supplier directly delivers the ordered goods (performance phase). The customer controls the delivered goods and pays (evaluation phase).

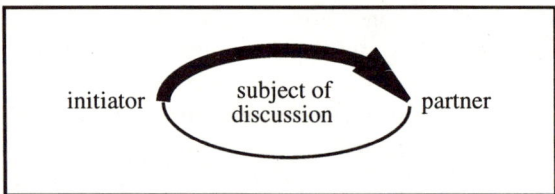

Figure 2-18: Representation of a declaration workflow loop with a missing continuation phase

The second exception concerns the missing of the second phase in the declaration workflow loop. This is the case when the partner in the discussion does not at all respond to the proposed subject by the initiator (see Figure 2-18).

Figure 2-19: Representation of an action workflow loop with an automated request phase

The third exception concerns the automation with information systems of one or more phases in the action workflow loop. The representation in Figure 2-19 means that the request phase is existing, but a technical system generates the request on behalf of the customer.

The resulting maps do not, and do not intent to, represent organisational structures (i.e., hierarchical relations), information flows (i.e., documents, forms, objects), or material flows. The scope is to represent *business processes* as a distinct perspective from information processes or material processes as a customer/supplier relationship or a chain of such customer/supplier workflow loops.

This questioning about customers, suppliers, conditions of satisfaction and relations among workflows leads to identifying those places where gaps and confusion lead to incomplete workflows, misunderstanding of results and ineffective information flow. The interpretation of these results can then lead to new forms of processes, instead of automating the old procedures. Furthermore, this approach to workflow analysis overcomes traditional methods which have been *production-oriented* (focusing on efficiency and control), by a *satisfaction-oriented* method (focused on commitments and conditions of satisfaction).

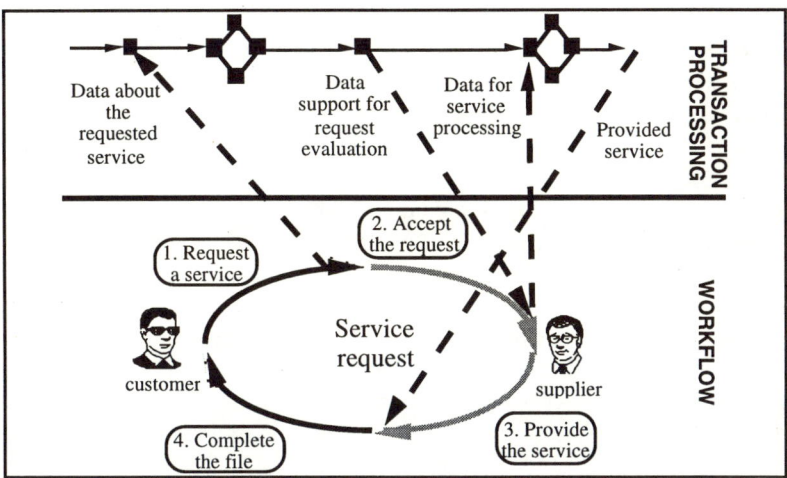

Figure 2-20: The workflow protocol integrates routines in a business process

The workflow protocol allows to integrate communication (parts of the so-called unstructured characteristics of the work process) as well as organisational or EDP procedure (parts of the so-called structured characteristics of the work process) into a common description. The routines are seen as constraints or supports to the completion of the workflow protocol. In the example described in Figure 2-20, a transaction processing application is updated by a customer's service request workflow step and supports the following supplier's step in evaluating the request and providing the service.

The use of the loop structure for workflow modelling has been shown to be promising in a number of cases, e.g., managing the review of job candidates for hiring personnel (Medina-Mora *et al.*, 1992); professional processes in advertising at Young & Rubicam (Marshak, 1993); curriculum management at George Mason University (Denning & Medina-Mora, 1994); remote sensing processes for rapid estimates of agriculture in Europe (Schäl & Zenié, 1994; 1995; 1996); the purchasing process in a municipal energy company (Di Stefano *et al.*, 1995).

In the following paragraph an example of a successful application of this concept in a chemical company conducted by the author is briefly described. It may illustrate the usefulness of the proposed concepts. Its importance for this research is in that it is the first study of applying the workflow concept on a process. The more detailed case studies in chapter 5 and 6 pick up the same concepts.

Case history 2: The workflow protocol for a distributed business process in a chemical company

The case history shows the difference between traditional organisational analysis and systems design, and the workflow approach as described before. The case concerns a chemical company with major production plants in several European countries and a world-wide marketing and sales network (Morawetz *et al.*, 1991).

The company has undergone an organisational change which emphasises the business rather than the previous functional organisation. The company created three business units organised around its major product lines: functional chemicals, resins, and advanced materials. Each business unit is composed of manufacturing, marketing, sales, logistics, applications development and technical services. Along with these business units go three functional groups: research and development, operations, administration and finance. The importance of certain countries is reflected in the presence of their country managers in the company's strategic development activities.

The advanced materials business unit generates specific products and services in a value-driven approach to customer's problems and requests pursuing economies of scope. Processes for advanced materials are self-configuring and adapting to constantly changing situations. Advanced materials sells mainly differentiated products or, as they are called in the chemical industry, specialities. Several processes in the advanced materials branch are not covered by EDP applications. The customer's complaint is an example of processes without IT support. A company's complaint initiates the procedure *Product Performance Investigation Request* (PPIR) in the company. The process is actually supported by traditional communication channels (mail, telephone, etc.) and paper-based. The information flow of the PPIR process is shown in Figure 2-21. This diagram shows the structure of the process as it ideally takes place.

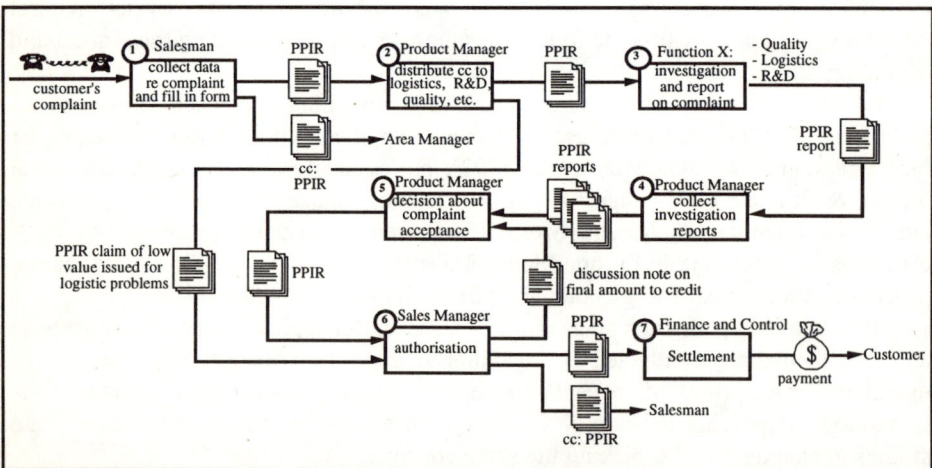

Figure 2-21: Information flow for customers' complaints in the Product Performance Investigation Request (PPIR) procedure

The salesman fills in the PPIR form which identifies whether it is a production or service complaint, or a customer relation issue with a critical or uncritical status. Additional information concerns customer and product specifications, possible complaint causes, the claimed quantity and the related invoice (activity 1 in Figure 2-21). This PPIR form is sent to the product manager Europe for advanced materials and a carbon copy also to other persons according to a distribution list, e.g. the area manager.

The product manager passes the form to the secretary who follows the procedure (activity 2 in Figure 2-21). The secretary sends a copy of the *Product Performance Investigation Request* to the respective responsible for possible faults as they are indicated by the salesman (logistics, R&D, quality, etc.). These persons have to investigate the customer's complaint and make a report expressing their diagnosis and corrective actions taken (activity 3 in Figure 2-21). This report is again passed to the product manager (activity 4 in Figure 2-21) who decides whether to accept or not the customer's complaint (activity 5 in Figure 2-21).

In the meantime the product manager can ask to withdraw all the claimed material or to take a standard sample out of the claimed batch. He sometimes discusses the importance of the customer for the resins business with the product manager for resins in order to have some more inputs for his future moves. The salesman might be asked for further information about the damage by the product manager.

The sales manager has to authorise the decision taken by the product manager (activity 6 in Figure 2-21) before the customer's claim can be reimbursed or a respective product delivered for the claim's settlement (activity 7 in Figure 2-21).

The closed procedure's documentation is sent to different persons in quality, logistics, sales, etc. according to a mailing list. There is also one person for every product to follow up complains in order to avoid continuing complains.

The procedure foresees a shortcut for low value complaints caused by logistical problems. In this case the product manager passes the *Product Performance Investigation Request* directly to the sales manager to authorise the settlement without activating the investigation.

The whole process lasts about one month and the division for advanced materials has about 50 complaints per year. The importance of the procedure does not consist in the total value but in the relation with a customer. Every damaged sack of material is as important as a contaminated or low quality product.

The company intended to develop an EDP-procedure to support the customers' complaints. This application followed mainly the information flow chart. The different actors involved in the process could write and read different fields of this database according to their organisational roles (salesmen, product manager, sales manager, etc.), geographical allocation and functional responsibilities (marketing, logistics, finance, etc.). The application reflected only the structured part of the process and was based on files which were saved on the mainframe.

The access rights for the new procedure have been defined. They foresaw a constant access for the product manager and limited access rights for all other persons directly involved or belonging to different functions. There are six status to identify the progress of the procedure:

1) the product manager has received the PPIR from the salesman
2) the PPIR is under inquiry by quality, logistics, R&D, etc.
3) the product manager is waiting for detailed information for defining the PPIR
4) the product manager is defining the PPIR
5) the PPIR has to be signed for settlement by the sales manager
6) the PPIR is closed, refused, etc.

The rational of this planned procedure is shown in Figure 2-21 without any reference to the question whether the different actions take place in reality to satisfy the customer who is complaining. No feedback links between the actors are shown. Thus, a fundamentally different diagram is needed corresponding to a fundamentally different view of the procedure discussed here. The main issue still to be addressed in the customers' complaints was to focus on *workflows* as a set of co-ordinated activities with the objective to produce customer satisfaction. The diagram needs to show for both, each actor and each action, how these actions are performed satisfactorily - as expected from actions concerning customer complaints. Thus, Figure 2-22 shows the current PPIR procedure as a workflow in the language/action perspective. It is based on a detailed analysis of the conversation flows in the advanced materials business. This analysis allowed to identify recurrent action workflows, the involved roles and actions to be done. Furthermore, in some instance the persons involved discuss generally their position or declare intentions for future actions. These communications between different roles are represented in the formal representation as declaration workflows. The existing phases of each workflow loop are represented in bold and grey arrows. The missing phases are indicated by a thin line where this is helpful to follow the conceptual flow; otherwise they are left blank. The representation of the workflow makes clearly evident that the PPIR procedure does not guarantee customer satisfaction.

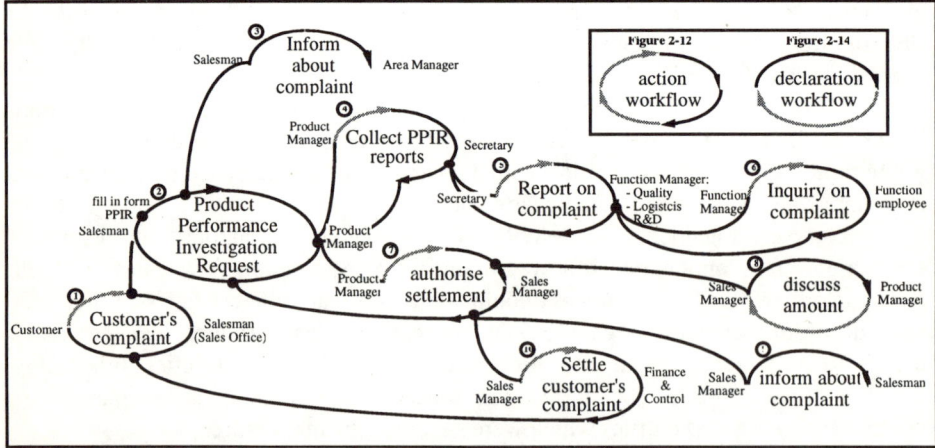

Figure 2-22: Conversation flows in the Product Performance Investigation Request (PPIR) procedure

The customer opens a relation with the salesman (workflow 1 in Figure 2-22). This relation, however, is not at all continued by the salesman. On the contrary, finance and control reports the possible settlement directly to the customer (return from workflow 10 in Figure 2-22). This leads to a difficult identification of the supplier for the customer; is it the salesman who listens to the complaint and takes notice of it, or is it finance and control who represents the organisation for the service delivery (settlement of damage)? This situation makes evident that processes have to be designed with a clear customer/supplier relation.

The salesman fills in the PPIR form and sends it to the area manager (workflow 2 in Figure 2-22). This information about complaints should induce a discussion about the implications and possible actions to undertake for recovery from a bad service in first place. This does not happen, because the monodirectional information flow of PPIR form to the area manager is seen as a bureaucratic action (workflow 3 in Figure 2-22).

Without having this fruitful discussion, the salesman sends the PPIR form to the product manager. Also this relation among the Salesman and his internal supplier, the product manager, remains without content (workflow 2 in Figure 2-22). The product manager uses the PPIR form to start the decisional process about faults and possible settlement of damage. However, also here the customer, i.e., the salesman, is not informed about the decision by his initial supplier, i.e., the product manager, but by the sales manager's authorisation (return from workflow 7 in Figure 2-22).

The most consistent customer/supplier relations are present in the PPIR investigation part. The secretary forwards the request for reports on the complaint on behalf of the product manager to the functional managers (workflow 5 in Figure 2-22) who delegate the inquiry to their staff (workflow 6 in Figure 2-22). Anyhow, the fourth closing phase is missing in all three workflows (workflow 4, 5 and 6).

The various shortcuts among workflows and roles lead to a situation where the mainly interested persons in the process, i.e., the salesman and the product manager, are the less involved roles. As a consequence, they do not know how the process evolves. The PPIR procedure is not centred on the external and internal customers and the completion of customer/supplier transactions, but on the PPIR form. This weakness of the PPIR procedure is not evident in the information flow diagram (see Figure 2-21).

Viewing the process in a business perspective in addition to the information process perspective gives more insight for shortcomings and possible improvements. This example makes the different process perspectives evident which have been discussed in chapter 2.4. A comparison of the two diagrams (Figure 2-21 and Figure 2-22) shows the fundamental differences of the two views. Figure 2-21 shows the ideal structure which resembles the linking of activities and data (in a certain sense the linking of machines). Figure 2-22 resembles reality more closely dealing with processes involving people. Software concepts modelled to support such processes are to be based on analysis and evaluation of such different views (and diagrams). These different views shape the software structure through all different layers of programs as shown by Tschiersch (1994). The system development and implementation in the

48   Chapter 2

case studies of chapters 5 and 6 are based on the second type of view - concentrating on people and not on data and activities.

In addition to the different view on processes, existing processes are improved by business process re-engineering. Figure 2-23 shows a re-engineered version of the customer complaints process. The main change concerns the fact that all workflows are closed. This makes clear who has what kind of relation and responsibility with other persons involved, i.e., as customers and suppliers. The same persons are customers for some workflows, while they are suppliers for others. The whole process is focused on the main customers who are the salesman as an *internal customer* (workflow 2 in Figure 2-23), and the company's *customer* as an *external customer* (workflow 1 in Figure 2-23).

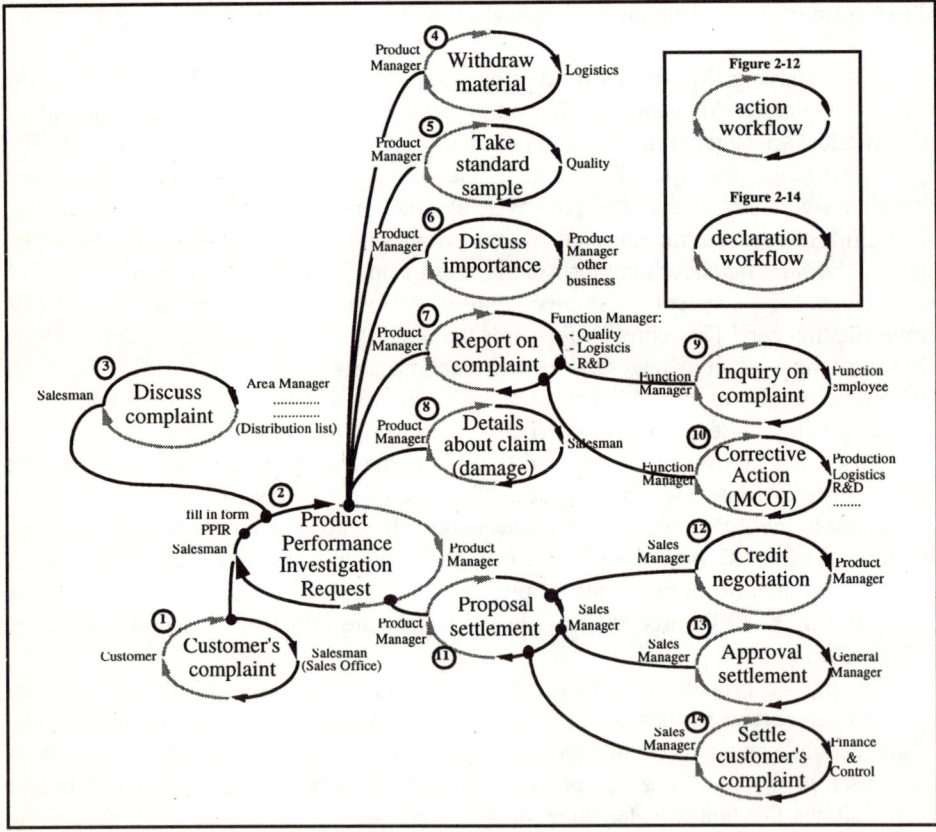

Figure 2-23: Workflow with completed customer/supplier relations to handle customer complaints

In this chapter the concept of *business process re-engineering* has been introduced. The focus on *business processes* supports the change from functional into process organisations. The analysis and design of *business processes* has been proposed as *co-operative workflows* modelling *customer/supplier relations* in the *language/action perspective*. For understanding the business dimension in process re-engineering, the differences between material, information and business processes have been outlined. The concept has been shown comparing data-flow diagrams with workflows in a case history for customer complaints in a chemical company. The illustration will be followed up in detail on business processes in training and financial services in chapter 5 and 6.

The following chapter discusses different approaches to co-operative work to understand the support requirements for computer systems. The subsequent chapter 4 introduces a specific computer support for co-operative work, i.e., workflow management technology.

3. Analysis and design of co-operative networks

This chapter introduces concepts of co-operative work and how it can be supported by computer systems. These concepts are related to the interdisciplinary research field of *Computer Supported Cooperative Work* (CSCW). The description of co-operative work and the design of computer support is an open research question in CSCW. This research wants to contribute to the field of CSCW with a taxonomy for co-operative work and deducted support requirements.

The scope of this chapter is to define co-operative work by different dimensions, i.e., as *co-ordination, collaboration* and *co-decision*. In addition, different dynamics in co-operative work are described (*co-operation in the small* versus *co-operation in the large*). On the basis of the set *taxonomy* for *co-operative networks functional requirements* for support systems are deducted. Beside specific functional requirements, *two general dimension of design* to support co-operative work are introduced (*activity synchronisation* and *information sharing*). These dimensions and requirements define a *service portfolio* to support co-operative networks. The research concentrates in the following chapters on one of the four support issues in the portfolio: *workflows* for *communication* in *domain services*.

The concepts for the analysis and design of co-operative networks are applied to two preliminary cases conducted for this research. Case history 3 explores the analysis of co-operative networks in software engineering. The following case history 4 shows the dynamics of co-operative networks for the example of working processes in the European Space Agency. The concepts of this chapter will be further applied in the extended case studies of chapter 5 and 6. This chapter prepares also the basis for discussion of the specific computer systems of workflow management technology, introduced in chapter 4 and applied in chapter 5 and 6.

Before defining co-operative networks, the overall importance of co-operation in work setting is explained in the first paragraph. In addition, co-operative work is defined in relation to work processes producing products or services.

3.1. The social organisation of work

Why do people co-operate? Why are processes performed co-operatively? Why spend the inevitable overhead cost of co-operation in terms of labour, resources and time for the joint effort of multiple persons? The obvious justification for incurring this overhead cost is that workers could not accomplish the task in question if they were to do it individually (Schmidt & Bannon, 1992). This is one point of view, which states that the individuals need co-operation in order to do what is expected from them.

In addition, work is seen as always socially organised. This implies a co-operative nature from a sociological perspective (Schmidt, 1990; 1991b; Hughes et al., 1991). The German discussion in sociology of work on the concept of co-operative work has in its core the notion of *interdependence of work* (Popitz et al., 1957; Dahrendorf, 1959; Kern & Schumann, 1970). *Social organisation of work* thus does not imply that people in a working process are mutually dependent on the activities of others; therefore they might not directly conceive the interdependency, but in any case their activities are connected by some *mechanisms of interaction* (shared resources, co-ordinated tasks, planned schedule, time dependency, division of labour, etc.). In co-operative work settings, people apply various *mechanisms of interaction* to reduce the complexity, and hence, the overhead costs of articulation of work, e.g., by:

- *organisational structures* in formal (explicit, statutory, legally enforceable) and less formal (implicit, traditional) allocation of resources, rights and responsibilities within the co-operative ensemble;
- *plans* and *schedules* e.g., such as master schedules and kanban systems in manufacturing companies;
- *standard operating procedures*; and
- *conceptual schemes*, e.g., such as thesauruses and taxonomies for indexing or classifying information objects which are manipulated by multiple persons (Schmidt & Bannon, 1992).

Furthermore, the co-operative workers have to articulate (divide, allocate, co-ordinate, schedule, mesh, interrelate, etc.) their distributed individual activities. Because of these interdependencies any process necessitates a number of secondary activities for maintaining, mediating and controlling the co-operative relationships (Schmidt & Bannon, 1992). In this social organisation, work is carried out by individuals in a complex interaction with others.

Hughes et al. (1991) argue that *all work is socially organised*. The problem in understanding the social organisation of work is only how to describe it. Hughes et al. (1991) take an extreme point of view claiming that:

> 'it may therefore make sense, as one approach to the analysis of work [...], to consider the ways in which work processes are 'individuated' - that is, translated into things that persons can do.' (Hughes et al., 1991: 311)

This argument is extremely critical with task analysis as developed and practised in Human-Computer Interaction (HCI) and related fields (e.g., Moran, 1981; Sébillotte, 1988). Such task analysis starts at a point where tasks are already individuated activities. Tasks are described in more or less detail/levels by a top-down model. The analytical task models likely miss the co-operative sense of the organisation of work, i.e., the overall relation of people doing tasks. The limits of task analysis in relation to co-operative work are discussed in more detail by Schäl & Shapiro (1992).

But what is co-operative work about in organisations? Is there a way to define co-operative work in the general setting of social life? Schmidt (1990) distinguishes co-operative work from social interaction at work in general by relating it to *content* and to *production*. Schmidt argues that co-operative work in real world settings requires some organisational form and does not occur by accidental relations:

> 'Cooperative work [...] is constituted by *work processes that are related as to content*, that is, processes pertaining to the production of a particular product or type of products. Cooperative work, then, is a far more specific concept than social interactionn in the system of work in general. The concept pertains to the sphere of production. It does not apply to every social encounter occurring during business hours, nor does it apply to every interaction pertaining to the running of, say, a company.' (Schmidt, 1990: 10)

The author extends the definition given by Schmidt (1990) for co-operative work also to the production of *services*. The main point for agreeing with Schmidt is the fact that *organisations exist because they produce something for customers* (products or services does not make a difference for the co-operative nature of work). Thus, the following definition can be derived.

Definition: Co-operative Work
Co-operative work is constituted by work processes pertaining to the production of a particular product, or type of products, or services.

The assumption that co-operative ensembles are generally *groups* is doubtful, in particular for the notion of a *shared goal*. The notion of group work does not encompass the rich and complex reality of co-operative work. As already pointed out by Popitz *et al.* (1957), the group is not the specific unit of co-operation in modern industrial plants. Here, co-operation is typically *mediated by complex machine systems* and often does not involve *direct communication* between agents. Instead, agents often co-operate via a more or less common *information space* without direct communication and not necessarily knowing each other or even knowing of each other (Schmidt, 1990). Co-operating ensembles are sometimes a *transient formation*, while in other cases they assume the character of a *stable formation*. Co-operative relations become stable because of the requirements of work being done.

First, the *task* or the *commitment* itself maybe a *continuous or recurrent phenomenon*.

Second, the *work environment* and the technical and human *resources* available at a given time may be relatively stable.

Third, *domain knowledge* is required and must be acquired by means of *participation* in the work process.

Forth, stable co-operative work patterns may arise from the *economics of co-operative work*, because the *overhead costs* for articulating co-operative work relations may be reduced by entering stable relations for co-operation (Schmidt, 1990).

* * *

This paragraph has shown that the phenomena of co-operative work is always present and has been discussed in sociology for a long time. A definition for co-operative work was given here; this definition is set in relation to Computer Supported

Cooperative Work (CSCW) in the next paragraph. The origin and historical development of field of CSCW which emerged less than 10 years ago, is explained.

3.2 Computer Supported Cooperative Work

3.2.1 The history of CSCW and groupware

The decade of the 1980s saw a massive rise in the importance of personal computing which was followed by a trend towards networking all the end-computing devices. As a result, there was a growing awareness of the possibility to work together over the networked infrastructure. Furthermore, the discovery of new possibilities by users generated a demand for specific applications which support group activities.

This was the context for the birth of the area of *Computer Supported Cooperative Work* (CSCW). The term CSCW was used to describe the topic of the interdisciplinary workshop in 1984, intending to discuss on how to support people in their work arrangements with computers (Greif, 1988). Irene Greif and Paul Cashman coined the initials CSCW. Greif and Cashman did not intend any special definition of a new field, but referred to a set of concerns about supporting multiple individuals working together with computer systems. The meaning of the individual words in the term were not especially highlighted (Bannon & Schmidt, 1989). Since then CSCW has emerged as a new interdisciplinary forum for research into the issues central to the design, implementation and use of technical systems which support people working co-operatively (Bannon *et al.*, 1991).

After the first successful workshop, a number of conferences have been held in the United States of America, Canada and Europe (CSCW, 1986; 1988; 1990; 1992; 1994; ECSCW, 1989; 1991; 1993). Beside the alternating European and American conferences there is a growing number of events with specific CSCW interest (e.g. IFIP8.4, 1990; COSCIS, 1991; IFIP8.5, 1992; COOCS, 1991; 1993; 1995; GROUPWARE, 1992; 1993; 1994; APPLICA, 1993).

Four years after the first workshop in relation to the second CSCW conference, Greif (1988b) defines CSCW in a book of readings on the topic as computer support for group work. The idea of *group* as the main unit to focus on is common to several approaches in CSCW and directly related to the term *groupware*, i.e., software for groups. Johansen (1988) defines groupware as:

> 'a generic term for specialised computer aids that are designed for the use of collaborative work groups. Typically, these groups are small project-oriented teams that have important tasks and tight deadlines. Groupware can involve software, hardware, services and/or group process support.' (Johansen, 1988)

Some groupware definitions take a workspace-oriented view where groupware is a support for people engaged in a common task by an interface to a shared environment (Ellis *et al.*, 1991). Groupware is often regarded as the technology-driven development of applications which represent a natural extension of software for workstations interconnected via a local area network, a development of *Office Automation* ideas and a significant extension to *Office Information Systems* (De

Michelis, 1990). Examples of existing applications with groupware features are *co-authoring systems* and *shared group calendars*. Another term related to the field of CSCW is *Workgroup Computing* which refers to the support provided by networked micro-computers. The author agrees with the definition given by Bannon & Schmidt (1989).

> **Definition: Computer Supported Cooperative Work**
> *Computer Supported Cooperative Work (CSCW) is an identifiable research field focused on the understanding of nature and characteristics of co-operative work with the objective of designing adequate computer based technologies to support such co-operative work.*

This definition focuses on the understanding of *co-operative* in order to support the work by taking into consideration the results gained in the design process. This research follows the idea of understanding first the nature of co-operative work with the final objective of designing computer support.

3.2.2 The role of computing in CSCW

Information systems play an important role in modern organisations; private and public organisations have always spent huge amounts of money on information systems: first in *mainframes*, then in *on-line computing* facilities and nowadays in *personal computing*. Nearly all this expenditure is made to manage information because there is a persisting perception that *controlling data* means controlling the private or public organisation's destiny. Most companies and public administrations have created EDP-centres, data-processing groups, information management systems and other constructs which are born around the idea of *information* to be managed and administered. All technology being bought and developed revolves around the same paradigm: hardware, software and networks are designed and optimised around *managing data* (Schäl, 1992).

But there is a missing perspective: organisations do not run on information, they run on *relationships*. Information is only exchanged within these relationships and determines the final result or the organisation, i.e., customer satisfaction. Unfortunately, most organisations have created information systems which do good information management (store and retrieve data), but do not support these manifold relationships.

The concept of *information to be managed* has to be replaced by *communication* and *information sharing* in order to reflect the fact that organisations are based on co-operative work and serve customers by satisfying their needs.

The necessity for rethinking the use of information technology is also shown by the findings of the MIT program 'Management in the '90s' that *investments in information technology do not guarantee success* (Scott-Morton, 1991). Instead, the expenditure in technology has to be aligned with strategies and the behaviour of the whole system. Information technology is embedded in more and more areas of the organisation, but not yet embedded in the business process management. It has developed from a long period when technology was risky and too often did not work, into a situation where we have more technology than we know how to use. It is shifting from:

> 'a tradition of computing, where telecommunication was an add-on, to integrated technology platforms, where telecommunication provides the highway system into which computing applications fit.' (Keen, 1991: 236)

At the same time, information systems can become an integral part of the strategic choice to re-design public and private organisations as a process-organised service provider.

The classic support provided by information systems to procedures in big organisations is *transaction processing*. Since the sixties, *electronic data processing* (EDP) has tried to automate and rationalise organisational processes and to manage the related data.

The counterpart to rigid transaction processing and mainframe applications was *personal computing* which has been successful since the late seventies. A number of flexible and individually usable applications have been developed. Especially professionals appreciated the use of word processors, spreadsheets, drawing applications and others. The main concern of personal computing was not the treatment of data, but of information as being the interpretation of data (e.g., by using spreadsheets) and the creation of documents (e.g., by using word processors which might integrate graphs, tables and other imported sources). The information is, however, kept *atomistic*.

The two worlds (mainframe-based transaction processing and personal computing) have shown big problems in coming together. They often still exist as two separated domains of computing. In addition, computer systems have not explicitly been designed to support co-operative work. Large-scale systems have primarily been concerned with optimising the highly structured procedures within organisations (transaction processing). Desktop systems for individual users have concentrated on personal productivity (De Michelis, 1990).

A new type of products and applications is emerging which fit in between the two levels of single-user applications (personal computing) and organisation-wide systems (transaction processing). Developments in the field of CSCW might become the glue for the traditionally separate aspects of computing in work settings (Schäl, 1992). This vision is represented in Figure 3-1.

Each ring represents one focus of computer development and of the principle customer or user of the resulting product. The outer ring represents *entire systems designed to serve organisational goals*. The inner ring represents *applications designed for individual users*. The middle ring represents *groupware, designed with groups in mind*. The middle ring is the focus of CSCW, but the field has also to interface with the previously existing rings or even integrate them into a more general view of computer technology.

Of course, at the same time previous information technology did also in some sense support certain groups in organisations. What has changed is that groupware is *designed with the explicit intention of supporting groups*. However, some people

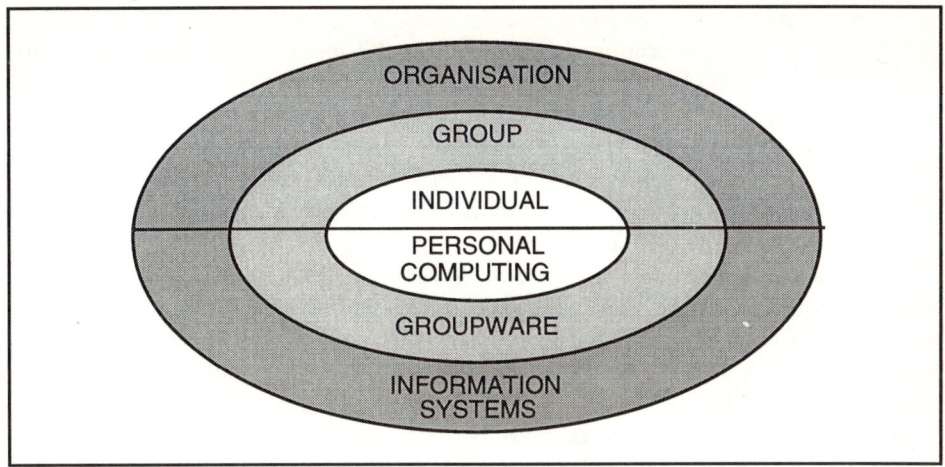

Figure 3-1: CSCW in the contexts of organisations, groups and individuals (from Grudin, 1994: 94)

still approach CSCW with a prior focus on large organisational systems and user organisations, while others still concentrate on single user applications (Grudin, 1991; 1991b; 1994). As explained before, one can allocate CSCW as a new field of research and development which relates to the area of software tools for managers and professionals. Are groupware tools creating a discontinuity with respect to the traditional well known personal computing tools most people use on their work-stations?

From one point of view, CSCW appears as a radical innovation with respect to previous approaches to *office automation* and *personal computing*. New theories of management and organisation have accompanied and founded its early developments, opening a debate, within the CSCW field and outside of it, that is still alive; most of the groupware tools which have been designed and developed in the last five years, appear radically new.

From another point of view, CSCW can be considered as an evolution of both *office automation* and *professional computing*, characterised by the conditions required to promote substantial research and development in the CSCW area:
• computation is so inexpensive that virtually all members of groups can afford to use computers;
• the technological infrastructure supports communication and information sharing, notably networks and software running over them;
• widespread familiarity with computers allows for a sufficient number of groups that are willing and able to try the software (Grudin, 1989; 1994).

The basic components for groupware tools are word-processors, data-bases, electronic mails, etc., as any office tool we have ever seen. The strength of the CSCW field relies on its ability to generate both new tools and new ways of using traditional tools. This development opens also a new space to support persons working together by increasing their threshold of sustainable complexity (De Michelis, 1996). This has a particular relevance, as it defines a limit which cannot be overcome through organisational means. CSCW systems might enhance the threshold of sustainable complexity of a co-operative ensemble as other technology improved the strength of men. By augmenting the physical and information processing power of the individual worker, technical innovations may dramatically reduce the need for and the scope of co-operative arrangements required to perform a given task. Thus one man, when equipped with a bulldozer, is capable of removing loads far beyond the capacity of an individual or even a handful of individuals equipped with shovels (Schmidt, 1990).

The time and place matrix in Figure 3-2 (Johansen, 1988, Johansen *et al.*, 1991), appears frequently in the CSCW literature to describe the approaches taken so far in the design of tools. The quadrants, however, can help to divide technologies and types of (individual and) co-operative work, rather than to support them in an integrated way. With the distinction of tools and situations represented in the matrix, users are left switching from work mode to work mode and from tool-set to tool-set, rather than moving smoothly from situation to situation and from need to need within an integrated co-operative environment (Hartfield & Graves, 1991). This requirement for CSCW systems has also been deduced from social studies on multitasking and channel switching (Reder & Schwab, 1988; 1990), and from technical work (Bignoli *et al.*, 1991; Agostini *et al.*, 1993; De Michelis, 1996; Schmidt & Rodden, 1993). Hartfield & Graves (1991) state that a CSCW system has to provide support for a continues transition between individual work and group work.

De Michelis (1996) argues for the main requirement of supporting the switching from routines to conversations within working processes, integrating different communication media:

> 'A CSCW Environment should support, without loosing effectiveness at the procedural level, a natural and immediate switch from the first system into the other one, and vice-versa, to accompany the user while his/her attention switches from the routine to the solution of the occurred breakdown.' (De Michelis, 1996: 17)

Therefore technology has to be capable to support co-operation in its manifold articulation and situations. The specific requirements and functionality for such a technology to support co-operative work are elaborated in this chapter. However, before looking at specific technical systems, the concept of co-operative work is developed as co-operative networks in the next paragraph. Subsequently, requirements are derived to enhance and support co-operative networks.

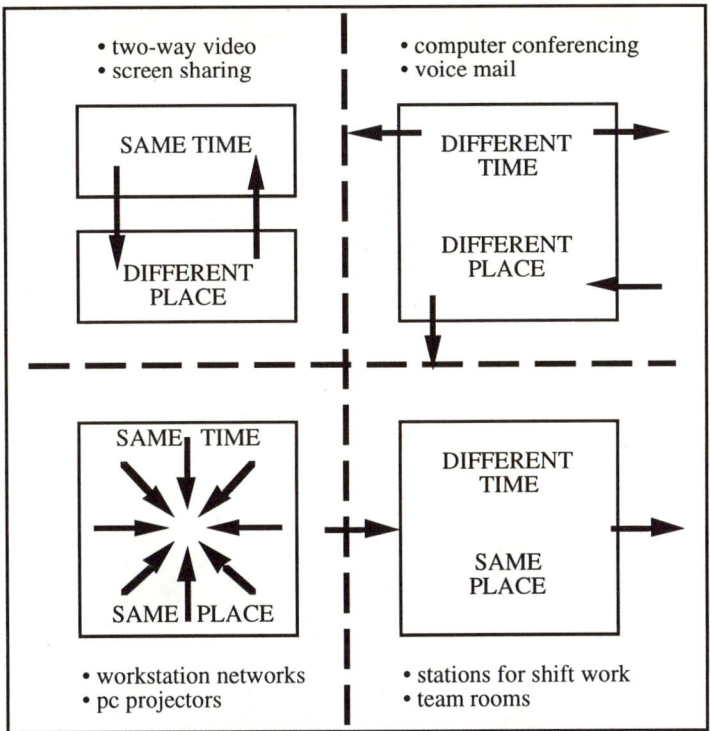

Figure 3-2: The 4-square map for groupware options
(from Johansen et al., 1991: 16)

3.3 Co-operative networks

3.3.1 Definition and components of co-operative networks

Supporting co-operation by computers requires a sound understanding of co-operation and recognition of the different spaces for design. For this aim, it is useful to investigate the forms assumed by the interactions among its members, critical situations in co-operation, the different nature of co-operative settings in relation to the permanent organisation, etc.

The concept of *co-operative network* is introduced to describe co-operative settings and ensembles. Developments in the systematic analysis of interactions in groups and organisations coming from the field of *network analysis* (Burt, 1982; Knoke & Kuklinski, 1982; Burt & Minor, 1983; Rice & Richards, 1985) are used for describing co-operative networks. Rice & Richards (1985) phrase the definition for network analysis as follows:

> 'The goal of network analysis is to obtain from low-level or raw relational data higher level descriptions of a system. The higher-level descriptions identify various kinds of patterns, or test hypothesis about those patterns, in a set of

relationships. These patterns will be based upon the way individuals and objects interrelate in a network [...].' (Rice & Richards, 1985: 106)

The analytical techniques in network analysis are *entirely independent* of the *subject matter* or the *context* to be assessed. This means that it can also be adopted to describe the phenomena of co-operative work. A network is defined by nodes and connections. *Nodes* can be individuals, offices, documents, machines or any other point capable of participating in a relationship to other points or combination of points. *Connections* can likewise take virtually any form that the analyst can define to be meaningful. This provides, of course, flexibility and power. In our case connections will be used for relations in co-operation. Figure 3-3 shows the principle elements of a network: nodes and connections.

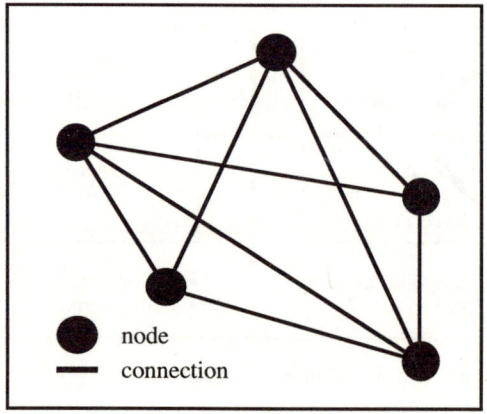

Figure 3-3: Nodes and connections constituting a network

A distinction is generally made between *positional analysis* (the assessment of positions which individuals or units hold in a social structure) and *relational analysis* (the assessment of interactions among those units) (Burt, 1982). The two models of analysis are complementary, but not overlapping; this means, that both are of help in gaining an appreciation of network structure, but they describe rather different things about how the network is put together.

As already noted, network analysis makes no a priori assumptions about what nodes and relationships might be. The analyst must define the *nature of the behaviour* which is of interest, the level of *aggregation* of that behaviour (across time and units) which is meaningful, the level of *interaction* necessary to constitute a significant relationship, and the *bounds* to be placed on the system under investigation. *Bounds, nodes, connection* and *behaviour* describe a *social network*. For the description of *co-operative networks*, four similar dimensions are introduced. Co-operative networks are described by *commitment, nodes, relation,* and *articulation*. The final scope is to identify *types of co-operation (co-ordination, collaboration* and *co-decision)* (De Michelis, 1990; 1996; De Michelis *et al.*, 1992; Schäl & Zeller, 1990) as co-operative networks in an organisation. This is accomplished by using indicators which show the most significant components (*commitment*, *nodes*, *relation* and *articulation*) of a co-operative network. The mapping of dimensions of network analysis and the adoption for co-operative networks is shown in Table 3-1.

Table 3-1: Dimensions of network analysis and the description of co-operative networks

Dimensions of Network Analysis	Components of a Co-operative Network
bounds	commitment
nodes	nodes
connection	relation
behaviour	articulation

Each co-operative network has a clear distinction with the rest of the world, both if it is steady in time as an office, and if it is temporary as a project team. It can be characterised by means of the *commitments* its members take one with another, and with persons not belonging to it. A co-operative network is, therefore, a collection of (completed and taken) commitments among its members and with the customer of the network's product. Commitments made and already completed define the organisational structure of the co-operative setting - in particular its members' *roles* and *responsibilities*. The roles of its members are defined in language, through the commitments they satisfy. The commitments already taken, on the other hand, contribute to the definition of the ensemble members' agenda, in terms of things to be done. Definitions for co-operative networks and the single components of co-operative networks are given as follows.

> **Definition: Co-operative network**
> *A co-operative network is defined by the pattern of commitments its members make among each other and with third parties, the roles its members play, the relation among its members of synchronisation or sharing, and the articulation of work characterising the networks behaviour.*

Commitments defining the bounds of co-operative networks

The *commitment* defines the *bounds* of a co-operative network. A *commitment* characterises a unit of work, i.e., a task, a set of related tasks, a process, with the final scope of a future action (the output of the co-operative network). This future action can be a *realisation* (a *product* or a *service*) or a *decision*, i.e., a new *possibility 'to be'* (e.g., new organisation, new structure, new business, new responsibility). There has to be a *customer* (internal or external) for each *realisation*, who defines the *customer satisfaction* for the *commitment*. The *decision* is defined by a *commitment* which will be expressed as an *explicit agreement*, i.e., a *conclusive declaration*. Every node necessary to achieve the commitment is part of the network. The achievement of the commitment can be more or less complex. The complexity depends, e.g., on the impact of a commitment on the overall organisation (company, division, office, group, etc.), its value (strategic, economical, etc.) and its risk (costs, return on investment, time, etc.).

Definition: Commitment
A commitment is a unit of work with the final scope of satisfying the customer of a co-operative network by its future realisation or decision of a certain complexity. The commitment defines the bounds of the co-operative network.

Nodes playing different roles in a co-operative network

Nodes can be *virtual units* (i.e., persons constituting an organisational unit) or *individuals*. A node co-operates with other nodes in the co-operative network within a commitment. As already noted, positional analysis assesses *roles* in *social structures* and the *equivalencies* among *roles* held by individual roles; relational analysis examines the *connections* between nodes and defines certain *properties* of individuals. Both types of analysis to describe nodes and their relation with other nodes in a co-operative network are used. Figure 3-4 shows a co-operative network with different nodes (a manager, three performers and an archivist), being connected by different relations (synchronisation and sharing).

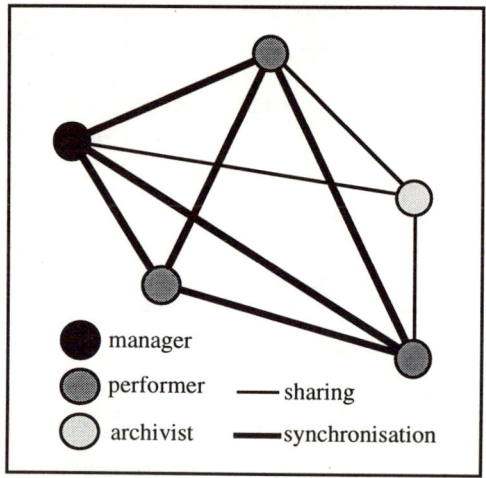

Figure 3-4: Nodes and relations in a co-operative network

Different roles are defined by the communicative behaviour of people managing their daily work (Mackay, 1988), and choosing communication channels (Reder & Schwab, 1988). Nodes are characterised according to Malone *et al.* (1987) by the different roles of *archivists, managers and performers* which they play in the network. Nodes are defined by their *communication roles* and *communication management*. Nodes can play *informative, operative* and *co-ordinative roles*, and apply different criteria for *archiviation, execution* and *delegation* for communication management. This differentiation depend on how nodes manage their *personal commitments* in the overall commitment (by *delegation* or *execution*), how they manage *information* (author, owner, administrator, co-administrator, co-author, user, reviser, reader, proof-reader, etc.), and their *audience* (vertical or horizontal).

> **Definition: Node**
> *Nodes are virtual units or individuals participating in a commitment as archivists, managers or performers.*

Relation of nodes in a co-operative network

The relation of nodes in a co-operative network is characterised either as synchronisation (e.g., of actions, time, space, etc.) or as sharing (e.g., of information, culture, knowledge, etc.). The relation can have a high or low variance (e.g., for reciprocity, motivation, qualification, etc.) within the commitment (see Figure 3-4).

> **Definition: Relation**
> *A relation connects nodes in a co-operative network by synchronisation or sharing within different degrees of variance among nodes participating in the commitment.*

Articulation defining the behaviour of co-operative networks

The *behaviour* of the network is expressed by the *articulation* being adopted or necessary to produce the commitment. The *articulation* depends on the *degree of structuredness* and on the number of units in the commitment. The final product or service can be *composed* of a series of identifiable components. Otherwise, it is unique without an internal structure. In addition, the commitment can be structured by time, space, specialisation, competence, etc.

> **Definition: Articulation of co-operative networks**
> *The articulation of a co-operative network is defined by the structuredness and composition of the commitment.*

Having defined co-operative networks and how to characterise them, the next paragraph introduces different types of co-operative work. The three distinct types of co-operation (co-ordination, collaboration and co-decision) can be isolated by applying a model built on the characteristics introduced in this paragraph. The model to characterise co-operative networks is presented in the subsequent paragraph.

3.3.2 Basic distinctions for co-operative work

Different types of co-operation have to be identified in order to distinguish different co-operative settings. Within a single organisation, there will be several types of co-operative work (De Michelis, 1990; 1996; De Michelis *et al.*, 1992; Schäl & Zeller, 1990). During the course of a process, three types of co-operation (*co-ordination, collaboration* and *co-decision*) may be needed. De Michelis (1996) distinguishes furthermore co-decision into two forms, one with equal and another with distinct roles. The three types of co-operation are briefly described as follows.

Co-ordination

Co-ordination is the first type of co-operation. Persons co-ordinate their activities to achieve a final outcome of a co-operative process. Everybody acts in a more or less planned and recognisable manner to the process according to skill, role and other specific attributes.

> **Definition: Co-ordination**
> *Co-ordination is a co-operative process where individuals need to co-ordinate their actions with those of others. Actions of individuals gives meaning to the action of others and the others' actions contribute to an individual action.*

The main problem in co-ordination is the *synchronisation* of persons, actions and the consistency of the individual actions with respect to the whole process. Therefore successful co-ordination depends also on breaking down the process into appropriate component actions.

Collaboration

The second type of co-operation is *collaboration*. It means to work together in the execution of a certain action. Collaboration requires, by contrast to co-ordination, individuals to work together in order to achieve a single common goal or result.

> **Definition: Collaboration**
> *Collaboration is a co-operative process where individuals need to work together in the execution of a certain action to produce a final product. At the end of the collaborative process the single contribution of individuals cannot be isolated because the final product is an entity as the unified result of all individual contributions of the co-operative ensemble.*

The success of collaboration depends on the contribution made by individuals to generate a *shared knowledge*. The success of collaboration depends also on having a common understanding of the goal and of the process for achieving it.

Co-decision

The third type of co-operation is *co-decision*, where the individuals contribute to take a joint decision. The decision can be taken by *equals* (all participants have the same qualification and position in the decision process) or by persons of *different status* (each person participates in the decision on the basis of his/her specific role). Credibility assessment, creating a common understanding and sharing a common knowledge, are important aspects in co-decision processes which, therefore, in general are similar to collaboration. Also the co-decision process frequently cannot be split into individual contributions because it is a result of the mutual inference among the participants' heuristics and decisional models.

Definition: Co-decision
Co-decision is a co-operative process where individuals need to take a joint decision. At the end of the co-decisional process the single contribution of individuals cannot be isolated because the final decision is the result of all individual contributions of the co-operative ensemble.

When considering tools for supporting co-operative work, it is important to understand that the three principal types of co-operation need different types of support. Therefore, information systems have to be designed according to the organisation of labour and the co-operative activities which they should support. This requirement is discussed in detail later in this chapter. The model to understand the three types of co-operative work is described in the following paragraph.

3.3.3 The model to characterise co-operative networks

In this paragraph the strategy to analyse an organisational setting in terms of co-operative networks is described. The strategy comprises the theoretical framework derived before. The four components (*commitment, nodes, relation* and *articulation* as defined above) are sufficient to describe a co-operative network. There are different types of co-operative networks, reflecting the types of co-operation given before (*co-ordination, collaboration* and *co-decision*). In addition to these three pure types of co-operative networks, there can be two mixed types of co-operative networks (*collaboration/co-ordination, co-decision/co-ordination*). This is the case when collaboration or co-decision is mixed with co-ordination over time or space, or when the complexity of a co-ordination-type network requires collaboration or co-decision. There cannot be collaboration mixed with co-decision, because the commitment determines a realisation (then collaboration) or a decision (then co-decision). As a consequence, we have 5 possible syntheses for co-operative networks based on the attributes of the four components. The model to analyse co-operative networks is shown in Figure 3-5.

The model can be used for different purposes. A first application is to describe (analyse) the type of co-operation occurring in a given situation. The coherence of an actual network with the ideal attributes for a desired co-operative network can be checked as a second possibility in a diagnostic use of the model. The presence of enharmonic indicators represents a possible space for action and design (organisational re-design, training or technical support). Indicators for co-operative networks and its components are elaborated according to the structure in Figure 3-5 which allows to calculate synthetic indexes at different levels.

The model to characterise co-operative networks will be applied to understand the type of co-operation present in the two case studies in chapter 5 and 6. A preliminary case history of its application is presented in the following paragraph for co-operative networks in software engineering.

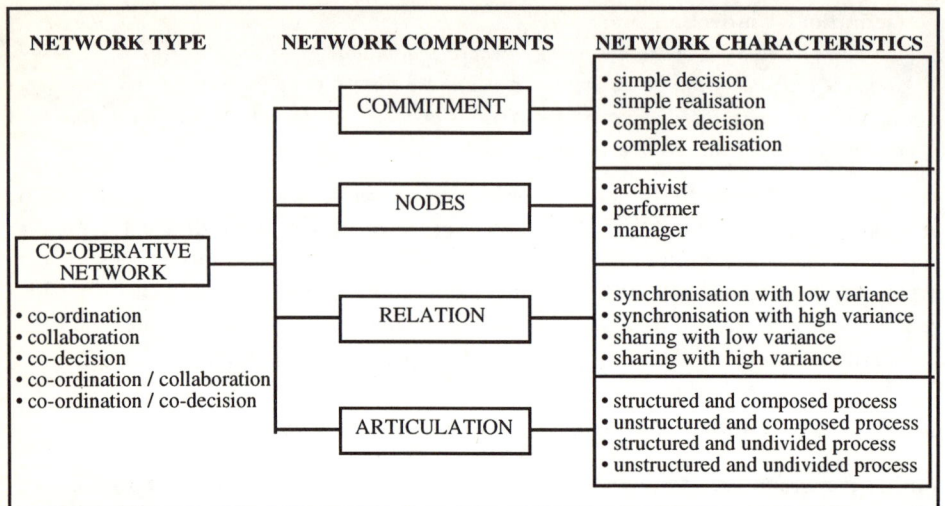

Figure 3-5: Types, components and characteristics of co-operative networks

Case history 3: Analysis of co-operative networks in software engineering

This case history presents the application of the basic concepts of the model to analyse co-operative networks in a medium-sized Italian company which develops telecommunication systems and provides network services for Italian banks (Schäl & Zeller, 1992). The company has ca. 250 employees working especially on feasibility studies, design, development and maintenance of telecommunication systems and services.

The model for co-operative networks was applied to analyse and improve communication management concerning a workgroup in a software project. Two phases of a software project were analysed as independent co-operative networks. These were the first phase of a developing project for a complex technical system, the *feasibility study* (preliminary studies, feasibility studies and approval) and the second phase of the project, the *realisation* (functional and technical analysis, development, internal and external test).

During a first step of the application, the model for co-operative networks has been developed. The top management and directors supported the proposed approach. Subsequently, the two project managers and all persons involved in the project were interviewed. The relation among nodes and the articulation of co-operation among individuals are summarised in Table 3-2.

The *feasibility study* of the software project is mainly characterised by *collaboration* with limited *problems of co-ordination*. This synthetic consideration results from the following facts:

Table 3-2: Analysed phases and components to define types of co-operative networks in a software engineering project

Phase of the software engineering project	Feasibility Study	Realisation
Commitment	complex realisation	complex realisation
Nodes	manager: FAT1, FAT6 performer: FAT4, FAT8 archivist: FAT1, FAT2, FAT5, FAT7 (see Fig. 3-6 & 3-7)	R1– R22 (for details see Fig. 3-8 & 3-9)
Relation	sharing with high variance	synchronisation with low variance
Articulation	medium structured and composed process	highly structured and composed process
Network type	collaboration + co-ordination	co-ordination + collaboration

- The *feasibility study* is a *complex realisation* of a fairly *composed product*, although there is only a medium *structured process* involved in the activities. The relation among people involved is of *great variance* and it is based on their capacity to *share competencies and information*.
- The persons' roles and activities are mainly oriented to information management. Information is also the source and final result of the *feasibility study*. The communication channels of the co-operative network are, besides *telephone*, especially *meetings, internal mail* and *secretariats* (offices). The basis of information produced and used are *working papers* and *minutes* of meetings. Most of the persons perform the roles of *co-administrators/co-authors* or *revisers/proof-readers* concerning these information resources.
- The roles of people does not show a homogeneous distribution. There are some cases of concentrated co-ordinative (i.e., roles FAT3 and FAT6 in Figure 3-6) or operative roles (i.e., roles FAT4 and FAT8 in Figure 3-6). This might be a problem for a collaborative network because a symmetric relation should be assumed among the various nodes in a collaborative network. However, the communication management analysis in Figure 3-7 shows a more even situation. This means that people use communication criteria independent from their communication roles.

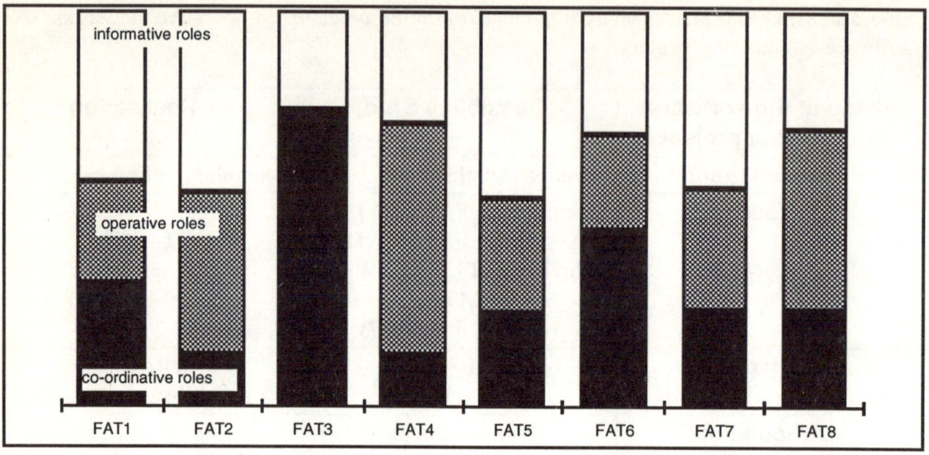

[Figure showing stacked bar chart with informative roles, operative roles, co-ordinative roles for FAT1-FAT8]

Figure 3-6: Roles in the 'feasibility study'[2]

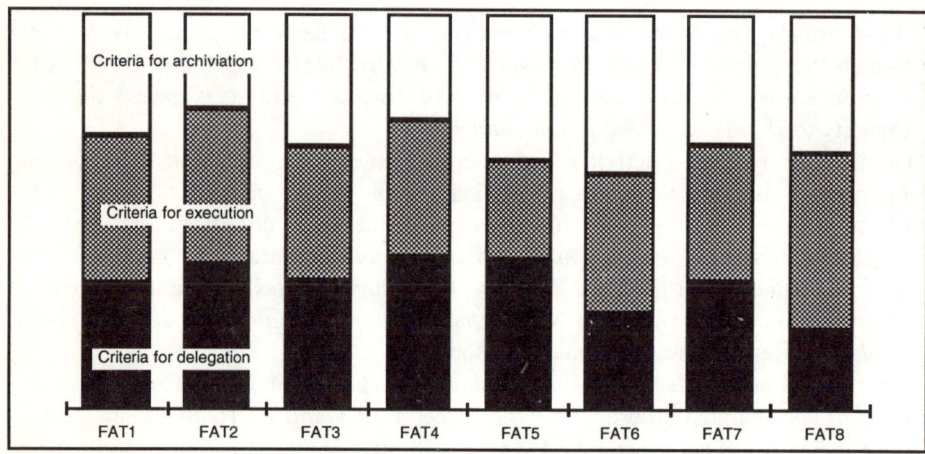

Figure 3-7: Communication management in the 'feasibility study'[3]

---

[2] The figure shows on the x-axis the 8 persons involved in the 'feasibility study'. They are represented by 'FAT1' to 'FAT8'. One can see on the y-axis the relative individual distribution of informative, operative and co-ordinative roles for every person and the general distribution of these roles in the project.

[3] The figure shows on the x-axis the 8 persons involved in the 'feasibility study' corresponding to the figure concerning roles. The figure shows on the y-axis the relative individual distribution of criteria for archiviation, execution and delegation, and the general distribution of these criteria in the project.

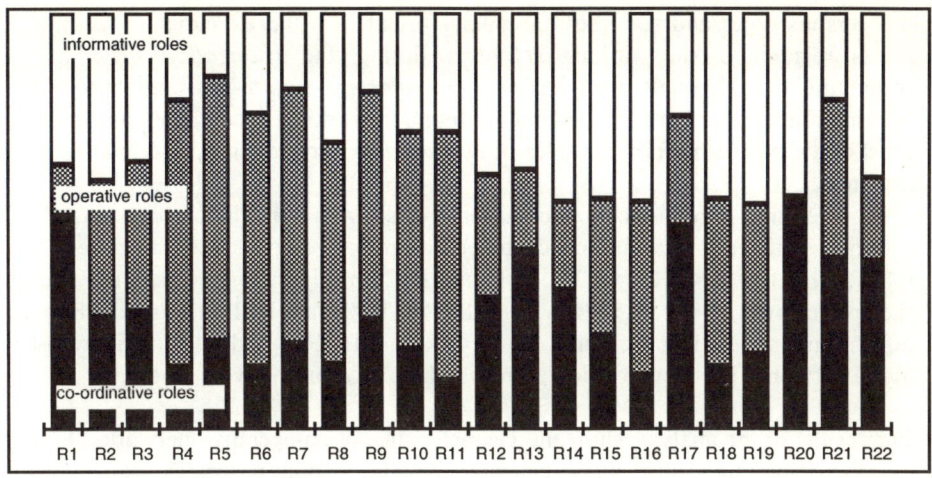

Figure 3-8: Roles in the 'realisation'[4]

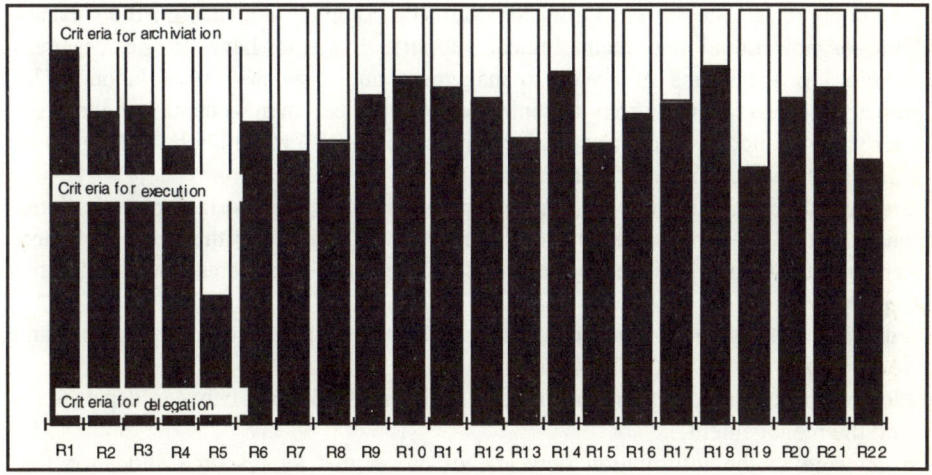

Figure 3-9: Communication management in the 'realisation'

The *realisation* of the software is mainly characterised by *co-ordinative aspects*. There is also a *significant collaborative aspect* in the network. This consideration emerges from the following facts:
• The commitment is, as in the *feasibility study*, a *complex realisation* of a fairly *composed product*. Different from the 'feasibility study', a more *structured process* is involved. There is only a *limited variance* and the relation among the persons is based on *synchronisation* of their distributed activities.

---

[4] The figure shows on the x-axis the 22 persons involved in the 'realisation' who are represented by 'R1' to 'R22'.

- The persons' roles and activities are mainly oriented to the execution of commitments related to the various activities during the *realisation*. The main communication channels are *telephone* and *informal face-to-face meetings*. The information used and produced is mainly found in working papers, data and forms. Most of the people perform the roles of *users/readers* concerning these information resources.
- Both, roles and communication management, show a very inhomogeneous distribution with very clear and concentrated co-ordinative nodes (i.e., managers are R1, R12, R13, R14, R17, R20, R21, and R22 in Figure 3-8), operative nodes (i.e., performers are R4, R5, R6, R7, R8, R9, R10, and R11 in Figure 3-8) and informative nodes (i.e., archivists are R14, R15, R16, R18 and R19 in Figure 3-8) in the network. This composition corresponds to a co-ordinative network.

The results of the analysis show the characteristics of co-operative networks. Problems concerning information management are relevant in both processes. This is true in general for the production, revision, filing and distribution of documents. This is also true when there is a high demand in a group for co-administration/co-authoring of the documents. The re-use of information in the company depends on the capacity of the organisational and technological support. Systems have to be designed according to the forms of project management and organisation of labour. The company has to change from a centralised to project management to the customer/supplier model which favours decentralisation of co-ordination by making individuals responsible for their commitments.

Hence, based on this analysis, the company introduced important organisational changes and a new procedure for the 'project flow'. Criteria for these changes were taken from the results of the analysed project. Changes to enhance co-operation in the company were:
- reduction of hierarchical levels combined with better indication of key positions and responsibilities,
- adoption of the customer-supplier model for internal relations between departments and the management,
- structuring of the information flow and of procedures for resource allocation and product acceptance.

The final scopes of the organisational change were to make the organisation more transparent in order to easily identify people and their roles in the company's organisation, to enhance quality of products and services, and to take advantage of user requirements for software development. In order to support co-operation in the company's projects, systems for electronic mail and shared data bases have been designed following this analysis. Today, an *electronic mail system* is used for *commitment handling* and an interface for *information management* was developed based on *hypertext models* (Schäl & Zeller, 1992).

* * *

In this paragraph different types of co-operative work have been characterised by applying a model on co-operative networks. In addition to this structural aspect of co-operation, dynamic dimensions have also to be considered. Therefore, a framework for analysing the dynamics of co-operative work is introduced in the next paragraph, to be illustrated by case history 4.

3.4 Dynamics of co-operative work

3.4.1. Co-operation in the small

Co-operative ensembles may be *ad-hoc* or *permanent*. Some will be engaged primarily in co-ordination, others in collaboration or co-decision. Many ensembles will combine the three types of co-operation, either concurrently, or at different stages of a process. The dynamics occurring in co-operative ensembles are developed here, taking the example of co-operation as it occurs in research activities.

Researchers interact with persons of two main categories:
- Persons belonging to one of the *groups* they are members of and the other persons in the research community. Scientists have an ongoing communication with persons belonging to the first category: every new conversation has some relation with the previous ones; there is a strong continuity in the history of their interactions.
- Scientists interact in an episodic way with others. There is no continuity. They sometimes need to open a conversation with one of them, but each new conversation with the same person has little to do with the previous ones.

Let us call the co-operation scientists have with persons of the first category *co-operation in the small*, and the other one *co-operation in the large* (De Michelis *et al.*, 1992). These two categories of the dynamics of co-operation are discussed as follows.

As already mentioned, *co-operation in the small* occurs within already *established ensembles*, which might be characterised by relatively well defined roles, rules and a common history. This creates a setting where each new conversation is related to previous ones, where relations between two persons assume meaning for other members of the ensemble and where people do things together.

The boundary between such co-operative networks and the rest of the world is generally well-defined. This is due to the fact that each network's member has a *role* within the co-operative ensemble and everybody knows what the network's members do together. There is also a continuity in the ensemble because its past experience influences its future.

Within co-operation in the small two kinds of networks can be distinguished, which cover most of the variety of the small groups researchers are members of: *stable organisational units* and *temporary project teams*.

Stable organisational units

Each experienced researcher generally participates in various organisational units which are stable. Examples are research units of a laboratory or department; divisions of a large research institution; committees guiding or controlling journals, other periodical publications or research programs; committees advising governments or intergovernmental institutions. Some of these stable groups' activities occupy most of the researcher's working time, while others are characterised by rare interactions; some of them have a deep influence on what they do day by day while others define a limited and well distinguished field of activity; some of them are fully transparent for them while others appear with a high degree of opacity; some of them are important while to others they pay little or no attention.

Temporary project teams

Each experienced researcher participates also in many different temporary teams, as in a small research project; organisational committees for conferences or program committees; selection committees for an academical position or a scientific award, etc. Temporary teams are different from stable organisational units. They are generally oriented towards actions. The team has one (complex) thing to do and every person has a task/role within the team. Whenever a temporary team does not do anything, its members likely lose interest and the team disappears.

3.4.2 Co-operation in the large

Co-operation in the large characterises interactions researchers have within their scientific community; experienced researchers interact not only with persons from groups they are a member of. Researchers frequently communicate and co-operate with other colleagues in an occasional manner during their activity. The community of the persons with whom they can have occasional interactions is very large, is loosely coupled and does not have well defined boundaries. The persons in those interactions can vary in time, a new interaction can enlarge their number without any formal agreement, and some of them can be abandoned due to loose relational patterns.

Interactions occurring within these ever changing communities are related to the subject and to the goals. The whole community is a world where people 'live' with or without any defined or specific roles to play. Researchers are looking for the right person(s) who can or want to do something with regard to their tasks. The community remains quite anonymous for the single scientist and there is no memory of past experience which might directly influence the future.

There are two main aspects to be addressed for co-operation in the large among researchers: The *establishment of co-operative networks* and *exceptional help*.

Establishment of co-operative networks

Whenever a single or several researchers want to start a new initiative – a journal, a research project, a research laboratory – they open conversations within their scientific community. Within these conversations they discuss the features of the new initiative, the conditions under which the contacted persons could possibly participate, the skills or profiles of other persons to be involved, etc. Generally speaking, the scope of their interaction is to generate conditions and co-operative ensembles, which make it possible to do something together in the future. While looking for people to create a new network it is possible that some conversations are opened without indicating the partner. This means that the call is addressed to everyone like a *broadcasting* message.

Exceptional help

Scientific work is characterised by a high number of *breakdowns* which a researcher has to face. An experienced researcher frequently discovers that something is missing to accomplish a specific task: an item of technical information, a scientific reference, a new paper, a name or an address of an expert in a specialised field, etc. In this case the concept of *breakdown* enters as defined by Winograd and Flores (1986):

> 'A breakdown is not a negative situation to be avoided, but a situation of non-obviousness, in which the recognition that something is missing leads to the unconcealing (generating through our declarations) some aspect of the network of tools that we are engaged in using. A breakdown reveals the nexus of relations necessary for us to accomplish our task.' (Winograd & Flores, 1986: 165)

As a consequence, the researcher opens conversations within the scientific community to overcome the problem. At the same time it can happen that someone discovers something which can help a colleague, or has been asked for before. In these cases the researcher opens conversations with other colleagues to distribute the information found. Also in the case of exceptional help some conversations are opened without indicating the partner (addressed to everyone). The conversations are accomplished in the researcher's *network of help*.

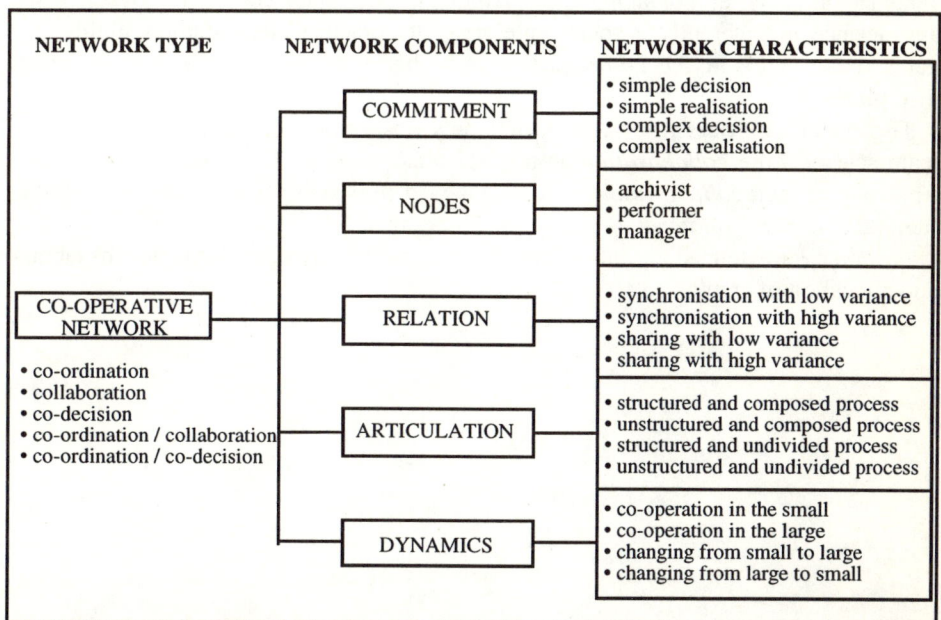

Figure 3-10: Types, components and characteristics of co-operative networks including dynamics of co-operation

The *dynamics* of co-operative networks has to be added to the other four components *commitment*, *nodes*, *relation* and *articulation* in Figure 3-5. *Dynamics* is a second component of co-operative networks which describes together with *articulation* what is called *behaviour* in network analysis. The resulting scheme to characterise co-operative networks is shown in Figure 3-10. All component to describe co-operative networks are applied in the two case studies in chapter 5 and 6. A preliminary case history is presented in the following paragraph for applying the new dimension of dynamics to co-operative networks. The case deals with co-operative networks in space science work.

Case history 4: Co-operative networks in space science work

The methodology which supports the identification of types of co-operative networks and their dynamics has been applied in the European Space Agency (ESA) (De Michelis *et al.*, 1992). The European Space Agency and European space research institutes are a networked organisation with highly qualified scientists working in different locations all over Europe and with tight collaboration with scientists in other continents.

Much of scientific research remains fiercely individualistic, with a single scientist displaying a high degree of creativity and versatility in the completion of a project from inception to tool-building, data collection and theoretical analysis. However, even the isolated investigator works within the *social definition of discovery* if only to demarcate what is *new knowledge*. Furthermore, what is discovered must meet some canonical criteria of significance. All this implies that a community of scientists and science is inherently a social enterprise. Its practice often requires highly organised *teamwork* in the *co-ordination* of highly specialised skills from different disciplines.

The scientific process, however, is not only *co-ordination*, but also a process of team science - the *collaboration* among scientists working on a common problem. This may be tacit *collaboration* of minds reached by searching and reading scientific literature, *explicit bilateral exchange* of ideas, tips, etc. It may be a *formal co-operation* over extended periods of time, with contractually agreed division of labour and allocation of credit.

Table 3-3: A sample of processes in the space science community

Process	Explanation
Experiment life-cycle processes	
Announcement of Opportunities (AO)	release of the AO by the Agency and user decision on participation
notification of interest	exploration of interest and opportunities for a possible experiment with a later constitution of a consortium in reply to a call by the Agency
payload selection	verification of resources availability and selection of proposals
payload design and development	development and initial testing of the payload
mission preparation	experiment plan conclusion and servicing and logistic aspects
mission operation	experiment performance on board, data capture and storage, preliminary analysis of experiments
Post-experimental processes	
research and study activities	process of modelling, data analysis, idea generation, etc.
development of special tools	software or instrument development
co-authoring	writing up experiment results for paper production and publications with well defined roles of scientists in the writing process according to his competence or special interest defined during the experiment life-cycle
Generic processes	
re-use of software and/or data	exchange of models and/or data among scientists
data research	looking for data on a specific issue
finding opportunities for co-operation	establishment of interest groups, consortia, etc.
looking for help	finding solutions to a problem/breakdown

De Michelis *et al.* (1992) identified a number of scientists' working processes. The material for the analysis was gathered from documents and interviews with system developers and scientists from the space science community. Table 3-3 gives a sample of processes which have been identified as a result of meetings with users and system developers; they cover a range of typical working processes in ESA's user community.

Table 3-4: Types and dynamics of co-operative networks in space science processes[5]

Process	Type of network	Dynamics co-operation in the small	Dynamics co-operation in the large	Dynamics changing small to large
Announcement of Opportunities	co-decision & co-ordination	-	+	±
notification of interest	co-decision	±	+	+
payload selection	co-decision	±	±	±
payload design and development	co-ordination & collaboration	+	-	-
mission preparation	co-ordination & collaboration	+	-	-
mission operation	co-ordination & collaboration	+	-	-
research and study activities	collaboration	+	+	+
development of special tools	co-ordination & collaboration	+	-	-
co-authoring	collaboration	+	-	-
re-use of software and/or data	collaboration	+	-	-
data research	collaboration	-	+	±
finding opportunities for co-operation	co-decision	-	+	+
looking for help	collaboration	±	+	+

Table 3-4 summarises the results of the analysis of the co-operative characteristics of the processes and ensembles in the space science community (co-operation in the small or in the large and the dynamics in changing from one type to the other). There are four very dynamic processes (notification of interest, research activities, opportunities for co-operation, looking for help). The greater part of processes remains usually in a defined domain and co-operation in the small is largely prevailing. This result should be taken into serious consideration because it implies a need for specific and limited workgroup domain supports rather than generic and undefined needs of communication and information search technology.

A framework to understand types and dynamics of co-operative work has been proposed in this chapter. These concepts will be used in the following paragraph to deduct support requirements for co-operative work.

---

[5] - means that the importance or presence of the process characteristic is low,
+ means that the importance or presence of the process characteristic is high and
± means that the importance or presence of the process characteristic is medium

3.5 Computer support for co-operative work

3.5.1 Relevant design spaces

On the basis of the introduced different types of co-operative work and dynamics in co-operation previously discussed, two design spaces for co-operative work are identified. These spaces are *activity synchronisation* and *information sharing*. They should be designed according to the dynamics present over time and space of the co-operative networks as open services for highly dynamic and large networks, or as *domain services* for more stable and small networks. The author sustains that:

> The main technique for co-ordinating the work of a co-operative ensemble is to provide facilities for synchronising the various activities performed by its members, whereas the main technique for promoting collaboration and co-decision between its members is to provide information sharing facilities. Co-operation in the large requires open services, while co-operation in the small has to be supported by domain services.

Striking the right balance between visible activity synchronisation and information sharing is critical to improve the productivity of co-operative settings (Figure 3-11).

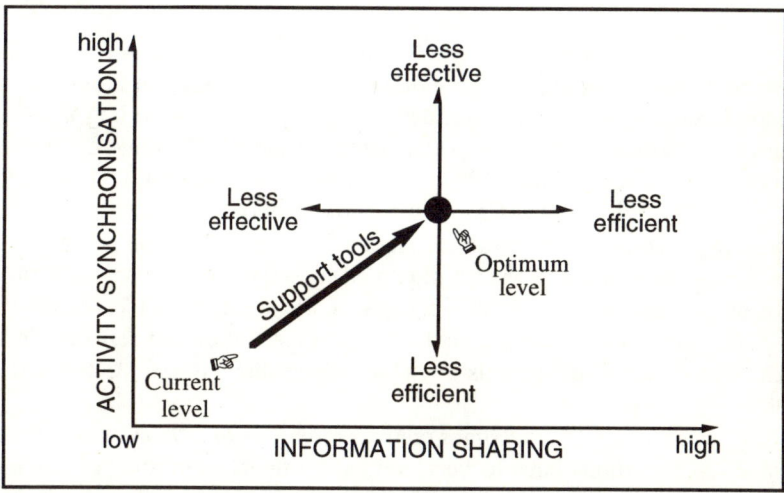

Figure 3-11: Balance between activity synchronisation and information sharing

Too little synchronisation makes the ensemble inefficient and often produce a duplicated effort, too much synchronisation can lead to over-formal communication between its members. This reduces the effectiveness of working as a group. Likewise, too little information sharing makes the co-operative ensemble ineffective, while too much sharing leads to inefficiency (De Michelis, 1990; Schäl & Zeller, 1991).

The first step in designing support for co-operative networks is therefore to identify the optimum balance between activity synchronisation and information sharing, which will vary according to the type and dynamics of co-operative networks and the capabilities of the individuals being part of it. It will also be necessary to assess the current levels of synchronisation and sharing (indicated in Figure 3-11 to be generally very low for the time being). The final stage is to identify the support tools which will provide the optimum balance between activity synchronisation and information sharing. Activity synchronisation and information-sharing are complementary critical factors for a co-operative process. The distinction of these two aspects is relevant for both, the analysis and the identification of appropriate design approaches and technical solutions, which should be conceived as parts of a single environment. They are leading to describing the support requirements of co-operative work.

3.5.2 Support requirements

Support requirements for co-ordination

There are two main requirements for the support of effective co-ordination. Firstly, the co-ordination support must reduce the *transaction costs* (Williamson, 1975; 1981; 1985; Ouchi, 1980; Malone *et al.*, 1987b; Ciborra & Olson, 1988; Ciborra, 1987; 1993; Schmidt, 1994) taking care of the management of communication for all persons involved. This means to support communication in a way which allows people to:

- *Distribute and select easily messages*: To satisfy these needs it is required that the system provides an *intelligent communication filter*. This filter should be applied to address, route and rank messages according to priority, providing a set of rules which can be defined by the user to manage the personal electronic communication (Malone *et al.*, 1986; 1986b; 1987; 1987b; Winograd & Flores, 1986; Pollock, 1988; Mackay *et al.*, 1989; ACM, 1992; Terry, 1993).
- *Link messages within a conversation*: The unit of communication is not a message, but a conversation, which is the set of related messages which can be identified by a subject. A conversation relates, e.g., to a commitment under negotiation or execution. People can better respond to a message if they can re-view the overall context – in other words, the history of a conversation (Bullen & Bennett, 1990; 1990b).
- *Record and classify messages/conversations with their current status*: Messages/conversations have to be identified by their commitments, their current status (e.g., started with a request, in a negotiation-phase, closed conversations, etc.;) and the categories which indicate main subjects (Flores, 1982; Flores & Ludlow, 1981; Winograd & Flores, 1986; ATI, 1987; 1988; 1988c).

These features of co-ordination support do not have the aim to reduce the number of group and/or *face-to-face meetings*, but to improve their productivity. Meetings might be instead supported for co-ordination needs to start them, to achieve process and to empower their effectiveness in building a common knowledge and understanding of current problems and activities (Whiteside & Wixon, 1988).

Secondly, co-ordination can be improved providing appropriate functionality to optimise the flow of activities in a process and to reduce the persons' effort to manage

their tasks and co-ordinate their actions with others (Winograd & Flores, 1986). A co-ordination support has, therefore, to help people to:
- *Model co-ordination*: The co-ordination system introduced to support a process has to be able to support as well centralised co-ordination functions as hierarchically distributed (delegated) and fully distributed co-ordination functions (Lai & Malone, 1988; Malone & Crowston, 1990; 1991).
- *Classify and select recurrent processes*: The co-ordination system has to be able to create categories for actions. These can be speech act types (commissives, directives, etc.) (Searle, 1969; 1975; 1975b) or other classes (requests, approvals, etc.) (Winograd & Flores, 1986; Medina-Mora et al., 1992). Activities can be seen as task types and conversation patterns which configure co-ordinated workflows in order to allow users easy access to current processes and make them considering their actions within a system of linked and co-ordinated workflows.

Support requirements for collaboration

Problems concerning *information management* are most relevant in collaborative processes. This is true in general for the production, revision, filing and distribution of documents (Greif & Sarin, 1986). This is also true when collaboration is not directly related with creating or modifying documents but people collaborate on a common task and need to share all the information characterising this task. In other words, knowledge workers collaborate via a common information space which is a public domain accessible to the collaborators.

A software product, for example, during the different stages of its development, can be described by a series of deliverables which are documents like product requirements, data analysis, functional specifications, design specifications, development plans, source codes, unit and integration test plans and libraries, certification plans and libraries, user manuals, beta test plans and libraries, etc. Deliverables associated to tasks are information which are related to both, the product and its development. Therefore, the information space is defined by the relationship of the information relevant either to the product or to the production process. Every change in the product or its production process requires its diffusion in the information space concerning information which is logically related to the change.

A tentative idea of an information space was already given by Bush (1945). Meanwhile models for information spaces have been developed (Engelbart et al., 1973; Engelbart, 1982; 1984; Trigg et al., 1986). New technologies, like *hypertext* (Conklin, 1987) and *hypermedia* systems (Gale, 1989), provide a useful approach to put this kind of model for knowledge representation into practice. The re-use of information in a company depends on the capacity of the organisational and technological support. Developing support systems for collaboration means to introduce tools which allow people to:
- *Structure information in a way that reflects how it was created*: When we access an information source for the first time, we adopt a 'logical' criteria of selection. However, when we access an information we have created together with others or we accessed before, the natural method is to reconstruct the process by which it was

created, or used for the last time. Concepts and techniques related to hypertext provide a promising model coping with this issue (Conklin, 1987).
- *Access each information unit with different rights depending on the different roles group members play in the process*: Collaboration does not imply the fusion of all group members' information. It is necessary to define for each information unit who can modify it, who can review it, who can merge different information units constructing new information units, and who can only read it (Begeman *et al.*, 1986).
- *Support questions and answers about the on-going task*: Any member of a collaborative network may need help to play the proper role in the process. The system must therefore provide facilities for individuals to ask ad-hoc questions that can be considered by the group as a whole. All group members must be in condition to provide help (Conklin & Begeman, 1988).

Support requirements for co-decision

When several persons participate in a decision process, *information sharing* has a prominent role, as in collaboration. But in this case it is possible to distinguish three different types of information: the information regarding the situation about which the decision has to be taken, the information regarding the criteria on the basis of which the choice can be made and, finally, the decisions that have already been taken, both concerning related topics, or steps towards the final decision to be taken.

In a co-operative decision process among two or more decision makers involved, a certain amount of time is spent to establish the degree of each others credibility in the delivery of information, statements of opinions, etc. Before taking any decision, various strategies are adopted and put into action by the group. In other words, the partners assess the level of credibility, that is, whether and how much they share a common background of agreed values. The *credibility assessment* is also directed to determine the reliability of information which the partners bring into the decision process (or hide in their agendas). If the credibility assessment yields a positive outcome, then information, solutions, suggestions and proposals put forward by whichever partner can be taken for granted without any further check (Bagnara *et al.*, 1991).

The co-decision support system must reduce the effort people spend participating in the decision process to share information, opinions and already taken decisions, in order to avoid both to continuously return on the already made steps and to leave some participants out of the process, as if they would not be necessary for reaching a 'good' decision. Supporting co-decision means to introduce tools allowing people to:
- *Share all information useful for the decision to be taken*: When a group opens a co-decision process it is necessary that all the information that is collected and created regarding the problem is made easily accessible to all participants in any moment of the process (during the meetings as well as when each participant is reflecting alone). Many of the features that make information easily accessible are similar to those pointed out with respect to collaboration requirements.

- *Share and make comparable the decision criteria*: The convergence of the opinions of the participants to a group decision is strongly improved if the participants can fully understand the criteria under which those opinions have been created. The sharing of the decision model, both if it is a spreadsheet table or an application of a more complex decision support system (Keen & Scott-Morton, 1978) used by another participant allows to understand better the person's reasoning.
- *Share the decisions already taken*: The decision process can become very inefficient if the participants start again and again the discussion from its very beginning, without being able to recognise the steps previously made. In this case, it is necessary that each meeting terminates with well defined minutes, fixing both what has already been decided (in terms of constraints and in terms of acceptable options) and what each member will do before the next meeting.
- *Manage conversations for possibility, clarification and orientation*: Co-decisions are taken as a result of a set of conversations for possibility, clarification and orientation (Winograd, 1986) for which each participant has to assess competence and credibility of the others. The effectiveness of those conversations is better when relationships are based on high reciprocity and professional, cultural and organisational proximity. These kinds of conversation can be improved by communication systems which help people to share proposals and opinions (Conklin & Begeman, 1988).

3.5.3 Development of a service portfolio

The problem of co-operation in the small and co-operation in the large has been outlined before. It is the ongoing process of large groups becoming small, the community dividing itself into sub-groups, and small groups growing up to large groups or looking for help (information). This dynamic has a certain impact on the development of IT systems and services provided to users, because it has to take into consideration the co-operation in the small as well as in the large. This requirement has to be combined with the general need for activity synchronisation and information sharing within co-operative processes.

A service portfolio has to be developed, taking into account the different dynamics of co-operative networks over time. Information system should support each of these networks and should integrate systems for *break-down resolution*. Some of these services will be general (standard applications for the whole network) – the *open services* – while others relate to sub-groups (customised applications for specific user groups or domains in the network) – the *domain services* .

Open services

Open services are aimed at supporting co-operation in the large (establishing groups, looking for help). Open services should be conceived as basic services to support communication and information retrieval in the co-operative network and its context. Open services like E-mail, teleconferencing and bulletin boards for group communication, and retrieval services for information management, are appropriately addressed by many present Information Systems. The best example for open services is the *Internet*. Open services are not further discussed in this research report. Nevertheless, the author puts emphasis on the need to integrate open services with domain services in a way which enables the users to shift from one type to the other, as is typical in the dynamics of change between co-operation in the small and co-operation in the large.

Domain services

Domain services are aimed at supporting co-operation in the small (stable organisation units, temporary groups). Domain services should be conceived as specific services to support communication and information sharing within specific groups or processes. This type of functionality is poorly addressed by present Information Systems.

A preliminary view of the functional needs for co-operative networks aims for the following correlation:
- open functionality is associated with work processes which are characterised by co-operation in the large or by highly dynamic co-operation in the small;
- domain and event functionality are associated with work processes characterised by stable co-operation in the small or by highly dynamic co-operation in the large;
- open search and event search functionality are associated with mainly collaborative or co-decisional work processes characterised by information-sharing needs;
- domain communication and event search functionality are associated with mainly co-ordinative work processes characterised by activity synchronisation needs.

The types of services and types of functionality can be crossed as described in Table 3-5, where some examples of possible functionality are reported.

Table 3-5: Functionality and service types in a service portfolio to support co-operative networks

Functionality	Communication	Information management
Open services	E-mail, Bulletin Board, Teleconferencing	Information retrieval
Domain services	Workflows	Hyper-links, Event research

In the following chapters, this research report will concentrate on domain services for communication. For this research task, workflow management technology is introduced in chapter 4.

4. Workflow management technology

Computer technology for process support has a long tradition. Information systems have tried to cope with this issue by *transaction processing*. Previous attempts to automate office work and increase productivity failed, because individual activities were automated without an understanding of how those activities fit into the entire business process. On the basis of past experience of procedure automation systems, new software products and enhanced office information systems' functionality are developed which fall under the new domain of *workflow management technology*. It is not a new technology for *procedure automation*, but takes the formal part of procedure processing applications and combines it with general communication and information sharing facilities. This added value to traditional *office automation* (Schäl, 1992) results from support requirements for co-operative work which have to be considered as explained in the previous chapter. Thus, computer systems have to support, and not necessarily to automate, predictable and formal structures of business processes, as well as the coping with unanticipated contingencies, dynamic change and breakdowns, to achieve the final objective of *customer satisfaction*. On this background, the limitations of procedure processing applications become obvious. The following paragraph discusses these limitations in more detail.

The subsequent paragraph introduces a new technology which should overcome the limitations of procedure processing applications. Workflow management technology is proposed to support business processes. Different commercial workflow management systems are presented and distinguished according to their main characteristics. Two tools out of the range of products are selected for detailed case studies. These tools are *The Coordinator* and *X_Workflow*. *The Coordinator* is described as an *ad-hoc groupware tool*. Several field studies on the use of *The Coordinator* are reported. The author applies the ad-hoc groupware tool *The Coordinator* in a training company in chapter 5. The second tool *X_Workflow* is a *business process automation system*. The system *X_Workflow* is applied in a bank in chapter 6.

4.1 Plans and procedures in process automation

Procedure automation has always concentrated on the predictable part of social work. It incorporates a model for task allocation, defined levels of responsibility, formalised patterns of communication, etc. The search for abstracted optimum sequences for co-operative work processes is understandable given the successes of *scientific management*, and the sequential nature of most computing machinery and programming representations (Robinson, 1993). In all these systems, *information* is treated as something on which office actions operate producing information which is passed on for further actions or is stored in data-bases for later retrieval.

While the information system may be designed to match the current social structure around the identified information flow and procedural working practice, the change of technology engenders a change of the social structure. An office is a social environment to which any introduction of procedural change, goal changes or automated equipment causes perturbations. This has been a bitter experience of office automation projects and installations, designed to match the traditional allocation of tasks in the office (Hammer, 1984; Suchman & Wynn, 1984; Schmidt, 1990). Many technologically successful systems have failed due to ignorance of human and social factors. For example, the mass movement of secretaries away from individual managers to word processing pools violated social maxims. In addition, if people who needed to exchange information are moved so that they are no longer close to the coffee machine, then information which was transferred in this informal way, may not longer be exchanged (Ellis & Naffah, 1987). As a consequence, computer systems have to be more than the rigid implementation of formal structure and control in the work process.

> 'The problem with incorporating models of plans (established procedures, organisational structures, or conceptual schemes) in computer systems is not that plans are fictitious. Rather, plans serve a heuristic function in action by identifying constraints, pitfalls and strategic positions in the field of work. [...] Procedures may of course codify 'good practice', recipes, proven methods, efficient ways of doing things, work routines. In flexible work organisations such procedures are of little value and may actually impede flexibility.' (Schmidt, 1991b: 13)

Organisations require to be able to cope with unanticipated contingencies in procedures. In this case, the perceived plan becomes a resource. In this ambiguous relation between plan and procedure, the organisation may still have the necessity to introduce some formal or statutory conditions, where non compliance of the constraints may evoke severe organisational sanctions. In any case, organisational procedures in computer systems cannot be programmed code, but rather heuristics and organisational statements that have to be interpreted to get the job done. Computer support of co-operative work should aim at supporting self-organisation of co-operative settings as opposed to disrupting co-operative work by computerising formal procedures (Schmidt & Bannon, 1992). This argument is enforced by Suchman (1987) who has analysed the role plans play in *situated actions*.

> 'Plans are inherently vague [... and] are resources for situated action, but do not in any strong sense determine its course. While plans prepropose the embodied practices and changing circumstances of situated action, the efficiency of plans as representations comes precisely from the fact that they do not represent those practices and circumstances in all of their concrete detail.' (Suchman, 1987: 52)

The value of a heuristic vision of procedures and the use of plans in its situatedness lies in two main issues.

The first issue relates to social processes in working together. In all social life, in societies as well as in groups and organisations, there are two basic social processes. One is the pressure to and striving for *uniformity* and *conformity*. The other process is *social differentiation*. Specialisation in skills and divergence in opinions and values are necessary for the functioning of most groups and organisations. The resulting conflict is beneficial for both, the social group and the individuals involved. Therefore, organisations can be seen as a framework for *co-operation* as well as for *conflicts* (Kensing & Winograd, 1991). These social processes occur via *communication* which should be supported by information systems, e.g., by functionality for *negotiation*.

Concerning the second issue, *change is frequent* and expected in many domains. An employee's vacation day, e.g., forces others to change their routines accordingly. Change also results from promotions, employee turnover, sickness, laws, etc. Some of these changes are short-termed and local, turning after some time into the initial state, while others are radical (e.g., a change in law might necessitate a new procedure with different personnel).

The occurrence of unforeseen events and the notion of *breakdown* and its implications is a fundamental concept in co-operative work (Winograd & Flores, 1986). Its implications are generally not taken into consideration by traditional office automation procedures. They rationalise the working process only by foreseen steps and do not support unpredictable events. The general meaning of breakdown implies that something which is missing in order to proceed, is needed. These missing items can be pre-defined as in the model of a *work breakdown structure* (WBS) in *project management*. This notion of breakdown implies a certain *recurrence* and possibility of *planning* for missing items (breakdowns) and *resolution*.

A second type of breakdown is an *unforeseen event* where something is missing for continuing a task, process, etc. Running out of ink while writing a report is an example of this second type of breakdown. Whenever we have this type of breakdown which we cannot overcome by ourselves, we look for help. We communicate with others requesting them to do something for us. This has already been discussed as the *network of help* for *co-operation in the large* (see chapter 3).

This final point concerning *exception handling* in a working process has especially to be supported by information systems which want to succeed in supporting co-operative work. This point is crucial for process support systems, because:

> 'it is impossible, both in practice and in theory, to anticipate and provide for every contingency which might arise in carrying out, a series of tasks. No formal description of a system (or plan for its work) can thus be complete. Moreover, there is no way of guaranteeing that some contingency arising in the world will not be inconsistent with a formal description or plan for the system. [...] *Every real world system thus requires articulation to deal with the unanticipated contingencies that arise.* Articulation resolves these inconsistencies by packaging a compromise that *gets the job done.*' (Gerson & Star, 1986: 266)

As a consequence, systems have inherently to be *open-ended* with escape hatches to handle unanticipated exceptions and emergencies. De Michelis (1996) argues that a CSCW system should support the user switching the attention from the routine to the solution of an occurred breakdown, without loosing effectiveness at the procedural level, and by a natural and immediate switch from the process-support system into another one, e.g. looking for help, and vice-versa (De Michelis, 1996). This is much more tenable than aiming toward notions of total automation of procedures, total removal of paper from the office (paperless office) or *peopleless offices* (Ellis & Naffah, 1987). That this scope is likely counterproductive has been explained in the second chapter. The following paragraph introduces the history and roots of *workflow management technology*. Different definitions and views of applications for workflow management systems are explained in the subsequent paragraph.

4.2 Workflow management technology

4.2.1 The history of workflow management technology

There have been a number of approaches to process improvement with information technology. Workflow management technology is claimed to be one of the innovative applications of the 1990s. Workflow management technology is a broad term, used in a number of different contexts and environments. Also known as *business process automation software*, it allows computer specialists to reflect the business process rather than to support or automate just discrete tasks. This will result into an improved productivity and flexibility needed for business competitiveness.

Workflow management systems have their origins in a number of different developments to automate and support business applications. In addition to *transaction processing*, in particular *document image processing* and *integrated office systems* have paved the way for the emergence of the workflow market. Initially the emphasis was on document storing, tracking and retrieval in working processes. Subsequently, workflow software has been introduced through integrated office systems. *Electronic mail* became the core of office systems and provided basic communication facilities which workflow systems need to transport messages and documents among its users and for file-exchange among component programmes.

Table 4-1: Generations of workflow management technology
(from Abbott & Sarin, 1994: 114)

Generation	Distinctive property	Major characteristics
First	application specific	• workflow capabilities expressed in particular applications (e.g., document management, E-mail) • hardcoded process definitions • closed and proprietary
Second	factored application	• workflow capabilities factored out from the application domain • workflow as a separate application, • limited selection of 3rd-party tools • process definition tailorable through script languages
Third (current)	tailorable service	• generic workflow services accessible to other applications through APIs • open standards-based architecture • full integration of 3rd-party tools • tailorable through GUIs, • proprietary workflow interfaces and interchange formats
Fourth (next)	embedded enabler	• workflow services fully integrated with other middleware services (E-mail, desktop management, directory) • standardised interfaces and interchange formats • workflow-enabled applications • ubiquitous but invisible workflow systems

A number of custom-built workflow applications have been developed using the companies proprietary electronic mail and office systems. Most recently developed *groupware* has begun to play a role in stimulating the development of workflow management systems. Current workflow management systems seem to resemble also previous work in *office information systems*. The pioneering work has been done in this direction by Michael Zisman in the SCOOP project (Zisman, 1977; 1978). Systems using hard-coded compiler languages evolved with the years into rule-based routing systems, like *Officetalk* (Ellis & Bernal, 1982; Ellis & Nutt, 1988). Officetalk was an experimental office information system developed at Xerox PARC which provided a visual electronic desktop metaphor, a set of personal productivity tools, a forms paradigm and a network environment for sharing information. Officetalk is based on *information control nets* (ICN) a simple, but mathematical rigorous formalism created and designed in the 70s to model office procedures (Ellis, 1979; Ellis *et al.*, 1979; Ellis & Wainer, 1994; 1994b).

A number of document imaging companies developed workflow management systems based on their experience on information management in the early 80s. One of the oldest document management products with workflow functionality that has reported some very large successful installations is *FileNet*. A typical large workflow application based on *FileNet* is reported in Davis (1991).

With the diffusion of the personal computer in networked environments, PC-based procedure automation software has been successful (e.g., *Staffware* and *Workhorse*). These groupware applications have been increasingly used to switch away from centralised corporate computing. They have been adopted mostly by large organisations to maintain or to define their internal procedures (vacancy request, travel reimbursement, invoicing, etc.). Some of these procedures are fairly small, while others may have hundreds of steps and people involved. Also big IT suppliers have adopted developments from these small software houses (Staffware is sold by ICL as *Powerflow* and by Unisys as *OfisProcedure*; Workhorse was used by AT&T for *Rhapsody*).

Workflow management systems use different methods for describing the process they support, from hard-coded *compiler languages*, to *rule-based routing mechanisms*, *PERT* and *CPM chart*-like graphical representations, *Petri-Net state-transition diagrams*, etc. The historical evolution of workflow management technology, its current status and next generation developments are shown in Table 4-1.

4.2.2 Workflow management systems and applications

Emerging *workflow management technology* in the area of CSCW addresses the different aspects of co-operative work in their temporal distribution in the process. In particular workflow management technology allows the re-integration of previously separate *communication*, *information* and *data flows* in a working process at any time and in its unpredictable complexity. In this sense workflow management technology combines *EDP procedures* and *organisational procedures* with *process management* and *exception handling* (see Figure 4-1). At the same time, workflow management technology is an environment which supports the integration of previously separate Information Systems (Office Information Systems, Electronic Data Processing, Telecommunication Networks, etc.) (Schäl, 1992). Meichun Hsu & Mike Howard (1994) underline the key-role for workflow management technology as the *integrator of disparate mainframe applications*. Often the interconnected applications are not relevant to the today's way of doing business. Custom-developed workflow management systems can meet newly identified business needs to accomplish specific integration purposes in business processes by using standard services (e.g., object request brokerage, name and transport services, message and data-interchange protocols).

As already claimed, *Workflow management systems* can be seen as the first tools facing the problem of offering integrated support to routine and non-routine work by providing their users with some *exception handling mechanisms*. Sometimes, exceptional conditions can be simply handled by a phone call to the right person. In other cases, activities must be cancelled or undone, rescheduled or new activities dynamically scheduled. Two different approaches have been followed in this respect (De Michelis & Grasso, 1993): either a communication system has been embedded within a workflow management system, or a workflow management system has been embedded within a communication support system.

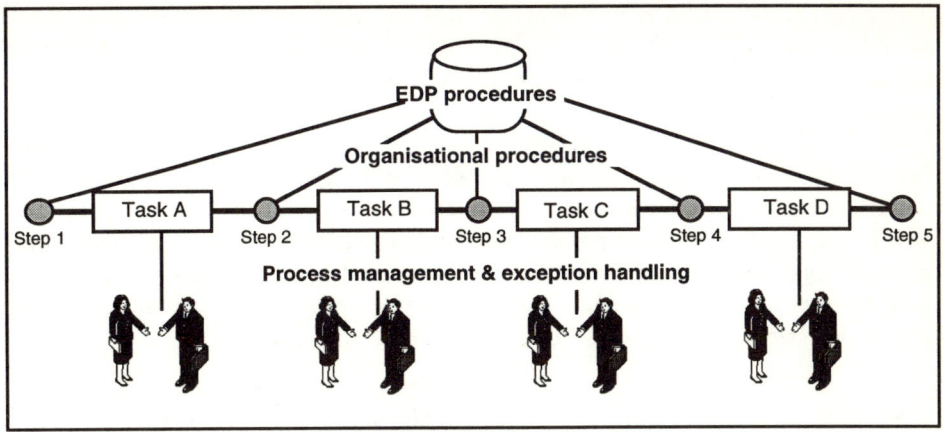

Figure 4-1: Different aspects of a working process

The relation between the communication system and the workflow management system tackles also the discussion about *mail-driven* versus *database-driven* workflow systems (Abbott & Sarin, 1994). The E-mail based approach has two disadvantages (Swenson *et al.*, 1994).

First, the E-mail in-box is private. There is no way for others involved in the process to know whether a request has been handled, worked on, delegated, etc. This might be counter to needs of co-operation in a process where it is important that others know this information which is useful for co-ordinating the activities and for status tracking.

The second disadvantage is that once a message is placed in a person's mail in-box, it cannot be removed except by the specific user. These messages cannot be re-addressed to other users according to changing roles and stages during the process which might require re-assignment.

The author has defined a new perspective for applications supporting business processes. These applications have been denominated workflow management systems. In the following, different definitions for workflow management systems are given. De Michelis & Grasso (1993) define workflow management technology as a tool for process modelling and automation:

> 'A workflow application is a tool for the specification and automation of cooperative office processes. The office work is made to flow as computer-based activities; workflow applications provide the means to both formally represent the processes as coordination procedures and to automate the actions that operate the relationships between the involved data.' (De Michelis & Grasso, 1993: 112)

Ellis & Wainer (1994) define workflow management technology as:

> 'systems that help organisations to specify, execute, monitor, and co-ordinate the flow of work items within a work group or organisation.' (Ellis & Wainer, 1994: 76)

The assumption that workflow management technology contains two basic components is a condition to differentiate it from traditional procedure automation: workflow management technology is composed of a *workflow modelling component* and a *workflow execution component*. The workflow modelling component enables administrators, users and organisational analysts to define working processes, so that processes and activities are defined, analysed, simulated and allocated to people (roles). The workflow modelling component is crucial for the differentiation of workflow management technology from procedure processing applications. This point will be explored for different process specification languages. However, some commercial workflow management systems have no model, so that this component is reduced to a *specification module*, and the execution component is referred to as the *workflow system* (Ellis & Nutt, 1993).

> 'A *workflow system* is an application level program which helps to define, execute, co-ordinate and monitor the flow of work within organisations or workgroups. In order to do this, a workflow system must contain a computerised representation of the structure of the work procedures and activities.' (Ellis & Nutt, 1993: 3-4)

However, the distinction between the workflow modelling component and the workflow execution component can induce a division of labour between programmers and users. The objective should be to make both components usable for a joint design of process support systems by users and programmers.

> 'The communality between all [...] systems is the separation of the planner from the user. The typical scenario involves an audit of the way the process is currently done and how it can be improved by interviewing a representative sample of the people involved in the work. Subsequently a programmer implements the process. Finally the process support application is deployed across the organisation. Inefficiencies and inadequacies of the process are fed back to the planner and some time later an improved process will be deployed.' (Swenson *et al.*, 1994: 16)

The missing perception of the workflow modelling component leads to procedure-like definitions for workflow management technology. One of the more procedural definitions for workflow management technology is given, e.g., by Hales & Lavery (1991). This definition lacks the organisational business perspective as explained in chapter 2 and defines workflow technology as being:

> 'a proactive computer system which manages the flow of work among participants, according to a defined procedure consisting of a number of tasks. It co-ordinates users and system participants, together with the appropriate data resources, which may be accessible directly by the system or off-line, to achieve defined objectives by set deadlines. The co-ordination involves passing tasks from participant to participant in correct sequence, ensuring that all fulfil their required contributions, taking default actions when necessary.' (Hales & Lavery, 1991: 5)

Instead, it is important to distinguish traditional office automation from today's business process automation.

'The emphasis in workflow management is on using computers to help manage business processes that may be comprised of many individual tasks, not on using computers to automate the individual tasks. The latter may be applied selectively to some tasks, but such task automation is not a prerequisite for using and benefiting from workflow.' (Abbott & Sarin, 1994: 113)

Workflow systems have to be programmed in order to be executed supporting a specific business process. The following paragraph introduces some workflow specification languages. An overview is given for the adequacy of these languages for process modelling. The procedure definition language *CoPlanS* is explained in detail, because *CoPlanS* will be used in *X_Workflow* for the case study on financial services in chapter 6.

4.3 Workflow specification languages

To support process design and definition, workflow management systems are equipped with a *procedure definition languages*. Petri-Net models have been primarily used to model structured systems such as computer programmes, factory production lines, etc. The outlined complexity of working processes raises new issues and challenges in the modelling of human activity in the workplace. This type of activities have a large component of unstructured, dynamic, and creative work. Therefore it is difficult to capture work via traditional modelling techniques. Most of the recent activity with Petri-Net models was motivated by Anatol Holt's work in applying Petri-Nets to modelling co-ordination in the workplace (Holt *et al.*, 1983; Holt, 1986; 1988).

Table 4-2: Language types and constructs in relation to perspectives for process modelling

Language Types and Constructs	Information Process Perspective	Business Process Perspective
State transition and Petri-Nets	X	X
AI languages and approaches [1]	X	(X)
Control flow	X	(X)
Events and triggers	X	(X)
Object modelling [2]	X	(X)
Precedence networks [3]	X	(X)
Procedural programming languages	X	(X)
Quantitative modelling [4]	X	(X)
Systems analysis and design [5]	X	(X)
Data modelling [6]	X	
Formal languages	X	
Functional languages [7]	X	

1   Including rules pre/post conditions.
2   Including class types and instances, hierarchy, inheritance.
3   Including *PERT* and critical path method.
4   System dynamics which applies feedback and control techniques to social phenomena to define a set of quantitative relationships among variables of interest that simulate the observed behaviour of social systems.
5   Including *DFD*, *SADT*, structure charts.
6   Including E/R, relations, structured data declarations.
7   A set of hierarchical decomposable mathematical functions depicting relationships among inputs and outputs.

Process modelling languages and representations can be evaluated by the extent to which they provide constructs which are useful for representing and reasoning about the various aspects of processes. Table 4-2 identifies language types and constructs supported by process modelling languages being explored in the research community. It summarises, furthermore, how these languages types and constructs are support for the two main perspectives for process modelling relevant for information system design as introduced in chapter 2. It becomes clear from this comparative table, that *state transition diagrams* and *Petri-Nets* are best suited as workflow specification languages; it is the only language type which covers best both, the information and business perspectives. The system *X_Workflow* models the process as state-transitions in a Petri-Net. From this point of view the specification language *CoPlanS* in *X_Workflow* is among the most appropriate ones. The *Information Control Net* model (ICN) (Ellis, 1979; Ellis *et al.*, 1979; Ellis & Wainer, 1994; 1994b) was one of the first proposed attempts to model co-ordinated procedures in organisational structures. In the ICN model each procedure is defined by a set of objects (e.g., persons, documents) and a set of relations (e.g., precedence and data access) which link these objects. A more recent example of a procedure definition language is *CoPlanS* (Co-ordinated Procedure Language), which was developed by GMD for the specification of office procedures in the DOMINO system (Kreifelts *et al.*, 1984; 1991; Kreifelts & Woetzel, 1987; Woetzel & Kreifelts, 1993). *CoPlanS* is introduced here, because it is used in *X_Workflow* for the case study in chapter 6. *X_Workflow* is the commercial system developed by Olivetti out of the research system DOMINO. (For a more detailed description of *X_Workflow* see paragraph 4.7. in this chapter).

The DOMINO system was developed in the mid eighties intended for the support of structured business processes in organisations. In DOMINO co-operation is modelled and supported by message exchange among actors which have to communicate about tasks to be carried out. An autonomous agent mediates these conversations and uses an input/output specification language of the procedure steps to co-ordinate the tasks.

There are four assumptions underlying the design of DOMINO (Woetzel & Kreifelts, 1993):
- Every office worker has a private working domain; co-operation takes place by *exchanging messages* rather than by *information sharing*.
- The messages exchanged are regarded as *speech acts*.
- An *autonomous agent* can use the *input/output relations* of the work steps to organise co-operation.
- The input/output relations of the steps define an *ideal procedure*; the mediating agent can handle *exceptions* from this procedure by means of *conversations*.

DOMINO offers some functionality for *exception handling* due to its support for informal communication; at any time, all persons involved in a procedure can send messages, optionally with enclosed documents. Breakdowns and exceptions from the pre-defined flow can be handled or recognised by the automatic agent due to the used message types, e.g., complaint, cancellation, delegation, forwarding.

DOMINO mediates and controls task related communication by notifying the participants about action which are due, by providing them with the information needed according to defined forms, and by routing the task's results to the defined responsible.

The procedure description language *CoPlanS* specifies which steps (*actions*) a procedure consists of, and what dependencies exist between these actions in the form of information (*forms*) needed and produced during their execution. A *role* is assigned to each action of the procedure. At run-time, DOMINO resolves these roles into responsible persons making use of an organisational database.

In *CoPlanS* a set of *actions*, a set of *forms*, a *need* relation between the forms and the actions, and a *produce* relation between the actions and the forms define a workflow. The first statement of the procedure specification language *CoPlanS* contains the forms needed to initiate the procedure and the forms which the procedure should produce. Then, for every action, the role and the forms needed and produced are given. *CoPlanS* allows alternatives for the set of needed or produced forms. This

94   Chapter 4

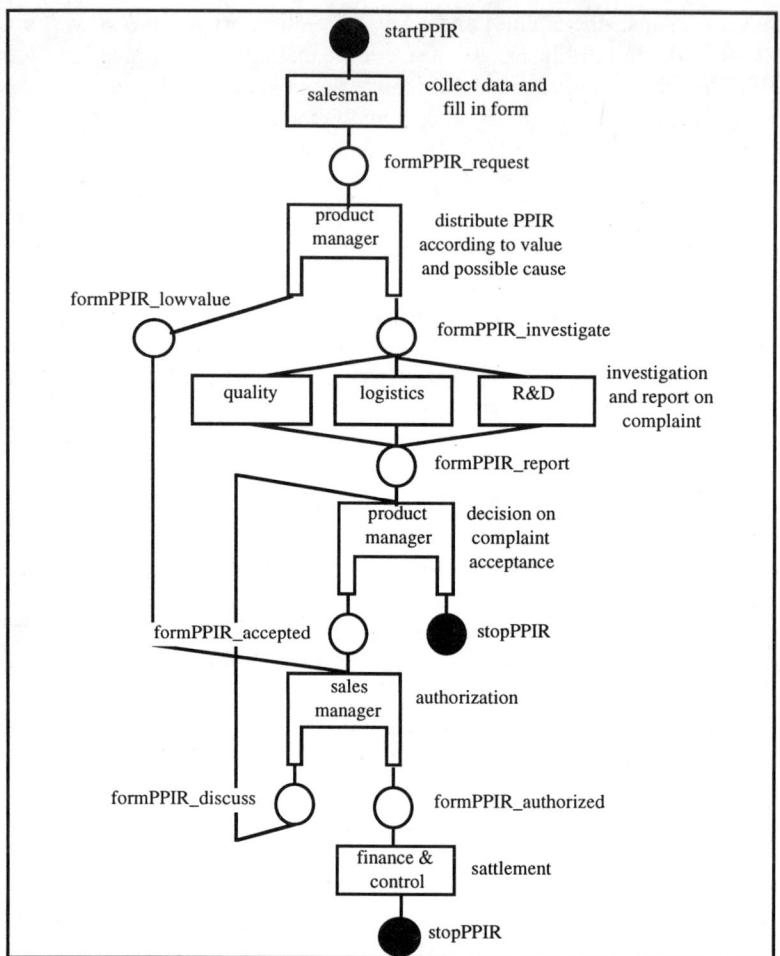

Figure 4-2: State transition diagram for the customer complaints process

makes the specification of alternative and concurrent courses of action possible. The description ends with a more detailed specification of the forms and roles used (Woetzel & Kreifelts, 1987; 1993).

The *need* and *produce* relations can be easily transformed into an informal Petri-Net; Figure 4-2 shows an example for the information flow diagram for customer complaints in the *Product Performance Investigation Request* (PPIR) procedure (see Figure 2-21 in chapter 2).

The boxes symbolise actions and the circles represent forms. Actions become due when all their needed forms (of one input alternative) are available. The person assigned to the role completes an action by making available all forms to be produced (for one output alternative). In other words, forms which have become available render further actions due, and action which have been completed will result in additional forms available. Eventually, the whole process finishes when all output forms of the procedure are available (for one flow alternative which leads to the end-form evidenced in black in Figure 4-2). For more explanation about the compiler, consistency, structure and behaviour checks on the Petri-Net see Woetzel & Kreifelts (1987; 1993).

According to *CoPlanS*, the workflow is treated as a process of interactive planning. A *plan* is a modified Petri-Net, representing activities, actors and objects. Every action in a procedure can be described via its input/output behaviour, i.e., by the documents it requires (input channels) and by the documents it produces (output channels). An action can have input and output alternatives which consist of input and output channels. This means that an action does not have to process all of its input documents and may produce only a subset of its output documents.

The *CoPlanS* specification defines an office procedure by its *name*. For every *action* is specified, as for the complete procedure, what documents are required and produced. The key-word *form* specifies a form that occurs in the procedure. for every form a list of attributes is specified. The last part of *CoPlanS* are *roles*. Roles are the actors of actions which occur in the procedure.

An example for the structure of *CoPlanS* would be:

PROCEDURE: PPIR
REQUIRES: startPPIR
PRODUCES: stopPPIR

ACTOR-A action1: salesman_collectdataandfillinform
REQUIRES: startPPIR
PRODUCES: formPPIR_request

FORM1: formPPIR_request
ATTRIBUTE1: value
ATTRIBUTE2: ....
ENDFORM1

ACTOR-B action2:
productmanager_distributePPIRaccordingtovalueandpossiblecause
REQUIRES: formPPIR_request
IF value FROM formPPIR_request CONDITION less than 100$
PRODUCES: formPPIR_lowvalue
ELSE
PRODUCES: formPPIR_investigate
.....

A different approach has been taken in WooRKS-UTUCS (Bicard-Mandel *et al.*, 1993; De Michelis & Grasso, 1993; Agostini *et al.*, 1993; Bignoli *et al.*, 1991), defining the *Activity Description Language* (ADL) in the Esprit project ITHACA. A workflow management system (COP) and a communication system (UTUCS) have been integrated into a common framework. The first is used to describe and support all routine activities in work processes, while the second helps the user to overcome *breakdowns* by retrieving the information required to solve the situation. ADL is used to describe how activities are connected to data and control links and who is an actor related to an activity (i.e., who has the responsibility to start and to execute an activity). The Activity Description Language describes each step of a procedure as follows:

STEP billing: ReviseObject	- - step name - activity type
RESPONSIBLE BillingClerk	- - role expression
INPUT Object	- - step input data
FROM OK OF evalOrder	- - step input links to design control flow
OUTPUT Object	- - step output data
END_STEP	

(from Bicard-Mandel *et al.*, 1993: 45)

The STEP key-word introduces both, the current step name (identifier) and the activity on which it is implemented. The RESPONSIBLE key-word specifies the role expression used by the role assignment mechanism. The INPUT defines on the first hand data taken in the procedure context and transferred to the specific step and, on the other hand, the links where the control flow is maintained from. The OUTPUT registers the data produced (newly created or modified) by the step (Bicard-Mandel *et al.*, 1993).

Beside the use of specification languages, workflow management systems have to be integrated into the general information systems architecture. A reference architecture for co-operative computing is proposed in the following paragraph. The use of workflow management systems as a specific layer in the architecture and the integration of other applications is applied in case study II in chapter 6.

4.4 Technological architecture for co-operative computing systems

The development of workflow management technology with the indicated functions and integration of data, information and communication flows implies a heavy use of a software layer which takes care of message exchange and routing. This software layer, below described with the name of *message control*, is a key component of a technological architecture which is the most appropriate to co-operative information services. These information service functions can be implemented in a technological architecture which, as a reference, is described in Figure 4-3 (Madnick, 1991).

Input/output systems and interface: this is the presentation layer in a client/server architecture and it provides the user interface and client's input/output functionality as the entry point to the information system. Input/output system are usually terminals and workstations, but also external networks sending and or receiving messages to/from the system.

Message control: message control co-ordinates the passage of messages between processing components; this involves routing, translation, sequencing and

Workflow Management Technology

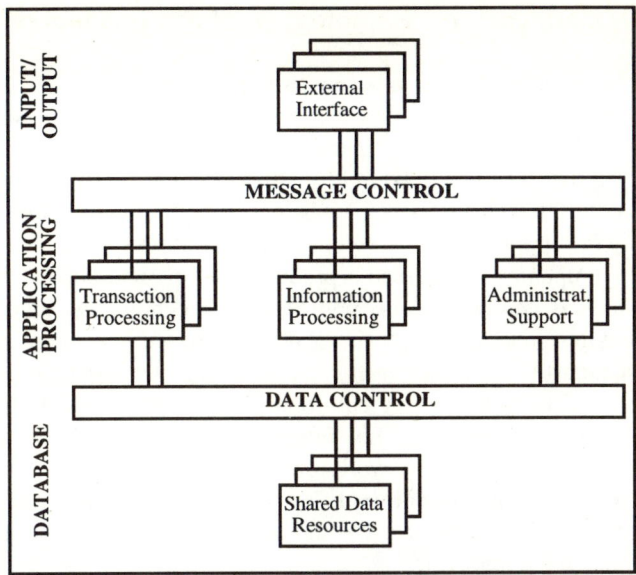

Figure 4-3: A flexible IT architecture for workflow system integration (from Madnick, 1991: 55)

monitoring. More specifically, *routing* accepts a request for delivery of a message to a particular logical function and determines the appropriate physical address; *translation* maps a limited number of protocols from one standard to another; *sequencing* determines the order in which messages are delivered to recipients on the basis of priorities; *monitoring* determines the state of the message within the system at any given time. Furthermore, message control co-ordinates the passage of messages between users; these messages are the relational communication layer necessary to run a business process.

Application processing: this is the server's (departmental or corporate) application layer within a client/server application model; it is composed of *transaction processing* (application that support specific operational activities), *information processing* (such as reporting, data analysis, graphics, etc.) and *administrative processing* (facilities for the performance of end user functions to maintain organisational, procedural or personal information, such as spreadsheets, word processing, scheduling, and so on).

Data control: data control co-ordinates access, format and passage of data between application processing functions and shared data resources.

Database: Shared data resources hold the information for one or more applications. They perform two basic functions: *information management* and *storage management*.

The components shown above should be logically separated, or can also be implemented on different computer systems. The more these architectural components are logically and (possibly) physically separated, the more flexible is the technological architecture.

4.5 Workflow management technology products and markets

Workflow management technology is a new issue for information systems people and managers. Nearly all IT suppliers have their workflow product for standard office systems on the market and have made it a strategic part of their product developments. These products will be fundamentally similar for the technical features, but suppliers will differentiate on the basis of support, training and value-added features. Some IT suppliers have developed their workflow products jointly with consultants or companies with ready products or methodologies for workflow technology. Lotus has enhanced *Notes* with Action Technologies' suite of workflow methodology and design components. Other might follow this strategy.

There is no standard for developing *Application Programming Interfaces* (API) for workflow systems. Therefore, for any call to or from a conventional programme, an API has to be inserted manually. This integration problem will remain for some time, as there is no standard for workflow systems themselves. The *Workflow Coalition* among the most important workflow vendors and users is working towards standards for interoperability, interchange and compatibility among the heterogeneous workflow systems on the market today.

However, workflow management technology is still an unfamiliar term for many users. Growth is currently hindered by a lack of knowledge amongst senior management about the concepts and benefits of workflow management technology. Up to now, the market has been supply driven. Very costly custom-driven workflow systems have been in use in the financial sector for many years, but the technology has only become widespread with the availability of standard software. The products available today are able to deliver the same functionality as an ad-hoc custom solution, but in a cheaper, faster and more easily re-programmable form. It is furthermore suited for use by business users rather than software professionals. The technical aspects of current workflow products will be improved in the short terms. Developments will include *graphical user interfaces* for process scripting and the integration of *multimedia* (e.g., voice messages).

The vast majority of the workflow installations in use are in the United States of America and in the United Kingdom. These were the home markets of the three suppliers which have driven the workflow market at its very beginning: *FileNet*, *FCMC* and *Workhorse*. At the early '90s, the number of installed licences count for 54% in the USA, for 38% in the UK, for 5% in France, and for 1% each in Germany, The Netherlands and the rest of Europe (Hales & Lavery, 1991).

The user base is polarised by geography as well as by industry sector. The majority of licences have been in the financial (17%) and public sectors (government and health care 50%). Other industries using workflow management technology are manufacturing (5%), advertising (3%), utilities (2%) and transport (2%) (Hales & Lavery, 1991).

Applications in widespread use include procurement systems, allocation of routine tasks to a pool of staff, and tracking of long-term activities. Government in particular, with its immense concentration of clerical and administrative tasks, was seen as an obvious candidate by the suppliers. The greatest business benefits are reached by tailoring tasks and processes to the unique way companies conduct their business.

A major benefit of workflow management technology is that, in many companies, it may be the first application jointly initiated by information system (IS) personnel and managers. Traditionally, the adoption of technology involved a top-down approach. Central IS was the gatekeeper of new technology and, commonly, the first user. It was only when technology became less expensive that it diffused down to lower levels of the organisation.

Most companies have recognised that they can no longer afford this approach, because the innovation cycle through centralised IS or outsourced services is too long. They want to apply discrete technology to specific business problems as quickly as possible. For this particular type of applications, the department, group or manager is commonly the cornerstone of the application content. Line people know the details of the specific business process and are in a position to analyse that process, recommend changes and evaluate the results. IS, however, must be intimately involved with the development of these applications to ensure that the company's technology infrastructure can balance the different single user or group requirements.

Therefore, the crucial point for success of workflow management technology is the proper process analysis before implementation. The simple mechanisation of steps in an existing procedure does not reach the potential benefits. Processes have to be analysed and re-designed by proper methods and skilled persons or companies (Keen, 1991; Denning, 1992; Hammer & Champy, 1993). The best implementations might be developed with the use of outside *consultants* or experienced *system integrators*. Workflow solutions cannot generally be bought from the package supplier. Therefore estimates in expenses for workflow technology foresee one third to be spent on consulting services – and the rest mainly for software and partially for hardware (Verity, 1993).

Table 4-3 gives some examples of current offerings for workflow management technology and for groupware products with workflow management functionality. The list does not pretend to be complete, but gives a hint on significant workflow products or developments from big IT suppliers. The offer is growing and, according to Marshak (1994), over 140 software companies are claiming that they provide workflow software. For market studies and product descriptions see, e.g., Hales & Lavery, 1991; White & Fischer, 1994.

Table 4-3: A sample of available and announced workflow products

Supplier	Workflow Management Product
Action Technologies Inc.	ActionWorkflow
Beyond	BeyondMail
Bull	FlowPath
DaVinci	The Coordinator
Digital	LinkWorks + TeamLinks
FCMC	Staffware
FileNet	WorkFlow Business System
Fujitsu Open Systems Solutions Inc.	Regatta
IBM	FlowMark
ICL	PowerFlow + TeamFlow
Olivetti	X_Workflow for IBIsys
Keyfile	JobMaker
Lotus	Notes [1]
MCC/Corporate Memory Systems	gIBIS/CM1 [2]
NCR/AT&T	ProcessIT [3]
Reach Software	WorkMAN
Recognition Equipment Inc./Plexus	ImageFlow + FloWare
Siemens-Nixdorf	WorkParty
Unisys	OfisProcedure
Wang	OPEN/workflow
Workhorse	Workhorse [4]
XSoft/Xerox	InConcert

1 Lotus *Notes* has poor workflow functionality. With *ActionWorkflow*, Lotus *Notes* becomes a full workflow system.
2 *CM1* has a specific workflow functionality for discussing design issues; therefore it is not a general process support system.
3 Previous systems have been *Rhapsody* and *Workflow for Cooperation*.
4 *Workhorse* was one of the first workflow products on the market, but did not succeed in business.

Workflow management technology can be divided into the three general categories of *document routing, ad-hoc groupware tools* and *business process automation*.

Document routing

At its simplest, document routing establishes the flow of information and routes documents accordingly. It represents, however, only a small portion of what is required to manage and track the flow of work in a process. Products in this arena are, e.g., **LinkWorks**, **WorkFlow Business System**, **FlowMark** and *InConcert*.

Ad-hoc groupware tools

Ad-hoc workgroup tools, such as *Notes, BeyondMail, JobMaker, Staffware*, or *The Coordinator*, provide some measures of workflow management technology through standard message based templates or forms. The flow component of such systems is generally a dedicated server which can either route messages addressed to general destinations (such as 'administrator'), or to a specific person (such as 'Mr. Smith'), or to automated agents that take action on behalf of people (such as processing information).

These tools show different views of the state of work depending on who does the inquiry. Although these capabilities can provide effective solutions to some users, they might not be adequate for organisation-wide workflow support. These products have to be modified for integration with existing information systems, especially if a mainframe is involved to track transaction across the enterprise networks. Chapter 5 explores the use of *The Coordinator* for process management in a training company.

Business process automation

Business process automation refers to the systems designed to define business processes and to implement them in software. At its best, workflow management technology encompasses both, a methodology for re-designing work and the means to automate and manage the resulting new workflows. In any case, without understanding business processes, it is impossible to build software to automate and manage workflows in a reasonable way. Systems in this arena are, e.g., *ActionWorkflow, X_Workflow, WorkParty, FlowPath, Workman* and *ProcessIT*. Chapter 6 explores the use of *X_Workflow* integrating concepts from *ActionWorkflow* for process management in financial services.

Two selected commercial products *The Coordinator* and *X_Workflow* are described in detail in the following paragraphs. Example of use from the literature and the author's direct experiences are reported for *The Coordinator*. The use of *The Coordinator* is illustrated by 6 short case histories, one of them (n° 9 on environmental control in a mechanical and civil engineering company) was conducted by the author. These case histories are followed by an extended report on an application of *The Coordinator* in a professional training company in Italy in chapter 5 (case study I).

The system *X_Workflow* is briefly described in paragraph 4.7. It is subsequently discussed in detail in chapter 6 (case study II). The case in chapter 6 on *X_Workflow* has been one of the first applications of this technology. Therefore there are no other reported experiences or case histories for this technology like for *The Coordinator*.

4.6 The Coordinator

The Coordinator is a workgroup productivity system currently used on IBM PC-compatible computers (ATI, 1987; 1988; 1988b; 1988c; Flores *et al.* 1988; Release

1.0, 1986; Seybold, 1987; Winograd, 1987; 1988). *The Coordinator* provides facilities for generating, transmitting, storing, retrieving and displaying records of *moves in conversations*. *The Coordinator* is a system for *action management*, grounded on the *theory of linguistic commitment* and *completion of conversations* in the *language/action perspective*. When opening a new *conversation for action*, The Coordinator provides options with different implicit structures (e.g., *request, offer, question* and *promise*), rather than providing an uniform command to initiate a message. The Coordinator applies language theories without attempting to automate language understanding. All of the interpretations (e.g., to open a conversation with a request) are made by the user, guided by appropriate menus. When the user has written the text, the system prompts up for three dates associated with the completion of the action: a *response by date*, a *complete-by date* and an *alert date*. Date entries are optional. When a user receives, e.g., a *request*, he has the option to respond by selecting an *answer* which can be a *promise, counter-offer, decline, report-completion* as significant *speech acts* in the conversation. Other answers, which do not advance the state of the conversation, are *acknowledged, free-form, commit-to-commit* and *interim-report*. By these choices *The Coordinator* provides a straightforward structure in which people can review the status of their communication with others (implicitly the *commitments* taken by themselves or others).

One has to note that the basic unit of work in *The Coordinator* is a *conversation*, not a message. In conventional electronic mail systems, messages in a conversation are often linked by conventions such as the use of *Re:...* in headers. For *The Coordinator* each message belongs to a particular conversation which can be based on the *conversation for action protocol* (see chapter 2.3.3) or a series of messages without structure. The study by Bullen & Bennett (1990; 1990b) on *Groupware in Practice* has shown that supporting conversations instead of simple messages is a major feature to improve co-ordination support systems.

The structure and status of conversations is the basis for organising retrieval and review of messages or conversations in the system. In the main menu under *organise* the user can define a *filter for the message retrieval*, such as *missing my response, my requests*, etc. in addition to the identification of *communication partners, time periods* and *key-words* associated with messages. Confirming the filter *The Coordinator* presents a list of messages matching the selected items. The retrieval structure has two levels, with the first identifying a conversation, then selecting for example particular messages within it or a report of the *conversation history* based on single messages.

The conversation handler is tightly coupled with a *personal diary*, where the user can read, for example, all the commitments he has to accomplish within one day, and all the conversations where his/her move is expected for that day. The user can enclose in any message within a conversation any file of any format.

Finally, *The Coordinator* allows to communicate both on *Local Area Networks* and on *Wide Area Networks* (messages are routed through a network of *hubs* to their destination).

Several studies have been conducted on *The Coordinator* (e.g., Johnson *et al.*, 1986; Bair & Gale, 1988; Carasik & Grantham, 1988; Ciborra, 1993). However, nearly all Coordinator studies refer to the first version which had a lot of interface problems and used a very *theoretical* wording for the menus (it has to be remarked that current version II of *The Coordinator* has strongly improved the previous release). The first version included a character-based interface which managed to keep up to 15 windows active, displaying or hiding part of them on the screen. The main functionality of managing conversations is implemented in the *converse menu*: The user selects from the menu to *open a new conversation for action* (having the choice between a *request* and an *offer*) or to *open a conversation for possibilities* (selecting *declare an opening*).The user actually has to understand the underlying philosophy for being able to use *The Coordinator* version I, e.g., choosing *open conversation for action* or *open conversation for possibilities*. The presented items on the converse menu are far away from daily used language and understanding in working environments. Furthermore, *The Coordinator* version I does not foresee any other message type than the moves in the conversation for action protocol represented in Figure 2-9 (*request, offer, delete, refuse, close, declare satisfaction*, etc.)

Action Technologies Inc. took critical studies and suggestions into consideration for the development of version II. The interface was improved by following recommendations as specified by IBM. Action Technologies Inc. followed the *Common User Access* standard, which represents a standard for *MS-DOS* software products. Beside pull down menus and function keys, *The Coordinator* version II can display up to four windows on the screen, managing up to 16 active windows in background.

The conversation for action protocol is still the core philosophy of *The Coordinator* version II, but the terminology and choices are more *wordy*. The user is not confronted with selecting a conversation protocol, but has seven choices to open a new conversation:
- *note* for quick, informal messages;
- *inform* for making reports or announcements;
- *question* for asking questions;
- *offer* for proposing an action or ideas;
- *request* for asking that things are done;
- *promise* for reporting plans to get things done;
- *what-if* for discussing topics and plans.

Each opening activates a relative conversation protocol. The associated set of rules are used by the so-called *Conversation Manager* to determine what kind of replies can be made. These possible moves are shown to the user in a context-dependent window when replying to a previous message. The shown alternatives are based on the kind of conversation, who started it, what moves have been made, etc. The moves in the protocol are enhanced by message types like comment, acknowledge receipt, ask about progress, report progress, etc. which are not part of the protocol and serve to reply without advancing the state of the conversation.

The first experience with *The Coordinator* is reported by Johnson *et al.* (1986). The trial in Aetna Life & Casualty Corp. was only short and for two small groups.

The results were preliminary and not representative. The doubtful seriousness of studies on *The Coordinator* has also been discussed in a workshop on *Evaluation Studies in CSCW*, organised by Liam Bannon and the author at ECSCW'93. In the following paragraphs, case histories on *The Coordinator* are reported. Four field studies are from the literature while two studies were conducted by the author.

Case history 5: Pacific Bell's applied research and development group

Pacific Bell conducted a trial of the first version of The Coordinator. The trial group in the Pacific Bell Applied Research and Development Division was dispersed across a variety of geographical locations and computing environments and the 15 persons had diverse job functions. The trial attempted to measure the effectiveness of *The Coordinator* Version I as a communication tool (reduce phone tag, replace company mail, individual organisation of work, quality of communication) and to evaluate the speech-act paradigm on which it is based. Only the first of these two objectives was achieved (Carasik & Grantham, 1988).

The 15 technical professionals had extensive training in computer science and programming. The group was characterised by less than 10 years job experience on average. The group was newly formed by members from several other functional groups within Pacific Bell. Therefore each of the members brought to the group different background, experiences and histories. All subjects volunteered to participate in the study.

The trial started with a four-hour training class about the theoretical background and practical instructions for use. The day-to-day user support burden after the initial training was more extensive than anticipated. The support person spent an average of extra two hour with each group member. The findings indicate the necessity for more intensive group training in the use of the product. Therefore co-operative work systems require a substantial investment in training and support. Furthermore, by their very nature, they imply a change in the way the company is organised, and a successful implementation will be affected by the existing co-operative culture.

The main finding of this study was that members of the group did not find that *The Coordinator* facilitated their interaction as a group. Furthermore, the implementation and support requirements for co-operative work systems are more difficult than anticipated by developers: the test group was not convinced that the offered functionality in *The Coordinator* was it worth the effort involved in learning to use the tool. Most of the study participants indicated a negative evaluation to the structured use of language incorporated in *The Coordinator* and to the nature of emphasising action in a collaborative work setting. Subjects reported to be restricted in 'how they can talk to one another' in the speech-act paradigm. Although, most of them admitted not having understood what the underlying language paradigm was; they felt that an intellectual understanding would not ally their felt emotional states (Carasik & Grantham, 1988).

Case history 6: Value Engineering in Digital Equipment Corporation

Manufacturing is an application domain rich in committed speaking. The *Contract* research project was developed within the language/action perspective for a value engineering team at Digital Equipment Corporation (DEC) by the Intelligent Systems Technology Group in 1985. The mission of the value engineering enterprise is to improve the value of an existing product or product line. Cost avoidance is the major value goal. Re-engineering is first done to particular parts in order to reduce their cost of manufacturing. These changes are then introduced somewhere in the life-cycle of a product.

Committed speaking was analysed within this context of value engineering computer products. The DEC experience suggests that computers are manufactured successfully only when there is committed speaking, and that a co-ordination system designed to support an enterprise must also support its committed speaking.

The engineering enterprise had created two separate organisations for engineering and manufacturing. The overall quality of action for the entire enterprise depended on the continual co-operation of its separate organisations to share their conversations. For example, it was observed that conversations about the engineering feasibility of a product change happened independently from conversations about the manufacturability of that product change unless people made an explicit effort to share them.

It was discovered that people were truly not aware that commitment was common to their conversations and that a co-ordination system could be useful to improve their awareness. This fact suggests that people are simply working and speaking being more or less being blind to the pervasiveness of commitment and to its essential dimensions. However, conversations in the workplace do not simply mean to exchange information. Instead they create commitments and actions. To make people aware of this fact requires training on committed speaking and a common culture together with good co-ordination tools (Marca, 1989; 1991).

Case history 7: Personal Financial Management Services at Guardian Royal Exchange

The Coordinator has been installed in every branch office of Guardian Royal Exchange (GRE) for its Personal Financial Management Services (PFMS). The application counts some 25 sites in the United Kingdom and a branch in Germany. The requirement was to provide a means whereby branch managers could carry out enterprise-wide conversations to facilitate implementation of policy decisions. A secondary requirement was to provide branch agents with a means of tracking progress on commission claims. Both these requirements are met by *The Coordinator*'s ability to initiate conversations designed to complete with an action. These actions can have completion dates associated with them and the progress of the conversation can be controlled by the use of reply dates on individual communications.

A typical example would be where a branch agent sends a request to head office to issue a commission cheque specifying a complete–by date for when the cheque should be issued and a reply– by date for the next day so the agent is informed of the status of the request. Head office may then reply to this by a counter-offer of completion on a later date as more information is needed before payment is made. The agent accepts this counter-offer and now has a record that payment will be made on a specified date. If such payment is not made the necessary proof is available from the electronic conversation. Again the whole process of communication is simplified for the user by the use of a workgroup name which ensures that the *Message Handling Service* (MHS) will deliver the message to the correct host, whether a host name has been declared or not (Schäl & Zeller, 1989).

Case history 8: Hewlett-Packard

Hewlett-Packard did a trial of *The Coordinator* Version I in-house and investigated in several business organisations for 3 years. Bair & Gale (1988) met 11 organisations and observed reactions to *The Coordinator* at 4 Hewlett-Packard sites.

In general users reported positive benefits as a motivation for overcoming difficulties such as learning and using a character-oriented interface. Despite criticism, *resistors* used it because of the *widespread connectivity* it provided in the larger installations. In addition to *being left out*, users reported they could not communicate with the large, geographically distributed community without *The Coordinator*. Reported benefits are often those identified with *electronic mail* and, in some cases, it is not possible to distinguish the value-added of *The Coordinator*.

The value of *The Coordinator*, particularly for *tracking commitments*, was indicated. The *visibility* of promises, requests, etc. was found to be a powerful management tool. Managers reported that they could keep up with management tasks better. This was particularly true when subordinators were geographically widespread.

Some companies reported that commitment tracking was a major value, others found it to be the major detraction. Tracking interpersonal commitments was socially unacceptable in a minority of the cases. However, those who reported this unacceptability tended to be users of traditional electronic mail systems.

General acceptance of the theory was reported to be important for successful use. The degree to which fully understanding the theory, i.e., the language/action paradigm, is a precondition for acceptance was not clear. The conversation structure had value in spite of the dislike for making commitments explicit. It was reported to reduce *junk mail*, because *The Coordinator* forced reflection and thoughtfulness in management and thinking.

Case history 9: Environmental control in a mechanical and civil engineering company

An Italian company for mechanical and civil engineering with about 500 employees introduced *The Coordinator* Version I in a pilot project for the protection of the civilian population in a valley of the Alps after a landslip in July 1987. A task force of the company had the task to monitor the hydrogeological situation of the valley and to manage the information system to take decisions to alarm or to evacuate people working or living in the valley. *The Coordinator* was adopted to handle the conversations the members of the task force had within it, and with other managers and professionals of the company, during their work.

The Coordinator was introduced about a year after the landslip. The situation in the valley seemed to be calm and the telephone infrastructure was again in use. 8 technicians and engineers used *The Coordinator* in the valley and headquarters. Each of them had a portable PC with an integrated modem and *The Coordinator* installed. The users had between 2 or 3 hours training on *The Coordinator* in different occasions (dates and place). The system was released on May, 2nd 1988.

The introduction of *The Coordinator* was difficult for many reasons, especially due to three main problems.

First, because of technical problems to connect the portable computers to a telephone in the emergency area. This was an additional handicap of the *store-and-forward mechanism* of the system. Only by connecting via phone to a hub, messages are sent and incoming mail is collected. The task-force members' attitude delayed their messages generally by half-a-day. This was due to their habit to connect most of them in the morning starting work and in the late afternoon before going home. The frequency of connections with the hub over a given period is shown in Figure 4-4.

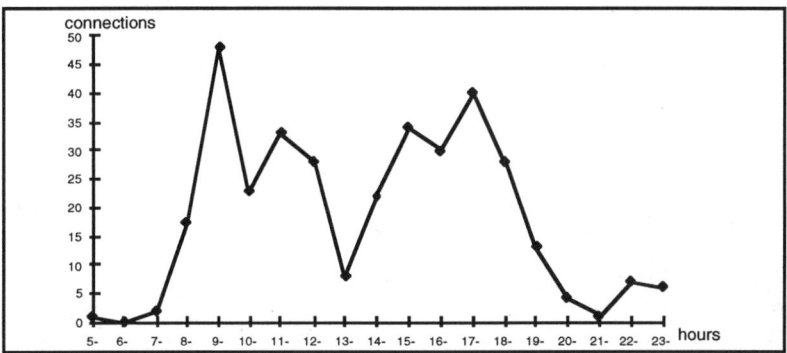

Figure 4-4: Frequency of use over day hours

The problem with the store-and-forward mechanism is, for example, who connects first in the morning deposits the messages for others, collecting only the messages from the previous day. Messages from other colleagues written and sent during the morning will be collected with the next modem connection – generally in the afternoon. The users understood this time-lack and did not use *The Coordinator* for urgent conversations. A benefit was the possibility to communicate with persons working at long distance (especially for different locations in the valley and between the valley and headquarters).

Second, because the introduction was not supported by an adequate information and education program, so that from the very beginning only some of the members of the task-force used it, and the other ones, among which there was one of its leaders, did not.

Third, the objectives of the experiment were not clearly stated, and no one of the involved persons had the responsibility for it.

The experiment was going on for some time with a gradual increase of use by the task-force members, but without changing the critical factors mentioned above. Figure 4-5 shows the usage of *The Coordinator* over time; the trial has been observed by the author from May, 13th to July, 22nd 1988 for a total of 71 days. Figure 4-5 shows only the working days of this period (without Saturdays and Sundays). There is a positive trend for the number of messages up to working day 21.

The use declines after working day 21, because a new landslip caused the end of the use of *The Coordinator*. It was clear at that moment that it was impossible to use it in critical situations, while it was a communication support not used any more by the whole task-force. In addition, it was not reliable from the technical point of view. Some users tried to encourage the use of *The Coordinator* again, before the task-force officially decided on July, 22nd (working day 53) to suspend *The Coordinator*. The introduction of a technology in a newly established group which worked on an emergency project under stress and uncertainty without an adequate organisational setting, was likely a good candidate for the failure (Schäl, 1988).

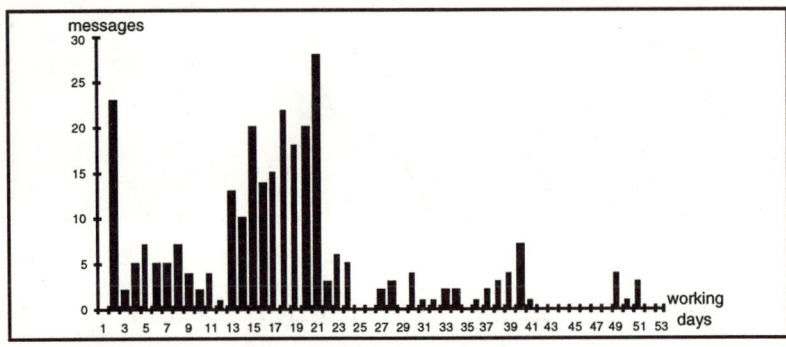

Figure 4-5: Exchanged messages per day during the trial

Case history 10: The Coordinator for defending human rights in Amnesty International

Amnesty International decided to adopt *The Coordinator* to link agents, regional offices and headquarters throughout the United States. Soon after the introduction of *The Coordinator*, a first case against the execution of a death penalty in Florida was supported by the new technology. *The Coordinator* proved to be a very effective means to keep track of all needed actions and information (organising meetings, involving personalities, co-ordinate press campaigns, organise the various tasks of the task force allocated to the mission).

At the beginning, *The Coordinator* confirmed and reinforced the existing organisational structure, being a functional hierarchy. Communication was mainly vertical: orders came from the top and reports on work accomplished or requests for more information came from the operative bottom. The lateral communication among branch offices and field agents working on the case was kept to a minimum by the users. Instead, they sent messages to headquarters, and from there directives would reach the relevant agent. This pattern of usage lasted for at least half of the campaign period, until a major press conference was held and the executive director was informed about its successful conclusion.

The Coordinator's use in the functional sense of the organisational hierarchy seems strange for a human rights organisation. Indeed, the use of the language/action structure is only part of the story. While messages were addressed according to authority ladders and channels, messages were copied by the *cc: functionality*[6] of the tool to all other users of the network. Thus communication in the structured sense of *The Coordinator* was at the same time formal and distributed informally.

In the subsequent period the users switched their attitude on the contrary: the hierarchical communication mode was replaced by direct communication among team members. Field officers communicated directly without sending up their messages the hierarchical ladder. Higher levels of management were called in only when necessary. Anyway, through the use of the *cc: functionality* they were always informed.

The case shows, that *The Coordinator* is successful when people use it without following only the strict rules of behaviour inherent in *The Coordinator*. Amnesty International used *The Coordinator* as a *conversation manager*, but at the same time as a *teleconferencing system* by the unanticipated use of the *cc: functionality* (Ciborra, 1993).

So far, experiences with *The Coordinator* have been reported to illustrate the range and success of its present applications. The system will be discussed further in chapter 5 based on the author's research in a training company. In the following paragraph the second commercial system (*X_Workflow*) is briefly described to prepare the field study II in a bank in chapter 6.

4.7 X_Workflow on Olivetti IBIsys

X_Workflow is an optional component of Olivetti *IBIsys* (Cavedoni, 1991). *X_Workflow* addresses the automation of multi-user office procedures based on the exchange of messages in a communication mechanism. It is based on the DOMINO project (Kreifelts *et al.*, 1991) which has been explained in chapter 4.3. for its workflow specification language *CoPlanS*. DOMINO is an office procedure system for modelling and monitoring structured processes in organisations. DOMINO is in itself form-oriented, i.e., each office procedure type corresponds to an electronic form to be filled in at the various stations it runs through during the procedure execution. It includes also informal and free-format communications in additional to the forms-messages. The procedure is viewed as a series of co-ordinated information exchange

---

[6] *The Coordinator* distinguished between the person to whom the message is addressed (To:...) and observers (Cc:...). The person to whom the message is addressed (To:...) is called a principle. Only principles can take actions and change the status of a conversation. Observers are recipients of copies of the original message. Observers can make comments during the course of a conversation, but cannot affect its status.

actions between several persons, who have the goal of fulfilling a certain task. Every action in the procedure is described by its input/output behaviour, i.e., by the documents it requires (input channels) and the documents it produces (output channels). An action can have alternative input and output channels which means that an action does not have to process all of its input documents and may produce only a subset of its output documents. The action is performed by a role to which a person can be assigned. This formal mechanism for modelling office procedures in *X_Workflow* is specified in the *Coordination Procedure Language* CoPlanS (Woetzel & Kreifelts, 1987; Victor & Sommer, 1989; Kreifelts *et al.*, 1991), which has been described in detail in chapter 4.3..

X_Workflow includes four applications: authoring, maintenance, user applications and auditing. With the author application, new procedures can be defined. The author describes procedure flows, steps and information received and generated in each single step. This is done using the description language *CoPlanS* developed in DOMINO. To define the presentation layout of the information displayed in each step, third party workstation tools can be used, i.e., word-processors, spreadsheets, form handlers, application builders, etc.

The maintenance application serves to install a procedure, and to define the users who can use *X_Workflow*. It includes also an *organisational handbook* to maintain an updated description of the company organisation providing a mapping between *users* and *roles* inside the organisation.

The user application allows the interaction of the individual with *X_Workflow*. A user can start a new procedure, becoming the *initiator* for that particular procedure instance. The initiator can inspect the *status* of the procedures started by the user, specify the *time constraints*, access the *history* of the procedure and *restart* it after withdrawal or cancellation.

A set of conditions can be handled according to the status of the procedure and the person's role in the procedure. Typical situations for exception handling taken into consideration in the *X_Workflow* design are e.g.:
- the wrong person is assigned to a specific role;
- the person assigned to a role is absent;
- a person discovers that an error has been made in compiling one of the received documents;
- the *initiator* is no longer interested in its completion and withdraws or cancels the procedure.

The following actions can be performed in the user environment on a pending task in order to overcome exceptions and advance the procedure:
- *delegate* the execution of an action to another user;
- *reject* the action specifying the reason;
- correct a mistake done by the previous actor by an *objection;*
- correct a mistake detected after the action has been completed by *withdrawing* the instance;
- *view, add and modify* attached documents (text, graphics, spreadsheets, etc.);
- *complete* the action compiling the foreseen forms.

The *auditing application* is a tool for controlling the status of active procedures. The possible auditors can be defined in the procedure and are not necessarily only the initiators.

Two of the commercially available systems (*The Coordinator* and *X_Workflow*) have been briefly described. In the following chapters 5 and 6 two field studies on these systems are reported on the basis of the author's own research.

5. Field study I: The Coordinator supporting distributed management processes

This chapter describes a case designing an Office Information System using *The Coordinator* to support a distributed business process according to the different types of co-operative work (co-ordination, collaboration and co-decision) in a professional training company primarily operating for the public administration in Italy. The author has been involved in the process analysis and the design and implementation of the computer system. Two years after the conclusion of the project, the author conducted a research to evaluate the usefulness of *The Coordinator* in supporting the distributed business processes for which the system has been designed and implemented.

At the beginning of 1990 the company started a project to improve co-operative processes within the organisation, especially for planning and realisation of training courses. This was achieved by encouraging communication and information sharing among all professional roles involved in these processes at all levels (directors, secretaries, teachers, etc.) within and among headquarters and the distributed training centres. The socio-technical solution (Butera, 1990) could not be modelled on the operation of bureaucratic organisations like public administration, nor on the operation of hierarchically or functionally organised companies. Therefore, the project took into account the specific institutional, organisational and cultural aspects of the company and started with an analysis of working processes in terms of co-operative networks. Critical aspects of the processes and types of co-operation were identified before specifying information technology solutions. Finally, a new Office Information System architecture was designed and implemented to support activity synchronisation and information sharing for the people co-operating in the work processes.

> *The scope of this case study is to verify whether the groupware tool The Coordinator can be used to support business processes. The technical system and its design theory of linguistic commitment and completion of conversations in the language/action perspective are evaluated.*

5.1 Company profile

The company discussed here is part of an organisation founded in 1951. It is a non-profit organisation which operates in the professional training sector and has local training centres (CPT - Centre for Professional Training) all over Italy and in several countries of the European Community. In 1980 the organisation adopted a distributed organisation structure and established regional headquarters with responsibility for defining and delivering professional training reflecting local requirements. The CPTs are autonomous from the regional headquarters with regard to the training courses they offer. The regional headquarters have the role of co-ordinating activities among CPTs and of dealing with the national headquarters in Rome.

The studied part of the company is the regional headquarters and connected CPTs in the Lombardy Region in Northern Italy. The regional headquarters is based in Milan and co-ordinates 24 CPTs which deliver nearly 300 training courses for 4500 students. These courses are funded by public money coming from the Regional Government and the European Community. This dependency on public funds generates some of the company's organisational problems in that the already complex structure comprises both political roles (regional and district presidents, board of directors and executive council), as well as professional roles (regional director, directors of the CPTs, teachers, etc.).

The planning and negotiation of activities and decisions concerning the distribution of resources is a complex process involving the directors in the regional headquarters and in the local CPTs. The whole process is also characterised by heavy communication flows between directors and their secretarial staff in both the planning and execution phases, while coping with the variability of the product *training course*.

The company's information system is characterised by an open and decentralised architecture. The company decided not to have a mainframe or another centralised system, and not to establish a Centre for Electronic Data Processing in the regional headquarters. Instead, they adopted a co-operative computing architecture at local and regional level, and installed personal computers and local area networks in the regional headquarters and CPTs. This choice was coherent with the decentralised structure and with the internal organisation which is not strictly hierarchical. The adopted architecture allows sharing of resources, while leaving autonomy to the network's nodes. The company's specific characteristics can be summarised as follows:

- managerial processes with a high level of complexity (management, planning and control);
- highly qualified personnel (mainly directors and instructors);
- information technology based on an open architecture with intelligent workstations and local area networks.

5.2 Analysis of co-operative networks in business processes

The project in the company started with a workshop to make the persons involved in the project aware of aspects of co-operation in their work processes and to define a cultural, organisational and technological framework for the project. In order to prepare the workshop, a first analysis was made concerning the principal managerial and professional work processes. The analysis was conducted applying the outlined methodology for *customer/supplier chains* in the *language/action perspective* based on design principles for *co-operative networks* (see chapter 2). The final aim was to identify characteristics of co-operative networks in the organisation before designing an appropriate information system.

At the beginning of the methodology's application it was necessary to identify work processes which were important for the organisation. This was done by interviews with managers having a general overview concerning the processes selected for analysis. These processes were the *hiring of personnel*, the meetings of the *board of directors*, the production of the *administration statement report*, the life-cycle of the

Table 5-1: Types and dynamics of co-operative networks

Process	Hiring personnel	Board of directors	Admin. statement report	Annual training programme	European training project
Commitment	simple decision	complex decision	complex realisation	complex realisation	complex realisation
Nodes	not analysed	not analysed	not analysed	not analysed	not analysed
Relation	sharing and synchronisation with medium variance	sharing with medium variance	synchronisation with low variance	synchronisation and sharing with low variance	synchronisation with high variance
Articulation	medium structured and undivided process	medium structured and undivided process	medium structured and composed process	medium structured and composed process	medium structured and composed process
Dynamics	co-operation in the small with a low changing of small/large	co-operation in the small with a low changing of small/large	co-operation in the small with a low changing of small/large	co-operation in the small and in the large with a high changing of small/large	co-operation in the large and less in the small with a medium changing of small/large
Network type	co-decision and collaboration	co-decision	co-ordination	co-ordination and collaboration and co-decision	co-ordination and collaboration

company's *annual training programme* and the conduction of *European training projects*.

The results of the analysis (summarised in Table 5-1; for a detailed description see Schäl & Zeller, 1991) were discussed with the project participants. This allowed to make persons sensitive for improvements in their professional and managerial processes. Furthermore, the participants appreciated the idea of introducing a system which would improve co-operation and communication in order to negotiate commitments and to take decisions. The discussions made also evident cultural and organisational problems in the working practice. There was a demand for more co-operative working processes among the different actors involved. Decisions, e.g., were often taken without a wide co-operation among the persons implied in the decision.

5.3 Analysis of communication flows

The most critical process of those analysed is the life-cycle of the *annual training programme* which includes mainly a planning and an execution phase. This process is traditionally characterised by an uncertain and ambiguous communication flow because formal and informal communication channels are used and redundancies are created by the interference of actions of different persons concerning the same subjects. The process' critical factors are also due to its variability and continually changes over time (target group of a course, number of students registered, etc.).

Therefore, a communication flow analysis was done for the life-cycle of the training programme following concepts from the language/action perspective. Persons and their communicative roles, actions and taken commitments, subjects and exchanged objects, relations among different communication flows and milestones (deadlines) were identified in order to analyse the critical factors and re-design the process' conversation space (Schäl & Zeller, 1990; 1991).

The communication flow analysis was done by interviews with persons in the regional headquarters and CPTs who are involved in the planning and execution phases of the training programme having a general overview of the process. The results were discussed with all people involved in the process in a one-day workshop. In that occasion critical factors were identified and solutions suggested in order to improve the process by appropriate Office Information Systems functionality.

The analysis helped to reduce the redundant conversations, to show the need for a more effective negotiation process among the regional headquarters and the CPTs, and to define a shared conversation protocol among the participants. Main problems identified in the process analysis were the undefined customers from the CPTs' directors point of view. They had no clear idea whether their customer is the regional director or the local government. A second problem was the unclear criteria for the evaluation of proposals for the training programme which made the decision process counter-productive for reaching a rapid decision. A continuous redundancy of plan modifications requested to the CPTs by the various directors in the headquarters generated the third weak point identified in the process. All participants had finally difficulties in assembling documents for the final training programme report. These problems have been addressed in the optimisation and re-design of the process. The results are reported in tables following the conversation protocol which reflect phases and objects of recurrent conversations in the process (for an example see Table 5-2).

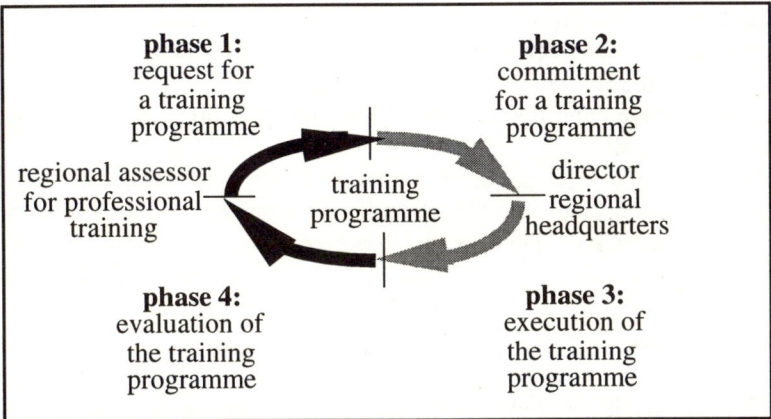

Figure 5-1: Basic workflow for the training programme's life cycle

The *conversations* are modelled according to the *language/action perspective*. The graphical presentation of the basic workflow is given in Figure 5-1. The overall process with the secondary workflows is shown in Figure 5-2. In the first phase the customer (i.e., the regional assessor for professional training) addresses his request for a training programme to the director in the regional headquarters. The director in the regional headquarters is the principle supplier for the assessor for professional training. He activates the persons in the training company to elaborate a proposal for an annual training programme in phase two of the basic workflow. This proposal is discussed among the director and the assessor to define a commitment of the director on behalf of his training company with the regional administration. In the third phase the training programme is executed. Therefore the director in the regional headquarters delegates the training activities to the local training centres. In the fourth phase the assessor for professional training evaluates the executed training programme.

Table 5-2 develops the main characteristics for a conversation about a certain subject. The first example treats the request by the Regional Director to the Functional Directors in headquarters to analyse the official call for training programmes by the Regional Government. Categories are associated with the recurrent conversations in order to classify topics and related conversations. These categories serve to identify process steps and phases in the life-cycle of the training programme, subjects and involved organisational units when this is helpful. The proposed category in this case is *call for plans* because the training company will deliver a plan with training courses to the Region. The principle participants in the conversation are the Regional Director (customer) and the Functional Directors

(supplier). The conversation has three steps which are modelled according to the *conversation protocol* in *The Coordinator* as *speech-acts*. These speech acts reflect also the four phases in the workflow loop designed.
1) the Regional Director *requests* one of the Functional Directors to examine the call;
2) the Functional Director *reports* to the Regional Director on the call;
3) the Regional Director *closes* the conversation with the Functional Director.

The step to 'agree' is left out, because generally there is no discussion or negotiation about the commitment in itself. The acceptance of the request is implicit for the actors involved and the Functional Director will directly respond concerning the contents of the call.

The second example models 4 steps in the conversation protocol, because generally there is a negotiation involved. The example concerns the request by the Regional Director to the local CPT's Director to run a specific training course. This recurrent conversation occurs after the general training programme has been established with the Regional Government. The proposed categories are the course's topic and the involved CPT's name.

Table 5-2: Example for modelling recurrent conversations

workflow	category	principle participants	from (role)	action (speech act)	to (role)
analyse call for training programmes	Call for Plans	Regional Director	Regional Director	request	Functional Director
			Functional Director	report	Regional Director
		Functional Director	Regional Director	close	Functional Director
execution of the training programme (a course to be run by a CPT)	course (topic)	Regional Director	Regional Director	request	Director of a CPT
	CPT (name)		Director of a CPT	agree	Regional Director
			Director of a CPT	report	Regional Director
		Director of a CPT	Regional Director	close	Director of a CPT

These identified recurrent conversations have been summarised in a manual which is used as a reference for recurrent conversations to be accomplished using *The Coordinator*. By doing so, it guides the work of all people involved in the process. People can follow in a correct way the foreseen process having the process conversation protocol as a general framework at hand.

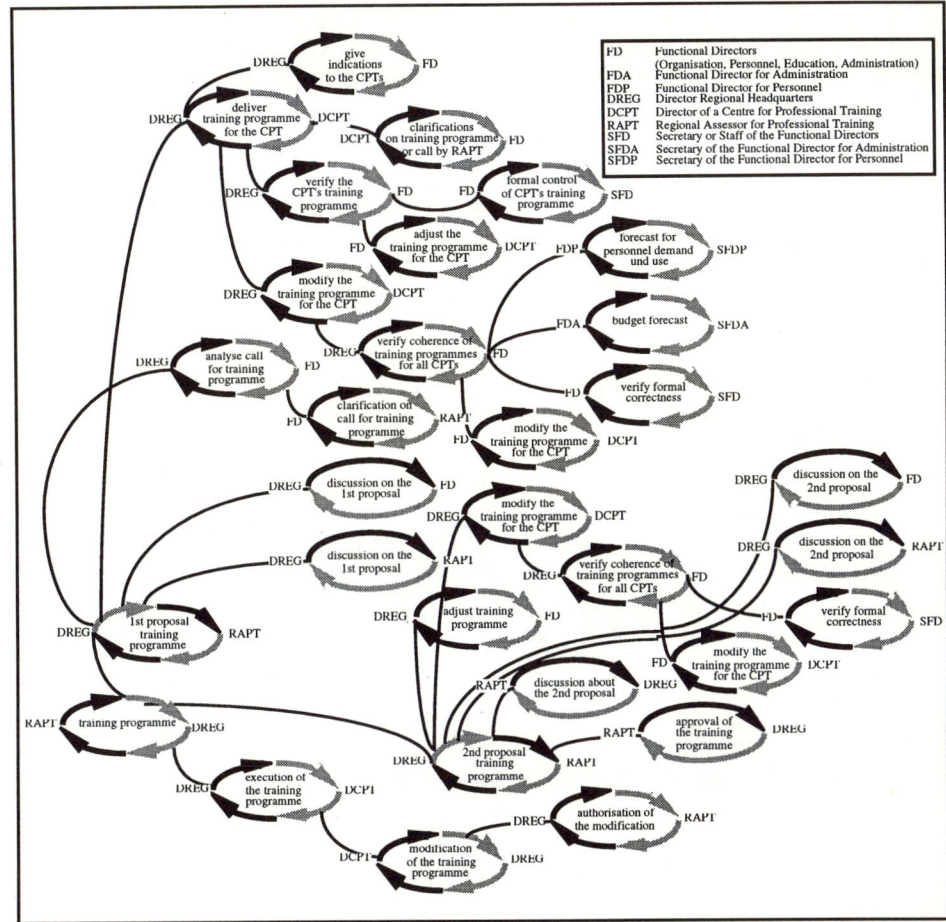

Figure 5-2: Workflow for the annual training programme's life-cycle

5.4 Introduction of The Coordinator

As a result of the described analysis, a new office system architecture was designed to give support for co-operative processes (see Figure 5-3). The basic concept was the integration of a communication system with the existing *Data Base Management Systems* (DBMS) applications to support the requirements concerning co-ordination (the specific system requirements are described in chapter 3.5.2; see also Schäl & Zeller, 1991). The communication system solution was realised by adopting *The Coordinator* Version II which is based on a diffused standard for *Message Handling Service* (MHS) (ATI, 1988b).

The software was installed in the Italian version on *Local Area Networks* (LANs) and stand-alone personal computers which are interconnected on a *Wide Area Network* (WAN) through public telephone lines. The LAN-server in the regional headquarters connects 30 personal computers. The CPTs have LANs or personal computers which connect to a hub-service via modem. The *geographical store-and-forward network* is actually based on public telephone lines which limits especially the transmission of big files due to the low transfer-rates (1200 bits/s). Large files are compressed before transmission to overcome this problem. The hub also connects to a public mail service by a gateway. This allows to receive and send messages from outside the company and to have access to an external data-bank on training issues (courses, projects, courseware, news, etc.) from the electronic mail system.

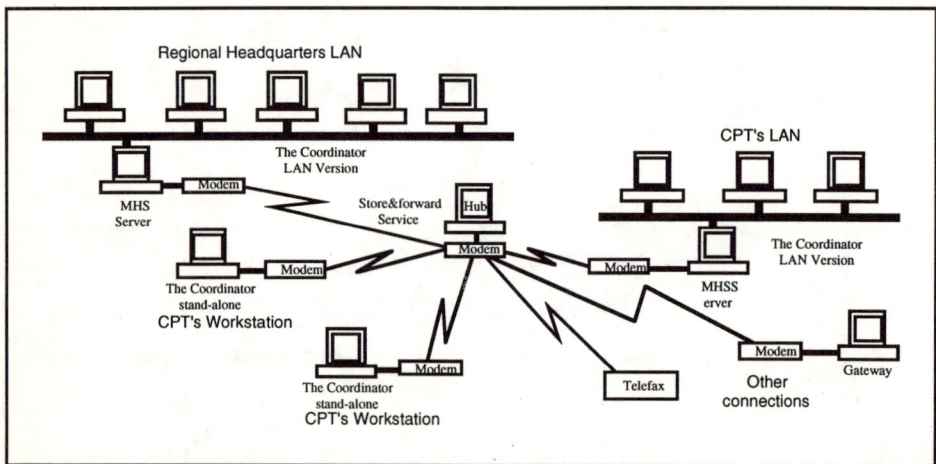

Figure 5-3: Distributed Office Information System Architecture based on The Coordinator and Message Handling Service

The global Office Information System architecture can be described as a three level structure:
1st level: DBMS applications and standard office productivity tools (e.g., word processing, spreadsheet, etc.);
2nd level: Communication software (i.e., *The Coordinator*, MHS);
3rd level: Personal computer's standard user interface.

Training

Users were trained in two distinct training courses. The first course was a full day training on basic functionality. The second course lasted half-a-day to introduce advanced functionality in relation to the working processes. Users had several weeks of personal experience between the first and the second course. This allowed for answering questions and repeating functionality in the second course on request from the users. The users were trained in two sub-groups in sequential editions of the training program.

The training courses did not explain the philosophical background of *The Coordinator*, but explained the language/action perspective as a functionality of the tool. The users practised the conversation protocol in several exercises in an interactive simulation (classes were trained on a local area network installation of *The Coordinator*). The examples used for explanations and exercises were taken from the previous analysis of working processes. This was in favour of a clear understanding for what purpose and how *The Coordinator* could be used in the trainees' daily work. The overall scope for the introduction of *The Coordinator* has been discussed in several workshops with the users (see previous chapter for the analysis of co-operative networks and communication flows).

5.5 Evaluation of The Coordinator

5.5.1 Method

Thirteen users were interviewed after two years that *The Coordinator* has been used in the company. The subjects cover personnel in the regional headquarters as well as in the professional training centres at all levels (directors, training staff and secretaries). Quantitative data were collected from system protocols. Qualitative data were gathered from semistructured interviews conducted with the users. The interviewees had no access to *The Coordinator* during the interviews and had to respond to questions about the software from memory and experience. During the interviews users have been asked about: the training perceived; the evaluation of the training courses; how and for what *The Coordinator* is used; which are the personal benefits from the introduction of *The Coordinator*; which functionality of the tool is useful or missing; what the person had read about *The Coordinator* and its underlying philosophy; which types for opening a new conversation exist in the menu of *The Coordinator*; which are the basic steps in a conversation for action; which message types the interviewee remembered from using *The Coordinator*; the person was shown the conversation for action protocol (Figure 2-4 from chapter 2 according to Winograd & Flores, 1986: 65) and was asked to explain it before being asked to show the basic steps in a conversation for action and the case of a negotiation; the use of the conversation protocol; whether the interviewee thinks that *The Coordinator* is adequate for the organisation and the personal work practices.

5.5.2 Results

The study makes clear that *The Coordinator* is heavily used in the company, but as an *electronic mail system* without an emphasis on the *conversation for action protocol*. The introduction of *The Coordinator* has brought benefits to nearly all users, mainly due to the distributed working situation of the company. In a certain sense, *The Coordinator* was a good solution for communication needs, providing some advanced functionality other electronic mail systems do not have (e.g., combining all messages with the same topic under a single conversation, tracing forward and backward through these conversations, allowing easy retrieval of messages in the conversation database, etc.). The core functionality of *The Coordinator*, however, is used by only a few persons. Users see a limited adequacy of the *conversation protocol* for their working environment. *The Coordinator* does not support sufficiently the perception of business processes in the organisation. We will concentrate on some findings to point out the most interesting interpretations of the results which are summarised in Table 5-3, Table 5-4 and Table 5-5.

Table 5-3: Training and background knowledge on The Coordinator

Subject	1	2	3	4	5	6	7	8	9	10	11	12	13
training course [1]	X		X			(X)	X	X	X	X	X	X	X	(X)
training sufficient [2]	X		X				X	X	X	X	X	X	
readings on the software product [3]	X		X	X	X	X		X	X	X	(X)		
readings on the underlying theory [4]					X	X							

1. X indicates that the person participated in the two training courses of one and a half days; (X) means that the person missed one of the two sessions; no entrance means that the person did not get any standard training.
2. X indicates that the person has been trained sufficiently to use The Coordinator; no entry indicates a not sufficient training for the person.
3. Some articles from magazines and books on The Coordinator and CSCW-related topics have been distributed as reference material during the training courses. X means that the person has read the distributed or other text on The Coordinator. No entry indicates that nothing has been read.
4. No material concerning the underlying theory has been distributed during the training courses. X means that the person has read the book by Winograd & Flores (1986) or other theoretical literature on his/her own. No entry means that the person has not read anything about the language/action perspective.

Table 5-4: Knowledge about the conversation handler of The Coordinator

Subject	1	2	3	4	5	6	7	8	9	10	11	12	13
message types for opening [1]			(X)		X	X	X	(X)	X	X	(X)	(X)	
conversation for action steps [2]			X			X		X	X	X	(X)		
conversation protocol [3]			X	(X)	X	X	(X)	X	X	X	(X)	X	
request [4]			X		X	X		X	X	X	(X)	X	
negotiation [5]			X		X	(X)		X	(X)	X		(X)	

1. The interviewees have been asked to name the seven message types which are proposed by The Coordinator for opening a new conversation (note, inform, question, offer, request, promise, what-if). X means that the person named them all; (X) means that the person named at least 4 of them; no entry means that the person named less than 4.
2. The interviewees have been asked to name the message types which are generally used for a conversation opened by a request (request, promise, report, close). X means that the person answered correctly; (X) means that the person knew principally the sequence and message types; no entry means that the person did not know the answer or made a logical mistake.

3   The interviewees have been shown the figure of the conversation protocol from page 65 in the book by Winograd & Flores (1986). The figure has not been shown during the training courses. They have been asked to explain the figure. The interviewees could take some time to think on their own before answering the question. X means that the person had no problem to explain the figure and to connect it to The Coordinator. (X) means that the person had some difficulties in explaining it. No entry means that the person had no idea about the figure or explained it wrongly.
4   The interviewees have been asked to explain the moves in a conversation opened by a request (request, promise, report, close). Using the figure from Winograd & Flores (1986), X means that the person explained the moves correctly; (X) means that the person had some difficulty in explaining the moves; no entry means that the person did know the moves or made a logical mistake.
5   The interviewees have been asked to show the moves in a conversation opened by a request in which the counterpart of the requestor does not agree and starts to negotiate the requested thing to be done (e.g., request, counter-offer, accept, report, close). Using the figure from Winograd & Flores (1986), X means that the person explained the moves correctly; (X) means that the person had some difficulty in showing the moves on the chart; no entry means that the person did not know the moves or made a big mistake.

Table 5-5: Use and benefits of The Coordinator

Subject	1	2	3	4	5	6	7	8	9	10	11	12	13
mail functionality [1]	X	X	X	X	X	X	X	X	X	X	X	X	X
mail services [2]	(X)		X			X	X		X		X		
other functionality [3]			X						X			X	
uses protocol [4]			X			X	(X)		(X)	(X)		(X)	
daily use [5]		X	X		X	X			X		X	X	
protocol is adequate [6]	(X)		(X)		(X)	X	(X)	(X)	(X)	(X)	(X)	(X)	
personal benefits [7]	X		X	X	X	X			(X)	X	(X)	X	X

1   The interviewees have been asked to name the most used functionalities of *The Coordinator*; X means that the person uses the general mail functionalities like creating and sending a message, replying to a message, etc.
2   The interviewees have been asked to name the most used functionalities of *The Coordinator*; X means that the person makes full use of mail services like categories for filing conversations, retrieval filters for consulting the conversation database, review the status of a conversation, trace the history of a conversation, etc. (X) indicates a limited use of these functionalities. No entry indicates that none of the mail services was named by the person.
3   The interviewees have been asked to name the most used functionalities of *The Coordinator*; X means that the person uses other than mail functionalities and services. These features are the integrated word editor, the agenda, filing functionalities and other tools and services (printing, administration, connectivity, operating environment DOS, etc.). X indicates that the person uses at least one of these additional functionalities (all of them named at least the agenda). No entry means that the person has not named one of these functionalities.

4. The interviewees have been asked whether they use the conversation protocol for their electronic communications on *The Coordinator*. X means that the person declares the protocol's use; (X) means that the person uses the protocol depending on the conversation; no entry means that the person does not use the protocol.
5. X means that the person makes daily use of *The Coordinator* (mainly to send or read mail); no entry indicates a non daily up to a de facto non-use of the software.
6. The interviewees have been asked whether they find the conversation protocol adequate. X means that they find it adequate; (X) means that they have some restriction on the adequateness of the conversation protocol for their working situation; no entry means that the person does not agree with the conversation protocol or thinks that it is not adequate at all for his/her situation.
7. X means that the person declared in the interview to have a personal benefit from the introduction of *The Coordinator*; (X) indicates a limited personal benefit for the person; no entry means that the person cannot see any personal benefit from the introduction of *The Coordinator*.

The Coordinator is training intensive

The Coordinator is a *training intensive* application. The users in this study got a total of one and a half days training. However, training was not sufficient to make them use the protocol. The best results (as far as the underlying model is concerned) are achieved by persons who had full training and have been using *The Coordinator* daily. The problem of training becomes severe for the CPTs where there is a *high turnover* in the personnel. *Newcomers* have never got a training course on *The Coordinator* and due to this fact they have difficulties in using it.

Subjects 2 and 4 did not perceive training and consequently do not know very much about *The Coordinator*. It is interesting to note that Subject 2 anyhow uses *The Coordinator* daily. At the same time Subject 2 is the only daily user who does not declare to have personal benefits from using *The Coordinator*. Subject 13 who participated only in one of the two courses, did not know very much about the underlying conversation protocol. Subject 5 missed the first training course and therefore had problems with *The Coordinator*. Nevertheless, Subject 5 and Subject 8 know the conversation protocol quite well, but do not use it. Subject 5 felt that more training is needed for its use. In general one can see that the knowledge about *The Coordinator* and its conversation protocol are highly related to the degree of use. This means that training is not sufficient for a successful introduction of *The Coordinator*, but rather a good starting point. *The Coordinator* has then to be practised to learn about its functionality and potential.

These findings confirm training issues outlined by Carasik & Grantham (1988) and already reported in case history 5. They report that their trial started with a four-hour training class about the theoretical background and practical instructions for use. The day-to-day user support provided after the initial training was more extensive than anticipated. The support person spent an average of extra two hours with each group member. Their findings indicate the necessity for more intensive group training in the use of *The Coordinator*. Therefore, Carasik & Grantham (1988) conclude, co-operative work systems require a substantial investment in training and support for groups rather than merely individuals.

The Coordinator is used as electronic mail

The Coordinator is mainly used as an *electronic mail system* without the underlying conversation structure. Only two of the 13 Subjects still use the conversation protocol. Personal benefits are mainly attributed to its mail functionality, i.e., reported benefits are often those identified with electronic mail, and in some cases it is not possible to distinguish the value-added of *The Coordinator*. This finding supports the study by Bair & Gale (1988). One Coordinator-specific functionality was appreciated by nearly all users: the concept of a *conversation* as being a series of *linked messages* and the possibility to *organise the conversation database* (Bullen & Bennett, 1990; 1990b).

5.6 Difficulties with the language/action perspective

Problems related to the use of the conversation protocol seem to be due to status differences (e.g., between directors and secretaries) and unclear working processes (i.e., without defined processes and roles there are no implicit commitments for persons involved which can be made explicit by using *The Coordinator*). This can be seen as a limit for using conversation tools in the language/action perspective in work settings as described in this case study. The inventors of *The Coordinator* already made clear that the tool has been designed for:

> 'settings in which the basic parameters of authority, obligation and co-operation are stable. [...] The Coordinator has been most successful in organisations in which the users are relatively confident about their own position and the power they have within it. This does not mean that the organisation is democratic or that power relations are equal. It means that there is clarity about what is expected of people and what authority they have.' (Flores et al., 1988: 173)

There was no clear negation about the *adequacy of the conversation protocol*, as in the study, where most of the participants indicated a negative evaluation to the structured use of language incorporated in *The Coordinator* and to the nature of emphasising action in a collaborative work setting (Carasik & Grantham, 1988). The single explanations of the interviewees are given as follows:

- Subject 1 does not use the protocol, but agrees in principle with it and sees a potential in using it. One of the problems for Subject 1 is that there are messages which remain without response. Subject 1 sees *The Coordinator* as useful where you have to 'make a point' in a conversation or to 'respond explicitly in a critical situation'.
- Subject 4 often has to organise meetings with participants from various CPTs. Therefore, Subject 4 uses *The Coordinator* to invite for meetings. The possibility to establish explicit deadlines is very useful for this activity. However, Subject 4 does not use the conversation protocol, because Subject 4 does not want to discuss the deadlines! 'This is fixed and cannot be negotiated'.

- Subject 5 sees one of the problems in the protocol for relations among persons on different levels in the organisational hierarchy (e.g., director and trainer).
- Subject 6 uses the conversation protocol and still insists to force others to use it. Subject 6 thinks that it is adequate. This is even more interesting taking into consideration that Subject 6 did not explore the philosophical background of *The Coordinator*, but appreciates its pragmatic utility in work.
- Subject 10 has to gather data and information from the training centres on behalf of functional directors in the regional headquarters. However, a request signed by a director is more respected than a request done by Subject 10 via *The Coordinator*. Therefore Subject 10 prefers to have an official letter signed rather than citing the director in an electronic message.
- Subject 11 manages *The Coordinator* for the general director who reads the messages as print-outs where Subject 11 also writes personal comments on. Subject 11 responds on behalf of the general director. Subject 11 does not use the conversation protocol, because Subject 11 does not feel like making a request on behalf of the general director: 'I mediate only the general director's conversations'.
- Subject 12 states to receive generally requests from the director with defined deadlines, continuing the conversation as foreseen in *The Coordinator* for the first steps of the conversation. At a certain point the protocol is not used any more, also because 'we don't negotiate'.

Taking into account these statements as some limits of tools in the language/action perspective, it becomes clear, that not all conversations seemed to be appropriate for the conversation protocol. This is confirmed by the statement that:

> 'The Coordinator was very carefully designed on the basis of a thorough, detailed analysis of a particular approach to conversation, speech act theory. However, the strength of its theoretical foundation also appears to be its Achilles heel. Its design is so heavily influenced by one perspective that it misses many of the important points about human communication and co-operation.' (McCarthy & Monk, 1994: 51)

Some other limits are mainly due to status differences and organisational problems already present in the training company before the introduction of *The Coordinator*. The existence of both, hierarchical and informal relations makes it difficult to intent the single communication according to the situation. This is similar to the case in Amnesty International (Ciborra 1993), where *The Coordinator* has been used formally and informally in presence of the functional hierarchy. Concerning the problem of status differences, the conclusion might be summarised as Suchman (1993) states:

> 'Rather than being a tool for the collaborative production of social action, in other words, The Coordinator on this account is a tool for the reproduction of an established social order.' (Suchman, 1993: 10)

Instead of seeing *The Coordinator* and similar tools as a general purpose *commitment handler*, we should think of specific process support in the language action perspective. The workflow in Figure 5-1 shows nothing else than commitments and the organisational roles being committed in specific transactions between customers and suppliers. However, it is difficult to overcome status differences without an explicit customer/supplier relation in a process support system. If, e.g., a director has to deliver something to a secretary (which means that there is an implicit request for the delivery to the director), it is difficult that the secretary would request it. The same counts for the negotiation of commitments because they are bound in the organisational context and behaviour.

In this sense, the language/action perspective is good for modelling existing processes and it reflects the business perspective in re-designing them. Commitments in processes are defined by the simple fact that somebody has to deliver something to somebody else as foreseen. This leads to the identification of customer/supplier chains in the working process. What has to be negotiated are the conditions under which the commitments among customers and suppliers are accomplished. This can well be done in the discussed perspective, as shown also in the *Contract research project* which was developed within the language/action perspective for a value engineering team at Digital Equipment Corporation (DEC) by the Intelligent Systems Technology Group in 1985 (Marca, 1989). The DEC experience suggests that computers are manufactured more successfully when there is committed speaking, and that a co-ordination system designed to support an enterprise must also support its committed speaking (Marca, 1989; 1991).

The language/action perspective and its implementation in *The Coordinator* has been discussed by many researchers (Bowers & Churcher, 1988; Malone & Crowston, 1990; Suchman, 1987b; 1993; Robinson, 1991; 1993; De Michelis & Grasso, 1994). Most work has been critical. In addition to the discussion of the language/action perspective, case study I has shown that there are limits to use ad-hoc groupware system to support complex processes. The experience of this field study on *The Coordinator* proposes to use the language/action perspective to design systems for clearly defined processes. One conclusion of the study reported here is that the overall business process needs to be taken into vision rather than the isolated commitment handling as in *The Coordinator*. Thus, the new design paradigm is the workflow paradigm for business process automation. It includes to make a wider use of the language/action perspective than in *The Coordinator*. Thus, this research report will show in the next chapter a possible use of the design paradigm for general workflow management systems in addition to commitment handling like in *The Coordinator*. The future use of the language/action perspective might be seen in the design of *business process automation* using process support systems like *X_Workflow* rather than ad-hoc groupware tools like *The Coordinator*. This new perspective in supporting business processes is discussed in the next chapter.

6. Field Study II: X_Workflow for overdraft management in a bank

This chapter describes the application of the organisational models and workflow management systems developed so far in this research report, in an Italian bank. The proposed approaches have been applied as discussed in the previous chapters for business process re-engineering, workflow analysis and design, co-operative networks and the use of workflow management systems. The author participated in this project for business process re-engineering from the very early analysis until the final implementation of the computer system. The objective was to guarantee the change of traditional structures and procedures of the bank into customer-oriented processes for financial services. The bank had to react to the changing competitive and financial situation due to the market liberalisation and to the stronger anti-crime control on financial transactions in Italy, by redesigning its market-oriented business processes. For this aim, first of all the customer related credit processes have been analysed using the method here developed. It is based on the customer/supplier model. Thus the credit management process was the target for a workflow-based reporting system. The system copes with events in the daily occurrence of overdrafts on current accounts which have to be managed by the agency director and the branch's staff. The reporting system developed is part of a global change from the centralised into a distributed credit management information system based on a client/server architecture. The functional architecture for workflow management technology defined in chapter 4 was applied to integrate the different functional modules (message handling, data management and document management) and, in particular, electronic data processing (EDP) on the mainframe with end user computing.

The scope of this case study is to verify whether the process automation system X_Workflow can be used to support business processes. The technical system and the application of the language/action perspective to the workflow specification language CoPlanS are evaluated.

6.1 Company Profile

The case is on a limited liability co-operative bank which was established in 1871. Its headquarters is based in a small city in North-Italy. The bank was the second co-operative bank to be created in Italy. The bank originated and grew as a local bank.

Initially its main purpose was to achieve widespread penetration in the province of its home base. The bank's regional character has been transformed with the passing of time. The bank tries constantly to reinforce its operating structure both by expansion and diversification of the markets, maintaining at the same time an equilibrium between the possible growth and the right dimensions sustainable for the bank. In addition to the local presence in the area of its headquarters, the Bank opened agencies in Milan, Rome and several locations in northern Italy. The bank's network currently numbers 70 branches, nearly all situated in the Lombardy Region. The bank has also taken advantage of its location on the border with Switzerland to expand rapidly its interbank and foreign currency activities; one of the bank's strengths is its expertise in currency intermediation on behalf of both, Italian financial institutions, as well as private individuals and companies. The bank is the 12th largest co-operative bank in Italy in terms of total assets.

In this context of growth and penetration into provinces other than the traditional home base, it should be noted that on 29 March 1989 the Banca d'Italia (National Bank of Italy) liberalised the opening of branches. Banks have been accorded complete freedom in deciding what dimension they want to have in the market. As a result, many other banks opened up in nearly all places the bank was present with its agencies. The mad dash to capture market share under the current regulations means that several banks changed their objective. Today one can observe the paradoxical situation of a small provincial capital with only 22.500 inhabitants, served in pre-deregulation times by four banks, now possessing seven banks (with 10 windows) and more to come.

Furthermore, the changing economical situation of industries as well as of private persons results in a growing credit demand on the Italian banking system. This is a positive development as far as business opportunities are concerned, but the number of outstanding credits is increasing, too. Furthermore, the complexity of the credit modalities and the customer's financial situation is growing.

Given this new competitive and financial situation, the small bank described here, had to act in order to stay profitable on the market place. The bank decided that re-engineering the credit process was required. The bank is in a process of change from a functional to a process organisation to cope with the new situation. Previously task driven activities with fairly fixed job descriptions have to be converted into goal driven processes where people have to show competence in coping with financial services and customer satisfaction.

The development of a workflow-based reporting system was a first step in a global change from the centralised information system into a distributed client/server architecture in order to align the information system to the required transformation of the bank. An end-user information system, layered on top of a mail-enabled workflow management system, was designed to provide users with real-time information on credits and to manage the credit process. The application was built to proof the feasibility of change by developing a workflow-based reporting system. The bank approached a consortium of three different companies to provide help and the right solution to the changed situation. The project was managed by the consultancy company RSO (Casonato, 1993; Schäl & Zeller, 1992b; 1993). The chosen IT supplier was Olivetti, primary because of its prior relationship with the bank (it is the branch equipment provider for specialised PC-based workstations). The designed and realised computer system was implemented in one of the bank's main branches using Olivetti's *IBIsys* as the *Office Information Systems* (OIS) infrastructure. The exchange of information and co-ordination of events in the process is based on Olivetti's *X_Workflow* (Cavedoni, 1991). The software-house ICON integrated the reporting pilot application on the platform using the expert system SECReTS (Chiopris, 1993).

The pilot project lasted nearly a year among analysis, design, development and implementation. The reporting prototype has been tested and installed as a certified application in the bank. There have been 15 persons directly involved (3 from RSO, 3 from Icon, 4 from Olivetti, an information systems manager and 4 users from the bank). The author has been mainly involved in the process analysis and re-engineering. Results from the process analysis have also been used to develop a different pilot for financial processes in the ESPRIT Project 2705 ITHACA (Agostini et al., 1993; 1994; De Michelis & Grasso, 1993).

6.2 Process analysis

6.2.1 Method

The author interviewed about 20 persons directly involved in the credit process and responsible for its financial success. The interviewees were bank personnel in local branches as well as in central offices. The described working practice was interpreted as the exchange of artefacts (documents, data, signatures, etc.) between customers and suppliers. For each transaction the customer's expectations from the supplier were characterised. The formal representation used to describe the financial process refers to the already explained workflow loops showing the customer/supplier chains, as explained in chapter 2.

During the interviews maps were drawn representing the identified customers and suppliers. The charts were directly discussed. As the interviewees looked at the paper-drawn sketches, they were able to validate the maps or they told the author how to alter them. The representation of customer/supplier relations in loops proofed to be of universal comprehension: none of the interviewees had problems with the representation and they continued for themselves in arguing according to the loop structure. The process analysis obviously contributed clarifying and making transparent the *real* business process to the bank's employees.

The questioning about customers, suppliers, conditions of satisfaction, etc., led to identifying gaps and confusion, incomplete workflows, misunderstanding of results and ineffective information flow. A large part of all communication occurs informally. Thus, its outcomes and resulting actions are frequently not transparent. They are neither reported, nor documented for further use by other bank employees necessarily concerned with these actions. In addition to the identification of *customers, suppliers* and *conditions of satisfaction*, the interviewees were asked directly to describe *breakdowns* and general *problems* in the credit process. The interpretation of these results led to the representation of the actual operative processes; re-engineered versions were discussed, instead of automating the old process.

The activities regarding credits are divided into two basic processes. The first process concerns the granting of credits to already entrusted or new customers. The second process is characterised by the management of all credits' life-cycles. This concerns, e.g., variations of existing credits, monitoring and review of the credit portfolio and the recovery of credits from revoked or expired credits. Table 6-1 shows the co-operative aspects of the two credit processes (for the explanation of the categories, see chapter 3). It becomes clear from the analysis of the two co-operative networks that the credit management process is the more critical process. This is due to the fact that the credit management process is concerned about breakdowns and undesired situations, while the credit granting process serves to avoid these situations in advance. Furthermore, the credit management process comprises many of the activities done also in the credit granting process. The following paragraph describes the credit granting process, while the credit management process is described in the subsequent paragraph.

Table 6-1: Analysed processes and types of co-operative networks

Process	Credit Granting	Credit Management
Commitment	complex realisation	complex realisation
Nodes	not analysed	not analysed
Relation	synchronisation with low variance	synchronisation with high variance
Articulation	highly structured and composed process	medium structured and composed process
Dynamics	co-operation in the small and in the large with a mode rate changing of small/large	co-operation in the small and in the large with a moderate changing of small/large
Network type	co-ordination and collaboration	co-ordination and collaboration

6.2.2 The credit granting process

Basic workflow: credit request

The bank's customer generally enters the bank and contacts a person at one of the counters. This front-office for general purposes (deposit, withdraw, etc.) does not handle new requests for credits and passes the practice to the director of the bank agency who is the bank's interface for all credit-related interests for the customer. Therefore, the basic workflow is the customer's credit request to the agency director. The graphical representation of the basic flow in the process is given in Figure 6-1.

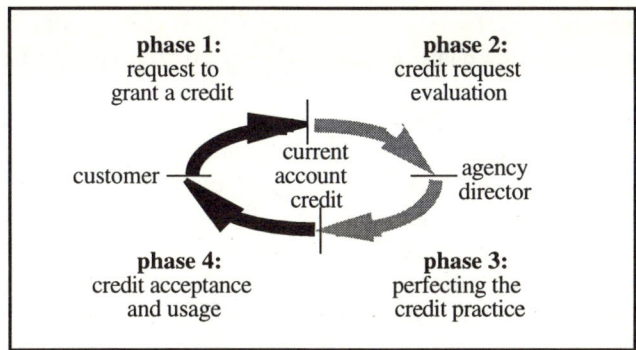

Figure 6-1: Basic workflow for granting credits on current accounts

In the first phase the customer addresses his request to the agency director and makes it explicit by using the foreseen application sheets. The customer generally gets these forms and first explanations for its compilation form the employee at the counter. The customer will present himself to the agency director with the filled-in forms.

According to the Italian law and rules established by Banca d'Italia, the request has to match some formal requirements. This means that it has to be a formal document which is signed by the customer. The document has to indicate the requested amount, duration of the credit and possible guarantees. The customer has, furthermore, to declare his passives at the date of signature if he is a private person. Legal persons (companies) have to annex the latest balance and their actual situation on all bank accounts.

In phase 2, the agency director evaluates the customer's request. The agency director consults the customer data-base in order to check whether the customer is already known or to control his financial position with the bank. After this first check, the agency director activates several secondary workflows with the customer, the clerks in the agency and central departments of the bank, in order to decide whether the agency director is in favour of the credit or not.

If the agency director is in favour of the customers request, he will activate the bank's internal procedure by using a form entitled *proposal for a credit concession*. The agency director fills in only some information. The form is then completed by the agency's credit secretariat (see secondary workflow D).

On the basis of these data, the customer's situation is calculated in tables on the same form. The final figures indicate the customer's total assets and the risk associated with the requested credit in the customer's actual situation. If the agency director sustains the credit request, he will sign it on the form *proposal for a credit concession*. His signature is sufficient to make the credit operative after the registration in the *book of credits*, if credit amount and interest rate are in his competence. Otherwise other organs of the bank have to sign the form (see secondary workflow F).

For some credits the practice might need some further work also after the credit is approved. This is done in phase 3, especially for credits with guarantees. These guarantees might involve specialist elaboration by different offices in the bank, like stocks, mortgages or foreign affairs. The customer might be informed about the agency director's decision informally but he gets in any case an official letter about the resolution of his request after it has been signed by the resolution body and all technical necessities have been fulfilled. This letter closes phase 3 of the basic workflow. The form indicates the substantial characteristics (amount and expire date) and encloses the general conditions of the contract. The customer has to sent a signed copy of the letter informing him of the granted credit back to the bank, in order to state his acceptance of the credit and the general conditions (which closes the basic workflow in phase 4). The basic workflow for granting credits and its connected secondary workflows are shown in Figure 6-2 (the secondary workflows are numbered with letters from A to I; the following description takes these letters as references in the headings of the paragraphs).

Workflow A: exploitation of the customer's motivation

The first secondary flow concerns the exploitation of the customer's motivation by the agency director. Therefore, workflow A is a declaration workflow in contrary to the basic action workflow. The final outcome are hand-written notes on the discussion with the customer by the director and possibly his own position.

Workflow B: documents for credit

After a first positive personal evaluation, the agency director, will ask the bank's customer to provide the necessary documentation for the procedure. These documents are, e.g., the customer's identity card, tax declaration, etc. In this case the bank's customer becomes a supplier to the agency director who becomes the customer. It is a general pattern of the workflow structure that the customer/supplier relationships can be reversed for certain business transactions as compared with the general perception of the words customer or supplier.

Workflow C: information about the customer

The agency director has then the option to involve other persons and institutions in order to get additional information about the customer. Possible information sources are, e.g., the agency's vice-director, the special credit office, the agency credit secretariat or other functions and personal in the bank. The agency director might also use external information sources, like the Chamber of Commerce, the Risk Centre at Banca d'Italia, a committee of local experts, consultants, etc. The directly in workflow C involved actors can make additional requests to third parties in order to investigate on the agency director's request.

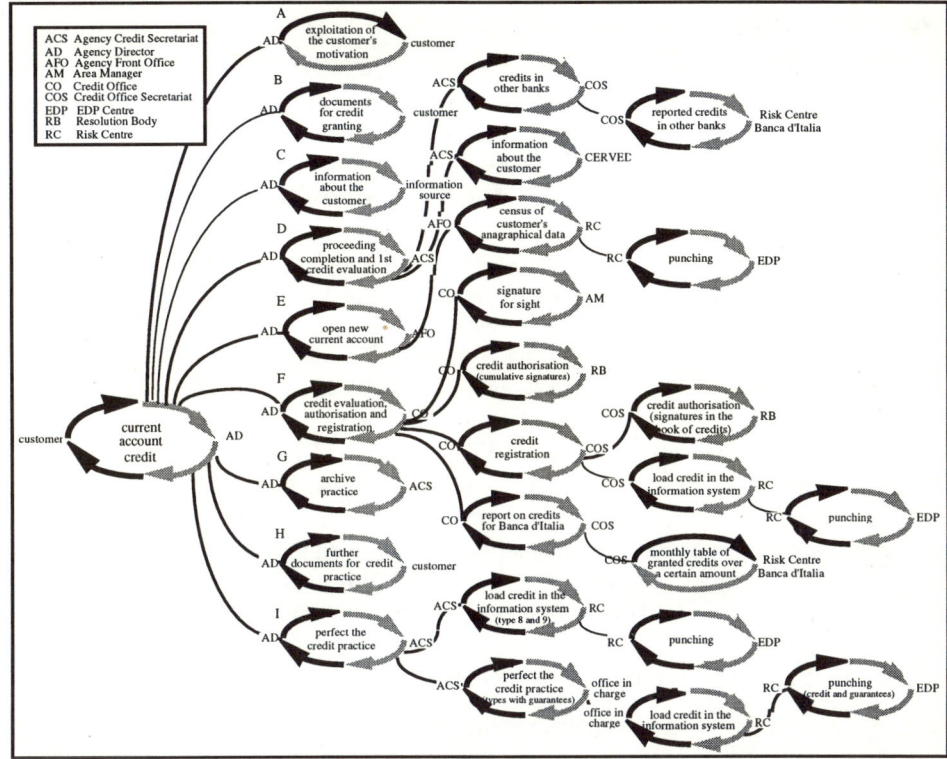

Figure 6-2: Workflow for granting credits on current accounts

Workflow D: proceedings completion and 1st credit evaluation

After the collection of documents and general information about the customer, the director passes the practice to his special secretariat for credits. He asks the staff in the agency's credit secretariat to complete the proceedings and to give a first evaluation of the credit's confidence.

The agency's credit secretariat compiles a new form *proposal for a credit concession* which in first instance integrates the information on the request forms and additional notes from the director's conversation with the customer and investigations on the customer. The agency's secretariat asks a special branch in the central credit office whether the customer has credits of more than 80.000.000 Lit in other banks. The central credit office forwards this request to the Banca d'Italia which has a *risk centre* with all credits over 80.000.000 Lit which have been communicated by law from the Italian banks. At the same time, the agency's credit secretariat makes an investigation on the public database of the Italian Chamber of Commerce (CERVED) about balances, protests, etc. This additional information from Banca d'Italia and Cerved is also introduced in the form *proposal for a credit concession*.

Workflow E: opening a new bank account

As the existence of a bank account is a prior condition to the whole process, the agency director will ask his counter staff to open an account in case the customer has not already got one. This bank account will not be operative until the final decision about the credit acceptance is taken. Therefore, the customer does not know about the opening of the bank account and does not receive any services related to the account (e.g., checks, credit card, etc.).

The agency director passes the customer's record to the counter staff who enters family name, first name and a reference number (equal to the later bank account number) into the procedure *general conditions*.

After this entrance to the Information System, the counter clerk asks the bank's central risk centre to register the customer in the bank's *customer database*. The central risk centre will check the input of the new account on the procedure *conditions*. It will then insert all data relative to the new customer into the customer database. In order to make the bank account operative, the EDP centre has to punch the information into the central bank account database.

The EDP centre produces every day a printed table with all variations in the bank's current account database. The table is given to the central risk centre as well as to the agencies. The account is operative after the punching in the information system.

Workflow F: credit evaluation, authorisation and registration

The agency director passes the practice to the credit office after he has decided to give a credit to a customer. His decision is made explicit by signing the form *proposal for a credit concession*. The agency director's request in action workflow F relates to different items. The first issue is the formal control and evaluation of the credit by the credit office. A second concerns the authorisation of the credit if the value or the interest rate is not in the agency director's autonomy. In these cases various persons have to countersign the proposal in order to authorise the credit within their specific competence. The third and final issue relates to the registration of the credit in the information system and legally required *book of credits*.

The credit office will control the formal aspects of the form *proposal for a credit concession* before it accepts the request and arranges for further actions. All requests are first passed to the respective area manager who has to sign the form, stating that he is aware of the credit request.

The credit office will then write an evaluation report on the credit request which becomes an integral part of the form *proposal for a credit concession*. If the credit is in the agency director's competence, the credit office will proceed directly to the credit's registration. Otherwise, different bodies have to authorise the credit. These resolution bodies can sign only to a maximum amount or for special conditions.

The credit office passes the credit form *proposal for a credit concession* to each of the required bodies in an amount-dependent sequence. Each body signs the request in order to authorise it and can give a personal statement relevant for the decision process (additional information regarding the customer, disapproval of the credit office's evaluation, etc.). These statements become also an integral part of the *proposal for a credit concession* as it proceeds in the signing process.

When all signatures for credits within an actual maximum amount of 1.500.000.000 Lit are collected, the credit office asks a special division in the credit office to register the credit in the *book of credits*. The already authorised credits under 1.500.000.000 Lit are at the very moment of their registration legally active; credits of higher value have still to be authorised. This is done by signing directly the *book of credits*.

In order to keep track of these three fundamentally different credit approvals, there are three *books of credits*. The first one is the list of all credits under 1.500.000.000 Lit in their temporal sequence reporting the authorisation in the *book of credits*. Each of the top highest resolution bodies (presidential committee and board of directors) has its own *book of credits*. The credit office will prepare for each meeting of the bodies a single page of the book with the respective credit requests. The page is then signed in the meeting for all listed credit requests.

After the credits have been authorised and registered, a copy is passed to the bank's risk centre for loading the new credit in the bank's information system. The bank's risk centre passes the necessary information to the EDP centre for punching the information. If there are guarantees for the credit, the bank's risk centre controls the formal aspects before it passes the information to the EDP centre. If the necessary documentation is still missing, the practice has to be made perfect in a subsequent workflow as far as guarantees are involved (see secondary workflow I).

The EDP centre inputs the data in the data-base for bank accounts and a daily print-out informs about changes in the data-base. These print-outs inform the director about the fact, that the credit is now operative on the bank's information system. At the same time the credit office sends a copy of the practice to the agency director.

Workflow G: archive practice

Finished practices have to be archived in the agency. This is done by the agency's credit secretariat. The practices are stored in a filing cabinet.

Workflow H: further documents for conclusion credit request

After the authorisation and registration of a credit, the customer has in case of some specific guarantees to hand over additional documents. These documents involve generally high costs for being legally valid and are therefore made only at this point. The agency director will request these documents from the customer for the perfecting of the credit's request practice.

Workflow I: perfecting the credit request practice

Action workflow I serves for making the practice perfect when there are guarantees involved. The director requests the perfection to the agency's credit secretariat. This secretariat can make the practice perfect for some credit requests (e.g., assignment current account credit and balances current account credit). All other type of credits with guarantees will be made perfect by the specific office in charge (stocks, mortgages, foreign affairs).

The agency's credit secretariat asks after the perfecting of credits the bank's risk centre to load the credit and guarantees in the bank's information system. The bank's risk centre passes the information to the EDP centre for punching. If there are guarantees for the credit, the risk centre controls the formal aspects before it passes the information to the EDP centre.

For all other credit types with guarantees, the agency's credit secretariat will forward the practice to the competent office in the bank (stocks, mortgages, foreign affairs) which will take care for the perfection of the practice and later registration.

6.2.3 The credit management process

Relevant activities regarding existing credits are characterised by the credits' life-cycle management. This concerns, e.g., variations of existing credits, monitoring and review of the credit portfolio and the recovery of credits from revoked or expired credits. The process is especially critical in the sense that the risks involved in all credits change over time and the bank has to perceive these dynamic changes in order to avoid losses. Different events, not always coming from the same parties, defined dates for revision, or a specific request, also from the customer, can give an input for a specific action within the managing process.

The basic workflow (Figure 6-3) can be identified in the area manager's relation with the agency director, asking to maintain all credits in the branch over their life cycle under established economical conditions (e.g., annual growth rate of the credit portfolio, no losses if credits cannot be paid back by customers, margins in the order of pre-defined interest rates, etc.). The agency director is the principle supplier for the area managers. The effective responsibility for the single credit is located in the respective agency where the customer has asked for the credit. This distribution of responsibility for credits reflects the decentralisation of the bank's decision processes towards the local branches. The agency director can activate a number of secondary workflows in order to guarantee a good performance of credits in his branch. These workflows are all in the third phase of the basic workflow (B-1 to B-8) and some of them are optional which means that they are activated by the director only in certain circumstances. The basic workflow for managing all credits' life cycle and its connected secondary workflows are shown in Figure 6-4.

Workflow A: indicating and recording various events

Workflow A is a declarative one and has only an indirect and informal relation with the basic workflow for managing the credits' life-cycle. Third parties who are mostly prominent persons, can give indications and hints to various individuals in the bank. This information is likely negative and has to be considered immediately for actions in order to prevent the bank from having difficulties with customers who might be in trouble or cannot pay back already used credits. Some of these declarations are already

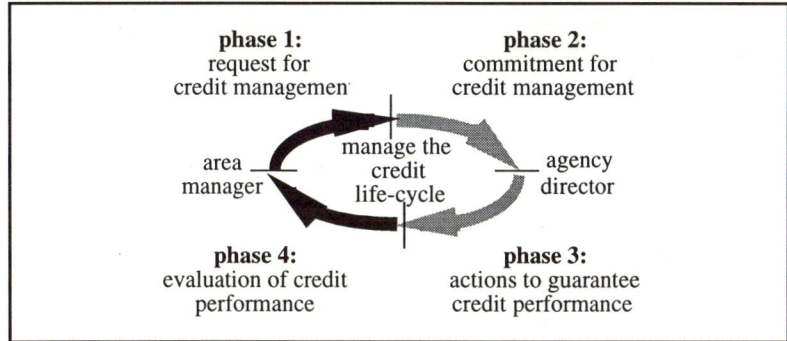

Figure 6-3: Basic workflow for credits' life-cycle management

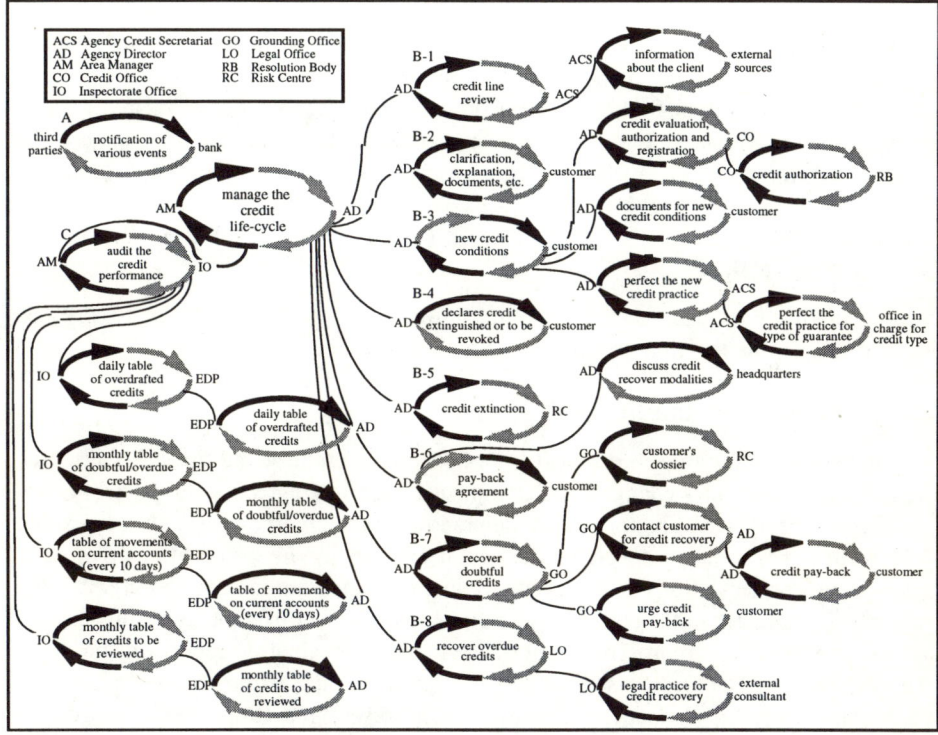

Figure 6-4: Workflow for the credits' life-cycle management

well-addressed (e.g., from the committee of local experts), others are regularly produced information which have to be addressed to the right person in order to generate a predictive action (e.g., reports from court or Chamber of Commerce), still others contain regularly produced information which has to be interpreted (e.g., newspaper and magazine articles).

There was no organisational process or information system which explicitly connected workflow A to the other processes identified in the analysis of credit processes. This implies that the organisation is inappropriate and reacts inefficiently and ineffectively to the notified events. The limit to support the credit management and review by a proper organisation and tools has been overcome by re-engineering process and designing the reporting system described in the following paragraph of this chapter.

Workflows B: guaranteeing the credit performance

Workflow B-1: credit line review

Workflow B-1 can be activated as a recurrent activity or on the bases of an exception. The first case refers to the annual revision of all credits over a certain amount and a revision every two years for lower valued credits. The revision is always done by the agency's credit secretariat. In the revision process the customer's total assets and risks are investigated. Information about operative credits on other banks (Risk Centre Banca d'Italia) and public available information (Chamber of Commerce) are always taken into consideration for the revision process. The second case is related to outstanding events which are, e.g., indicated in workflow A. In such circumstances the director can initiate workflow B-1 in order to predict the bank from possible damages.

Workflow B-2: request for clarifications, explanations or documents from the customer

The agency director can ask the customer in order to proof a doubt or to provide information for the revision process.

Workflow B3: new credit conditions

The agency director might decide to propose new credit conditions because the credit's confidence has changed. After the customer has agreed with possible new conditions, the agency director passes the practice to the credit office. The credit office will control the formal aspects of the credit request for new conditions before it arranges for further actions. If the credit is in the branch autonomy, the credit office will proceed directly to the credit's registration. Otherwise, different resolution bodies have to authorise the credit. The credit office writes an evaluation report on the credit request. The credit office passes the credit request to each of the required resolution bodies in an amount-dependent sequence. Each body signs the request in order to authorise it and can give a personal statement relevant for the decision process (additional information regarding the customer, disapproval of the credit office's evaluation, etc.). These statements become an integral part of the credit dossier. When all signatures are collected, the credit is registered in the legally required *book of credits*.

The customer has to supply all the necessary documentation for the procedure, such as identity card, tax declaration, etc. The customer has to hand over additional documents in case of specific guarantees. These documents involve generally high costs for being legally valid and are, therefore, made only after the bank's credit authorisation. The agency director will ask the customer for these documents for perfecting the credit practice.

The director requests the perfection to the agency's credit secretariat which perfects the practice for some credit types (assignment current account credit and balances current account credit) while other types of credits with guarantees will be made perfect by the specific office in charge (stocks, mortgages, foreign affairs).

Workflow B-4: agency director declares credit extinguished or to be revoked

The director writes a letter to the customer if he intends to revoke a given credit. This might be foreseen because the credit's duration was limited when signing the contract. Otherwise, the director might revoke the credit because he decided that the customer is no longer in a condition for having the credit. The customer might respond to the revoke letter or simply accept it by not acting. In discussing the possible revoking of a credit with the customer, the director might also decide to not extinguish the credit but keep it as it is, or he might offer new conditions.

Workflow B-5: credit extinction

After the final decision to revoke a credit, the agency director requests the extinction of the credit from the information system.

Workflow B-6: pay-back agreement

The agency director proposes the customer a modality under which a suffering credit could be paid back. The director discusses possible modalities for credit recovery also with headquarters.

Workflow B-7: recover doubtful credits

If the customer does not pay-back his credit according to the agreed modalities or he does not pay-back anything at all, the agency director will ask the grounding office to take care of it. The grounding office will insist with the customer and might also ask the agency director to urge the customer to pay.

Workflow B-8: recover overdue credits

If the customer is not willing to pay or he cannot pay-back a credit, the agency director will ask the legal office to open a legal practice. It is, however, doubtful that the bank will recover these overdue credits. The legal office inputs all the data in a specific application (CRESO) and delegates the legal practice to an external lawyer. Every six months the legal office produces a report for the agency director in order to explain the progress of the recovery process.

Workflow C: auditing the credit performance

Workflow C helps the area manager to evaluate the credit management by requesting an audit on all credits to the inspectorate office. The inspectorate office consults a number of reports from the EDP centre which permit analysis of the critical factors. These reports are:
- daily table of overdrafts;
- monthly table of doubtful/overdue credits;
- table of movements on current accounts (every 10 days);
- monthly table of credits to be reviewed.

A copy of these tables is also sent to the single agencies which will analyse them for their own dependencies in order to predict difficulties. Workflow C is perceived as a control function for the area manager related to the agencies' credit management, instead of being actively used to prevent the agency from damage. Re-engineering the process and implementing a *workflow-based reporting system* changed this perception of information for control into information for action. The prototype shifted the perception of data and information in the sense that information is only useful because someone can do something with it. The developed workflow-based reporting system is action-oriented. The main purpose for using information technology is to allow the user to understand the significance of information in a specific context. In this sense, reporting systems should be seen as information systems which allow the identification of *breakdowns* in the organisation and not as big warehouses for data storage and retrieval, used in this case mainly for control purposes.

6.3 Workflow-based reporting system for credit management

6.3.1 Requirements for the credit information system

It became clear from the analysis of the actual process that the bank had to develop an integrated information system for the whole credit process. The analysis provided some considerations about the main needs for new information systems functionality. The main weaknesses of the previous situation were:
1. Work was mainly done by using paper forms. There was a significant work load for re-writing information on different information systems or internal paper forms. The re-use of once gathered data or information was poorly developed, i.e., the same type of information (name, address, account number, credit request number, etc.) was repeated many times in the process by different persons.
2. The available information was mainly used for administrative control, instead of a pro-active use of data for, e.g., marketing. The managed data were not integrated and information about the history of the customer's relation with the bank was not available.
3. Process control was based on information reported in the standard print-outs produced overnight through the central mainframe-based procedures. This mainframe-based data processing is common to banks in general, because all banking data need to be centrally processed, correlated and compared. For the

agency director, however, the whole management process could not rely on real time information (e.g., status of the credit process, statistics, etc.).
4. Informal communication which takes up a large portion of all banking actions, is not reported or documented even if needed for further decisions. This type of information is hold personally in mind or annotated on personal agendas or paper. Thus it has to be retrieved informally, which indicates a high cost (i.e., to identify the right person, high telephone bills, disturbance, etc.).

The actual credit granting process as described before modelled also the data-entry and punching activities. Due to the possible automation of the mainly paper-based credit process, a number of activities can be taken over by the computer system. A hypothetical computerised credit granting workflow is outlined in Figure 6-5; the number of customer/supplier relations is notably reduced. This implies already in its own nature of a reduced number of transactions less cycle time and costs.

Considering the present limits in the process, the bank decided to explore new concepts for its information system development. The bank identified the reporting

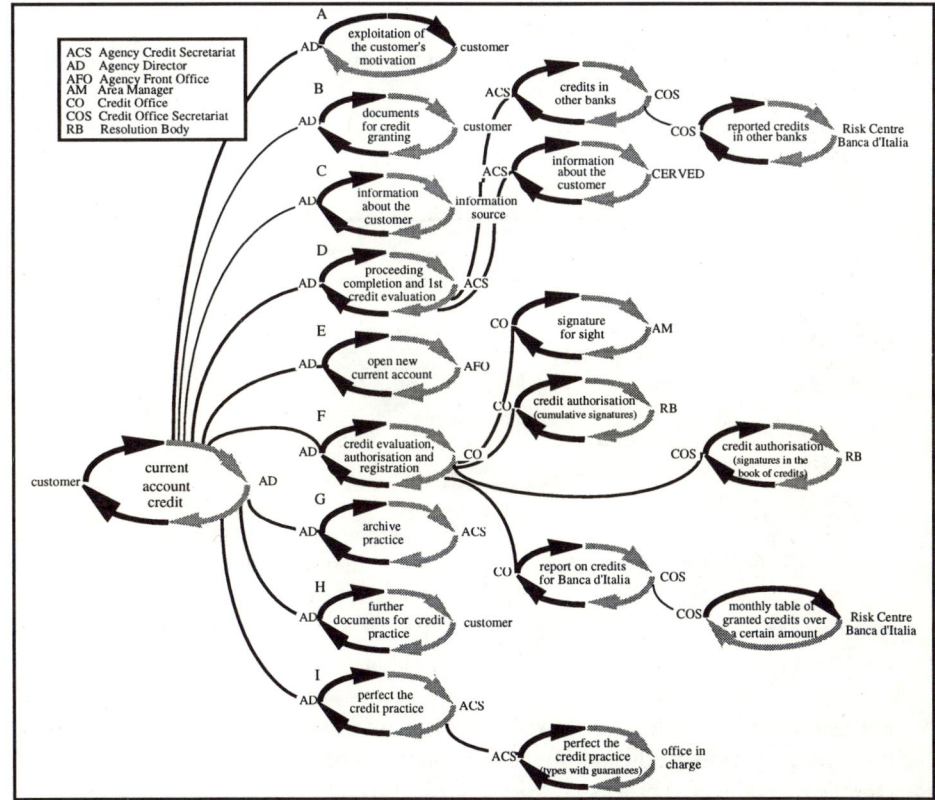

Figure 6-5: Reduced number of customer/supplier transactions in a computerised workflow for granting credits

process of critical events (i.e., unannounced overdrafts of customers) in the single branches as an adequate pilot application and as a first step in the development of a new overall information system.

6.3.2 The re-engineered credit management process

The development of the reporting system for critical events (e.g., overdrafts) went along with an organisational re-definition of the basic workflow for credit management. The main organisational objectives were to keep track of the various events which might be lost after some time without taking care of them. The re-engineered process had to take into consideration that:
- the whole business process for credit management and credit decision making should become more transparent; all communicative business actions should be visible, documented and traceable;
- the loosely coupled workflow A should be linked for certain events to the credit management process;
- the auditing workflow C should shift from a bureaucratic control process into a support function for the agency director;
- the agency director's responsibility for the credit process should be reflected in a more central role of the branch in the entire process;
- the decision-making process on credits should be supported by information technology and fast data processing.

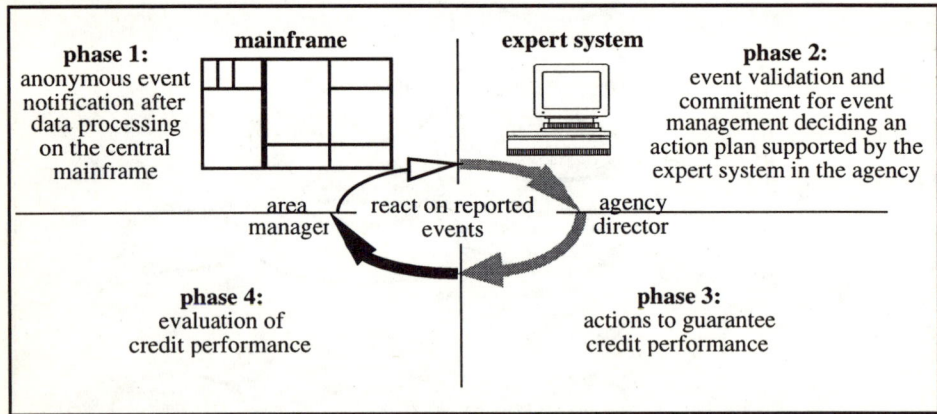

Figure 6-6: Basic workflow for the event-based credit management

For these aims the basic workflow for credit management has been re-designed on the basis of the previous considerations in relation to the existing process. The main idea for the re-engineered process is to see critical events (e.g., sudden overdrafts) as breakdowns which generate an explicit request for credit management. Therefore, the event notification by the reporting system becomes part of the first phase of the basic workflow in Figure 6-6. Instead of being merely informed about certain events (orally or by information printed on tables in the disconnected workflow A or the secondary loops of workflow C), the agency director is explicitly asked via the workflow system to evaluate and where necessary take care of the notified situation. This means that the request *to manage the credit life-cycle* to the agency director in the first phase of the basic workflow in the previous situation is enhanced and specified by being asked anonymously to react on reported events; the event evaluation becomes then part of the second phase which did not have any secondary workflows in the previous situation.

The first phase, however, is triggered by the supporting event reporting system which monitors all financial transactions of the branches on the central mainframe database. The expert system is based in the branch itself, to be used for decision making by the agency director. The system offers in a transparent way all information needed by the agency manager to decide on risk or no-risk events. Thus, the first phase represents basically the request for action of the area manager as the person who is superior (in banking terms) to the agency director. The area manager is the person finally responsible for all business actions in the branches of his area. This request, however, is anonymous. It is a token action, because this specific action is merely a computer message (or frame) which the agency director is requested daily to call up and respond to.

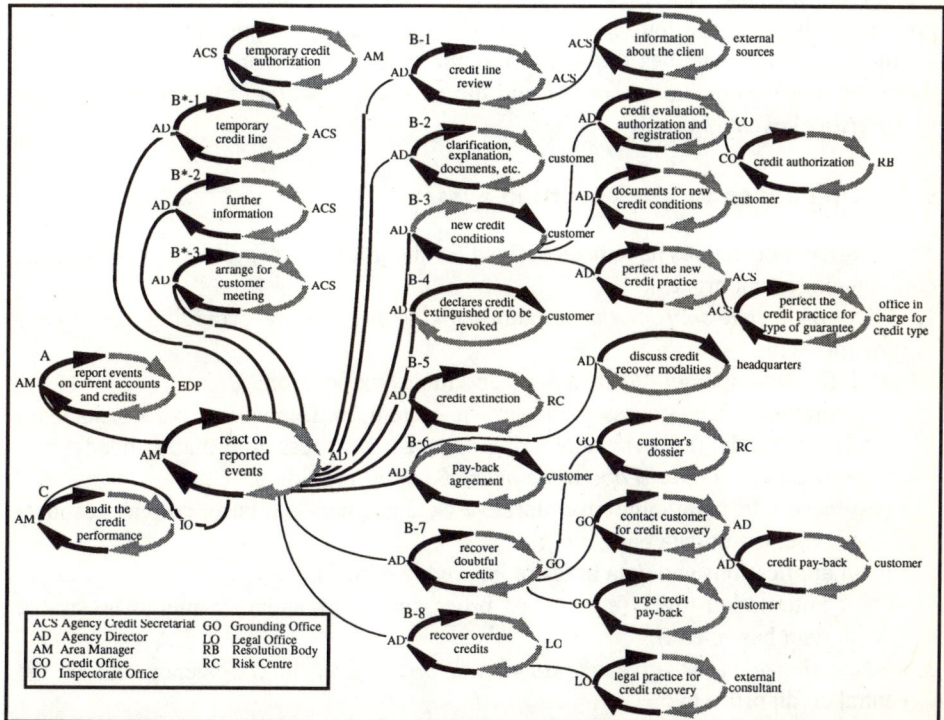

Figure 6-7: The event-based credit management workflow

The new workflow for the event-based credit management is described in Figure 6-7. It is a reinterpretation and rationalisation of the original credit management process. Now responsibilities are more appropriate and support systems are available. In the first phase, the bank (represented by the area manager through the anonymous computer link) asks the agency director to react on the basis of a critical event which is identified by the computer based reporting system (new workflow A). In the second phase, the agency director performs a series of activities to make a proposal for an action plan which depends on the notified event of phase 1. The agency director does this on the basis of a detailed computer supported case analysis using the expert system in the branch, and possible interaction with other agency personnel and the bank's customer. The follow-up workflows in the second phase (B*-1, B*-2 and B*-3 in Figure 6-7) include *requesting a customer profile or other information* from the agency secretariat, producing forms to *activate a temporary credit line* for the customer (which is prepared by the agency credit secretariat), and asking the agency office to *organise a meeting with the customer*. Only after these actions to evaluate the notified event, the agency director commits to manage the event by an action plan, or decides that the event is not risky and thus, does not need to be followed up. In phase three, the agency director initiates operative procedures in the bank involving other offices (central credit office, inspectors, area manager, board of directors, etc.). These processes remain the same as already identified in the previous process analysis. In the fourth phase, the area manager - as being finally responsible for the business – examines the result after the completed actions. The area manager thus evaluates the credit performance and the adequate reaction of the agency director to the critical events initially reported.

6.3.3 Objectives for the reporting system

The following objectives have been defined for the information system supporting the credit management process:
1. *decentralise and shorten the decision-making process* by providing the agency directors with:
   - all information about the customers and their risk position;
   - a computer based process management system, reflecting the bank's standard reference model (i.e. evaluation criteria, decision process, information needs).
2. *decentralise the standard operative procedures* by providing:
   - easy access to mainframe procedures (e.g., customer data base, current accounts data base, credit data base, etc.);
   - local applications and data bases (e.g., credit scoring);
   - office automation tools (e.g., word processing, text and data merge integrated with data bases, etc.).
3. *reduce the administrative workload and paper flow* in the agency and in the central credit office by:
   - automating the information exchange flow (i.e., the reporting process of critical events monitored by the information system);
   - automating the batch procedures launch.

4. *support informal communication and interactions* within the process, in particular:
   - transparency and reversibility of the workflow (e.g. between agencies, central credit office and resolution bodies for credit authorisation);
   - workflow auditing by the workflow initiator as well as by other management roles (i.e., the agency director and the area manager);
   - integration with other workflows (involving, e.g., special loans office; legal office; caveau).

6.3.4 Reporting on overdrafts

The analysis of the main critical events concerning the customer accounts has been done together with the agency director of one of the bank's main agencies. The overdraft on a given credit line has been identified as the most critical event. Furthermore, the Banca d'Italia does not admit the existence of overdraft and requires that banks cover it immediately by a regular credit line. Other significant events concern the dynamics of the customers current account utilisation, the quantity of unpaid checks, the delayed payment of pending debts, etc. The overdraft situation has been chosen for the pilot project for the following reasons:
   - it was given priority by the agency director (main user);
   - the elements to characterise the event are identified and the necessary information can be gathered from existing sources;
   - the process is relevant in terms of its articulation of co-operative work and its interrelation with other workflows in the bank.

An overdraft can occur after a financial transaction has been completed in another bank (e.g., a check is cashed in another bank), or when a customer makes a financial transaction at the bank's windows. Currently, the agency director gets the notification of a transaction in another bank which caused an overdraft each morning from a huge data sheet produced by the EDP Centre, including a few data about each of the overdrafts without any evidence of serious cases. The agency director has to analyse the cases personally and has to decide how to recover from the situation. In the case of the customer's overdraft at the agency's window, the agency director has to authorise the transaction.

In both cases, the agency director is in a critical situation because of the short time available to evaluate the seriousness of the overdraft. The agency director has immediately to start a procedure for bringing the customer's exposition *back to normal*. It is difficult for the agency director to get all the information needed in order to understand the customer's position. This means, that the agency director can manage properly only those cases where the customer position is well known. However, the agency director has to take relevant decisions also in all other cases without detailed information which implies a significant risk for the bank.

To manage overdraft situations, the agency director spends almost one hour every morning analysing the EDP reports, using selective criteria to focus his attention only on the most serious cases. He applies criteria to select two types of overdrafts:

- relevant overdrafts (i.e., where the amount exceeds 20 per cent of the customer's current credit line);
- minor but persistent overdrafts (i.e., where the overdraft is reported for more than 10 days).

The number of these cases occurring in a single medium-sized agency are:
- relevant overdrafts: 10 cases a day;
- persistent overdrafts: 20 cases a day.

These cases account for an estimated 20 per cent of all notified overdrafts. For each of the selected cases, the agency director starts a work process of data gathering and deep risk analysis to decide how to manage the overdraft. The agency director's decision and implied actions may involve several organisational roles in the bank (i.e., agency credit secretariat, central credit office, area manager, legal office, inspectorate office, etc.). Because of the inefficiency of the previous process, the agency director cannot manage all overdrafts. As a consequence, inspectors from the internal inspectorate office and, even worse, from the Banca d'Italia discover overdrafts controlling the branches.

6.3.5 The event-based reporting system

The reporting system for critical events is part of a strategic credit information system. The *event management function* in the reporting system serves to empower the management in the branch (i.e., the agency director) to take timely decisions when certain events occur. The system reports relevant events, e.g., the request of credits out of agreed margins or high-value movements on current accounts, in order to cope in an efficient way with this type of unforeseen event. The person in charge will then activate the appropriate working process, e.g., reviewing the actual credit line, agreeing with the customer a plan for credit pay-back, or to activate a legal practice for credit recovery.

With respect to the whole process, the pilot project covers the first and second phase of the action workflow in Figure 6-6: It is opened by the automatic event notification and stops actually with a proposal for an operative procedure (e.g., credit review). The whole credit life cycle process has already been analysed, but the information systems design for phases 3 and 4 will be done as part of a general credit management system in the near future. The workflows B-1 to B-8 are done with poor support by conventional systems for the time being.

For building an event-based reporting system, a logical architecture with 7 layers has been identified. These layers from transaction processing to end-user computing and their interdependencies are represented in Figure 6-8.

All *transactions* done on the mainframe are stored by up-dating a *customer database* (step 0). The reporting of critical events is initiated automatically by a *workflow co-ordinator* which starts a periodical polling on the *customer database* and verifies the existence of certain critical events (step 1). The request about existence of certain events is passed to an *expert system* which supports the event diagnoses (step 2). The expert system has access to the *customer database*. Specific events are identified by correlation among data produced in various procedures on the transaction side. These *evaluation algorithms* are applied to the *customer database* and, in case of matching, the event is stored in the *reporting database* (step 3). As soon as the workflow co-ordinator gets a positive result from its *polling* on the customer database, the event is checked on the reporting database (step 4). In case of matching the *event-based reporting workflow* sends a message to the person in charge (in general the agency director) (step 5). This message corresponds to the request for action in phase 1 of the workflow between the area manager (symbolised by this computer generated anonymous request) and the agency director (see Figure 6-6). The agency director can use the system for *data analysis* with *end-user computing* tools (step 6). This is phase 2 of the workflow where the agency director activates the discussed *follow-up workflows*.

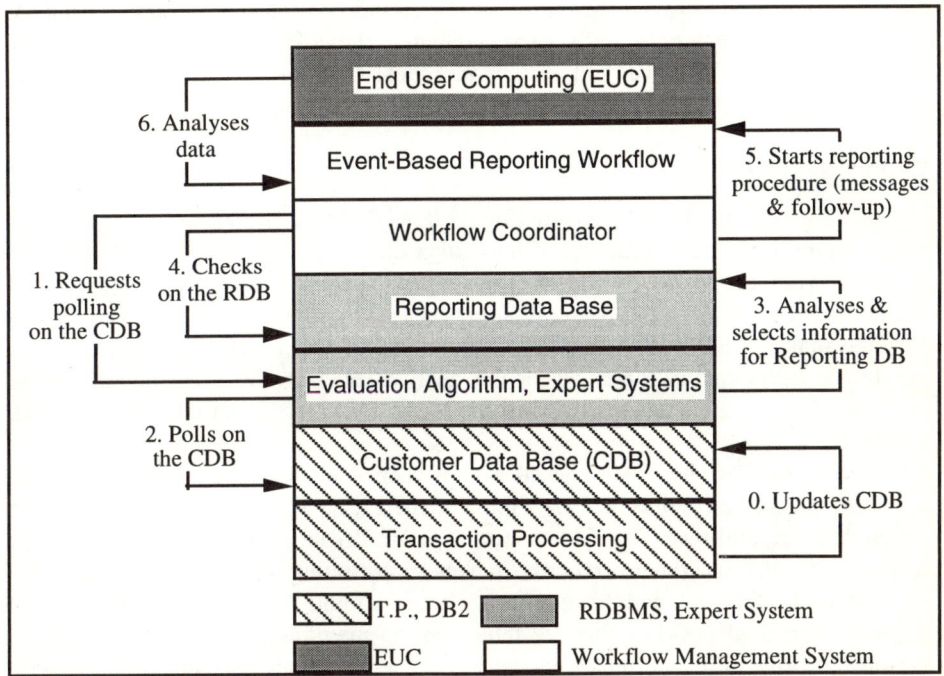

Figure 6-8: Logical architecture for the reporting system

6.3.6 Description of the application

The development of a reporting system which supports the communication among persons and different applications involved in the event-based reporting system implies a heavy use of a software layer which takes care of message exchange and routing. This software layer, below described in detail with the name of *Workflow Management System*, is a key component of a technological architecture which was already described in Figure 4-3 in chapter 4. The application has been implemented on the following components: a data base management system, an expert system, a workflow management system and an user-interface.

Data base management system

Data are held on the mainframe and on local servers. A *reporting data base* has been designed and implemented to store all the agency's customer data relevant for the analysis of an overdraft event and for the decision of an appropriate action. The reporting system accesses the *reporting database*. The design objective was to develop also an integrated *customer database*. The customer database manages customer and market information integrating it with the customer related transaction processing operations, e.g., movements on accounts. An overnight batch procedure has been developed to gather data from various mainframe based information systems: an existing DB2 data base and several sequential files. The procedure transfers the data to the agency file server and loads it on a local Oracle RDBMS. The size of the agency DB is ca. 120 Mb. Every night ca. 2 Mb of records are transferred.

Expert system

The message control layer is covered by *X_Workflow* and *X.400 mail* in the *IBIsys* environment. End-user computing of the *IBIsys* office environment is made available together with the expert system. The expert system has been designed and implemented to analyse the overdraft situation and to support the agency director's decision making. Such a system is an evolution of SECReTS, an expert system previously developed in the bank for the analysis of data about customers' credits given by Italian banks and recorded in the Risk Centre of Banca d'Italia (Chiopris, 1993).

A knowledge-base has been created after a deep analysis done together with the users. An Inference Engine has been implemented as a Prolog-meta-intepreter with explanation capabilities. The system acts as an "artificial actor" which identifies an overdraft on the customer's records, makes a reasoning about it, evaluates the seriousness for the bank and the appropriate action should be taken to recover it. The expert system analyses data from 29 tables on the mainframe. Analytical reports are provided for overdrawn current accounts, existing credits, statistics on the customer's relationships with the bank for the last 3 months. Similar analysis are provided on other current accounts which are connected to the overdrawn one. Possible decisions are suggested ranking from action for events with a low risk up to a very risky situation: modify the current accounts passive interests; issue a temporary credit line; negotiate a financial plan for credit recovery with the customer; review the current credit line; start a legal practice. Such analysis and the related explanations are provided in a report which will be forwarded to the user (the agency director) through the workflow management system.

After a decision is taken – e.g. to give a temporary credit line to cover a short period for overdraft recovery – the expert system monitors the customer's current account and signals any change until the workflow procedure is completed with a positive (i.e., overdraft recovery) or negative (i.e., legal practice) conclusion. This allows for a full range workflow management support until final resolution. On average, some 400 positions are analysed every night.

Workflow management system

Both, "artificial" and human actions are triggered and managed by the workflow management system. The workflow procedure is automatically started by an *artificial actor* providing the report. The report is forwarded to the agency director for analysis and decision making. At this point the agency director can ask the area manager to comment on the situation or ask for more information from the agency credit secretariat. The agency director has to decide the action to be taken. The workflow procedure supports further actions by the secretariat to manage the temporary credit approval, the area manager to authorise it, the agency director to monitor the overdraft recovery and to take further actions until the workflow will be completed. The workflow system allows for a temporary loan procedure activation and supports communication, notification and meeting scheduling with customers. Figure 6-9 shows the workflow steps implemented in *X_Workflow*. Three of them are monitored steps by the expert system.

User interface

Due to the gradual evolution of the bank's technological platform, a first prototype has been developed using the character based *MS-DOS* user interface. This affected the usability of the application and the concrete exploitation of its potential benefits in terms of managing complex information sets (e.g., expert system reports), multiple data and application integration. The bank decided to overcome these limitations by making the end-user environment evolve for all clients into *MS-Windows*. After the testing of the first prototype with a character-based user interface, the application has been implemented on the standard *IBIsys* and *MS-Windows* environment. The workflow management user interface is the *X_Workflow* one; the forms and application specific menus have been implemented with *Visual Basic*. The different users are represented at the input/output layer in Figure 6-10. The reporting system covers the grey parts of Figure 6-10; the agency director, the agency office and the area manager are using the reporting system, while the central credit office is not yet using it.

The bank's information system is based on an IBM mainframe (TP-CICS 9000 620 82Mips) with a MVS-SE operating system. The logical architecture's core is a VSAM database called CEFI (CEntral FIle). The central file CEFI contains for each customer an unique number with related pointers for active relations the customer has with the bank. The details of these relations are stored in separate VSAM files. The central unit has 200 Giga of disc space. The banks network connects 950 PCs and terminals by 12 X.25 nodes.

The bank, in consultation with the software house and the consultancy company RSO, decided on Olivetti *X_Workflow* to fill the Workflow Management System layer. This decision was supported by Olivetti which got interested in doing a pilot project of their new product in the financial market. The pilot project verified the

152   Chapter 6

technical feasibility of connecting the traditional information system with *X_Workflow* on a UNIX server.

The resulting hardware and software platform is shown in Figure 6-11.

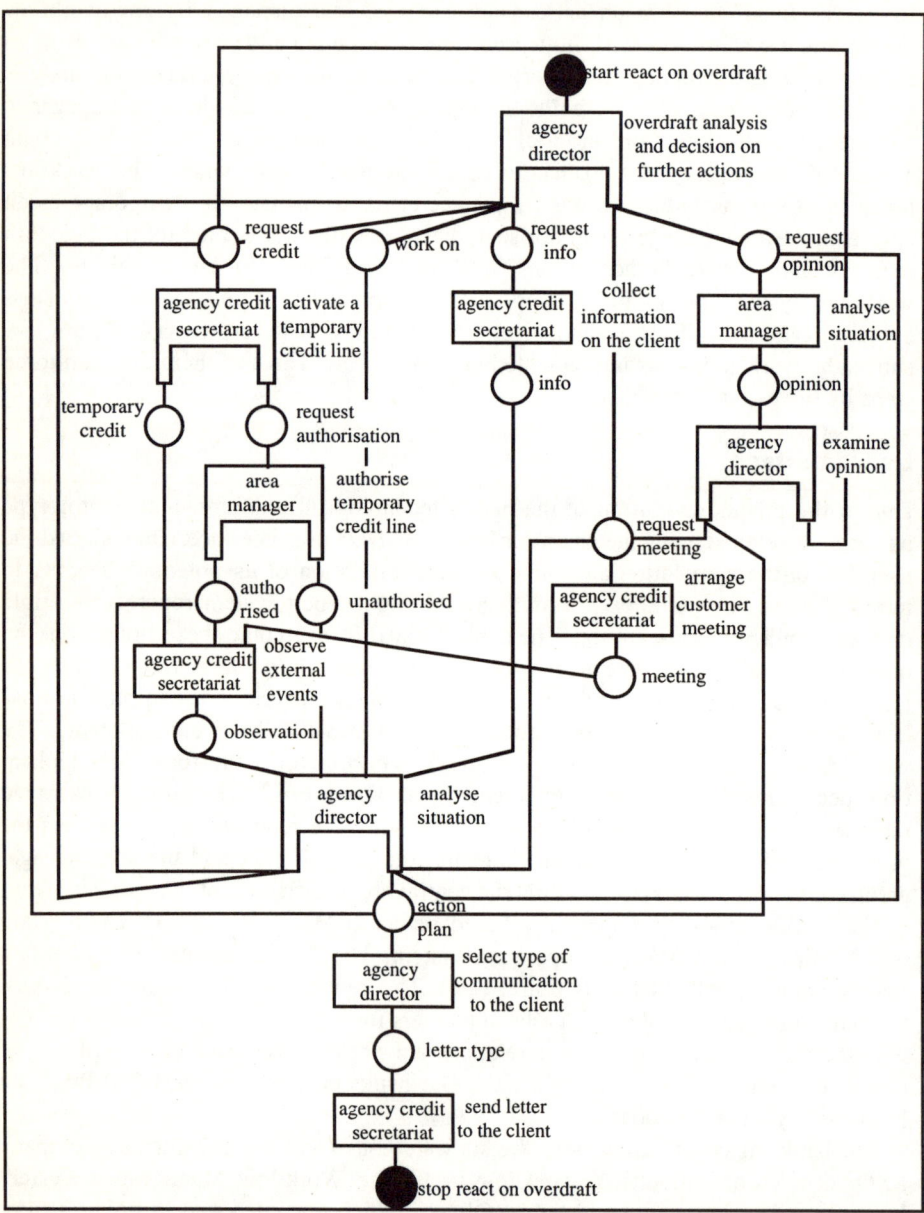

Figure 6-9: State transition diagram for the reporting workflow

Field Study II   153

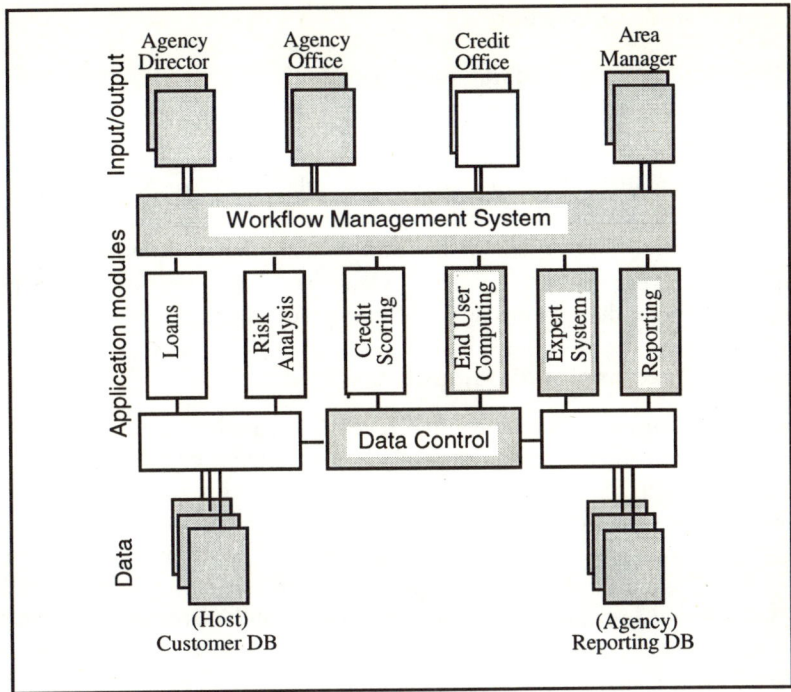

Figure 6-10: New information system architecture

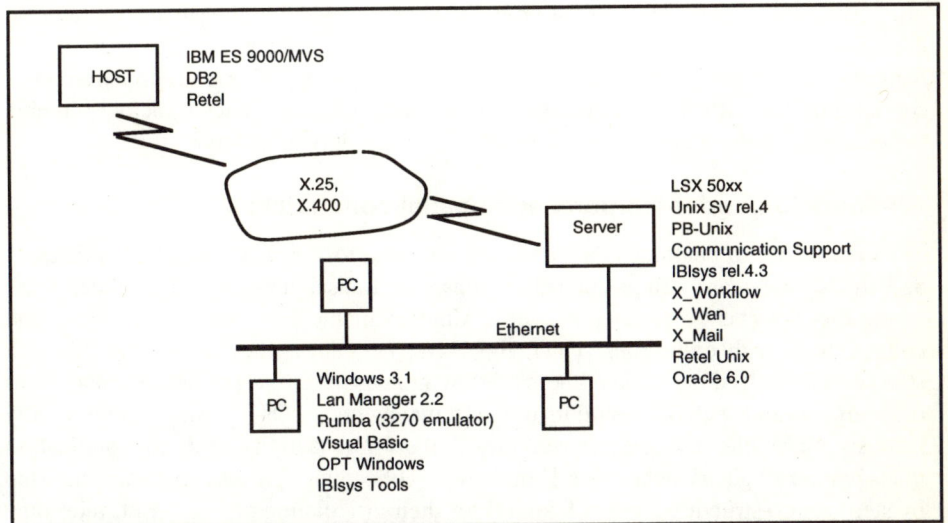

Figure 6-11: The new hardware and software platform

6.4 Results and consequences

6.4.1 Main benefits perceived by users

Definition of responsibility

In the previous situation, the area manager was able to shift responsibility for badly managed credit actions fully to the agency director, because no clear rules for responsibilities were laid down. In the new system the workflows represent in a transparent way responsibilities. This view has been worded as a positive achievement by both, the area manager and the agency director.

Evaluation of professional competence

The agency director perceives the evaluation by his superior (i.e., the area manager) in the new situation as a recognition of his professional competence in handling critical credit events, because the evaluation is based on well-defined criteria of performance which are incorporated into the reporting system of critical events.

Furthermore, with the new system, the evaluation is based on his handling of *all* reported critical events, while in then previous work situation sporadic evaluation was done by inspectors looking for isolated errors in credit management of the agency director for keeping track of critical events and the follow-up actions on already identified critical events.

Transparent criteria for risk management

In the previous situation objectives and clear cut criteria for credit management did not exist. This caused problems for both, the area manager and the agency director, in handling critical credit events. For implementing a transparent support system, the bank was forced to lay open their criteria for credit handling. These criteria were used for defining the critical credit events. Now the users (i.e., the agency director) perceive the existence of these criteria as a release from uncertainty in acting.

Co-operation under temporal and spatial constraints

The complexity of banking is growing, in part due to the new market liberalisation and the stronger anti-crime control on financial transactions in Italy. Under these conditions the agency director has little time available for deep data analysis and collaboration with colleagues. Thus, the users (i.e., the agency director and branch staff) acknowledged the value of the workflow management system because it reduces the temporal and spatial constraints of credit management. Only during the very early analysis phase the users perceived the *X_Workflow* activity and communication management (e.g., asynchronous E-mail with colleagues; process management step by step) as too structured and not natural for their articulation of work. But, after they have used the application, they reconsidered their day to day problems.

Completeness and usability of information

Data and information gathering from the different sources (transaction processing procedure, data bases, paper documents, etc.) was a time consuming and inefficient practice. The reporting application produced a significant benefit by providing the information required, both at a general and a detailed level, in addition to a first evaluation by the expert system.

Treating more overdrafts with the event-based reporting system.

The reporting system allows the analysis of an elevated number of overdraft cases which are risky for the bank. The event-analysis gathers information on cases which might not be taken into consideration otherwise because they are of small amounts or overlooked by the agency director on the print-outs. The agency director appreciated the systematic analysis of overdrafts, also because the total value of 'less important' overdrafts is considerable.

Managing the total process life-cycle

With respect to the traditional way to manage information through TP data sheet printouts, the workflow procedure allows the agency director to consistently monitor all events related to a specific event. This approach provides a relevant added value where the effectiveness of a decision is based on the completion of commitments taken with the bank's customer. In the case of overdrafts it means a radical shift from the conventional practice of repeated temporary credits to a more consistent and effective management of the evolution of the customer along with managing the credit recovery process.

6.4.2 Office procedure limitations

The case has shown that *X_Workflow* has still some limitations similar to those of traditional office procedure applications (as discussed in chapter 4.1). The results of this case study are similar to the previous experience done on the DOMINO office procedure system (Kreifelts *et al.*, 1991) from which Olivetti developed *X_Workflow* (see chapter 4.3 and 4.7). The main points for improvement of *X_Workflow* are:
- *exception handling facilities* (send back and cancel procedure features are not flexible enough);
- integration of *informal communication* or *ad-hoc comment features* (lack of the possibility of having another arbitrary person for having a look to a form or step; getting back his comment in an informal way);
- *integration of other tools* (this relates especially to electronic mail because *X_Workflow* messages are treated separately from ordinary E-mail in the *IBIsys* environment; therefore the user has to quit *X_Workflow* in order to send an E-mail message concerning an office procedure);
- *visibility* of the process (which is the next or previous step, who exactly is receiving comments and complaints).

6.4.3 The business process approach

The current results of the pilot project seem to be of considerable relevance beyond this project. The application of the customer/supplier model in process analysis and re-design has helped to develop a more market-oriented view of the bank's operations.

Prior to the pilot project, reporting was seen as a control function inspectors did in headquarters. The application of a workflow-based reporting system gave a new dimension to executive information systems the bank did not think of before. The project is a promising candidate for a high return on investment, because the bank will have an effective tool to cope with complex problems related to its business. Both, the new process organisation and the concept of work as entire processes rather than discrete functions are now better supported by the workflow concept. The future integration of the credit management process with other operational processes will be concluded by the consequent application of the customer/supplier chain in all business processes. The reorganisation of the bank will be supported by applying innovative technology.

6.4.4 Transferability of the customer/supplier model

This case has shown that the customer/supplier model is easy to introduce with workflow management systems, although they are not explicitly designed that way. Also the language/action perspective cannot be fully implemented by using *CoPlanS*, because *CoPlanS* is sequential, while the explicit communication structure of workflows in the language/action perspective is circular. As a principle, the input-output relations in *CoPlanS* can be sequenced in *X_Workflow* in a way that after each *customer's request* the supplier delivers his output again to the initial customer. In the case of closed customer/supplier chains all deliveries are *evaluated* by their customers. Thus, in a sequential model following the customer/supplier chain the customer should act in the last step of the sequence to close the customer/supplier relation. In this way, the circular structure of the workflow model can be transformed into a sequential structure in more procedural specification languages. This mapping is shown in Figure 6-12 for the specification language *CoPlanS* used in case study 6.

Also the difficulty of using all *message types of a conversation for action,* as included in the language/action perspective (e.g., reject, counter, renege, withdraw; see Figure 2-9, Figure 2-10 and Figure 2-13), can partially be overcome – as shown by the author in the frame of this project – by using the message type *objection* implemented in *X_Workflow*. This function allows the user to move the process back into the previous phase of the workflow. This is a necessary option for the second phase (commitment phase) and the fourth phase (evaluation phase) of the workflow loop. In *X_Workflow* the *objection* message brings the process back into the previous step (see Figure 6-12). By objecting the user can step back in the process and disagree with the specific deliverable from the previous step (i.e., the supplier disagrees with the customer's request, or the customer disagrees with the supplier's performance). In this sense it can be used as a modality for *negotiation* and *evaluation*.

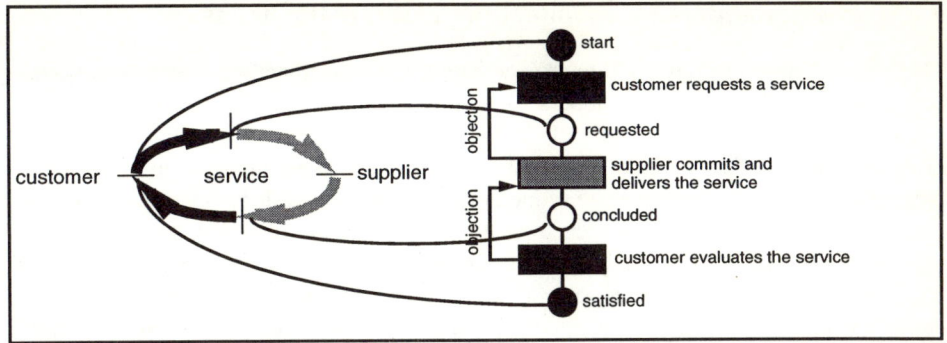

Figure 6-12: Mapping the customer/supplier workflow onto the specification language CoPlanS

6.4.5 Decision Support Systems (DSS) in process management

Decision making is one of the fundamental activities in managerial work which has been widely recognised as a complex and co-operative process. Many researchers observed that managers' work cannot be represented as that of a solitary mind, studying complex alternatives (Mintzberg, 1973; 1979). Managers make most of their decisions in order to cope with contingent and ill-defined problems (Keen & Scott Morton, 1978). Therefore, decision making in such a context cannot be approached only by the *bounded rationality theory* (Simon, 1957; 1976), but should also be seen as an exploratory process based on a cognitive and social domain (Winograd & Flores, 1986).

Thus, Office Information Systems should be designed as an information and communication network to improve the effectiveness and the responsiveness of people co-operating in such a social and organisational environment rather than as a means to automate structured procedures or to support rational decision-making (Schäl & Zeller, 1991). This approach requires new office models to appropriately analyse and understand the co-operative nature of the management process. One of these models of transforming the business is the workflow model integrating an appropriate decentralised decision support system.

The pilot project showed the huge potential of integration of expert and decision support systems within workflow management systems to assist managers (i.e., the agency director) in making appropriate decisions in the work process. The result has been strongly acknowledged even by the developers of DSS and expert systems involved in the project. The bank's MIS department experienced previous developments in this area which showed a limited benefit of expert system in banking processes (Chiopris, 1992). The idea of a DSS and an expert systems both integrated in a workflow management system has been acknowledged as an effective solution to explore the potential of such intelligent tools in a more practical way.

6.4.6 New paradigms for architectural and functional design

The design methodology of the project had a strong impact on the conventional design practice of software developers. The software developers did not accept at the beginning of the project to shift their view of data management and transaction processing from a functional to a process model. On the other hand, the expert system designers saw an opportunity to integrate an expert system in the workflow procedure. Their previous experience with the introduction of expert systems in the bank were partially frustrating because users had to explicitly decide when and how to access the system. Now the expert system is one of the automatically accessed applications within the workflow management system. Due to this integration the expert system is used more frequently than previous systems and with a precise scope.

These strategies have had repercussions on Olivetti as the system supplier. The described pilot project has been the first business case for Olivetti's *X_Workflow*. Therefore, this case study gives more insights into the possibilities of its use than previous test-beds in research environments (business trip, order purchase, etc.). Olivetti received beneficial feed-back from the pilot project in the bank for the future development of *X_Workflow*. These results refer mainly to the evaluation of already developed functionality and user requirements identified in the test-bed which may not yet been included in the current release of *X_Workflow*. This application stresses the value that workflow management systems may add to conventional information systems. This is due to the fact, that it is applied to an economically relevant business process which is critical for the bank's revenue and customer relationships. Furthermore, it implies the integration of a wide range of information technologies, such as transaction processing, expert systems, relational database management systems and office automation tools.

6.4.7 The ambivalence of information technology: support versus control

This case has shown one of the general problems for the implementation of information technology. The need for *transparency* and more information as a support functionality of the new system can likely be used against the potential benefit of user as a *control function*. The changing competitive and financial situation, and the new anti-crime legislation made it necessary to formalise the work practice of all actors involved in the credit process. Informal communication structures have been rationalised by showing the existing, but previously hidden customer/supplier relations. All these information about the process, informal structures and relations, have been implemented in the reporting system. Thus, it is potentially accessible to control people. One such control function is already used by the area manager who controls the agency director for performance evaluation.

This new situation might trigger new strategies to develop informal communication channels, because humans want to have freedom for communication without being continuously observed. This is a potential problem in the attitude of users, when in the future all business processes might be supported by workflow management systems. New informal relations between people will probably emerge.

7. Conclusion

The aim of this research was to design and test concepts of *Computer Supported Cooperative Work*, especially concepts for *workflow management systems* in order to fundamentally improve business processes in enterprises. In this research report, these concepts were applied to *administrative processes*. These principles for *Computer Supported Cooperative Work* and *workflow management technology* can be used for manufacturing and other application areas. This research starts, therefore, from the hypothesis that on this level of abstraction, the structures of manufacturing and administrative processes can be considered comparable.

The first scope of this research was to develop a framework for problem solving in complex organisations to improve their ability to survive in current market conditions. The arguments were given for organising enterprises by process rather than by function in order to respond to new market and customer requirements. The market-orientation can be achieved by working towards *customer satisfaction* in *customer/supplier chains* as suggested. *Co-operative networks* and *workflows* following the *language/action perspective* were proposed to model the resulting *process organisation*.

The second scope was to show that *workflow management systems* are useful to make the *process organisation* happen. The application of two different workflow management systems (*The Coordinator* and *X_Workflow*) in two different Italian companies showed that this type of information technology and its underlying concepts can successfully support *business processes* in organisations. Both companies gained substantial benefits from the use of these workflow management systems for administrative processes. The two companies were, firstly, a company regionally providing training, and, secondly, a bank with many branches. The solution with *X_Workflow* in the bank case seems to be more promising than *The Coordinator* used in the training company.

It follows that it seems to be feasible to also apply the concepts developed here in order to support *administrative processes* accompanying *manufacturing processes*, i.e., the material exchanges and linking of *production islands* or *semiautonomous working groups* in production chains can be seen as *co-operative networks* in *business processes* supported by *workflow management technology*.

These and other research results indicate, however, that current workflow management systems still lack a number of essential and useful functionality. Therefore, new functions have to be developed for workflow management systems from the results of previous experiences.

In addition to the more technical aspects, critical success factors and the problem of *change management* are open research questions to guarantee the success of *business process re-engineering* projects using workflow management systems. These issues define an outlook for future work related to this research.

Bibliography

Abbott, K.R.; Sarin, S.K. (1994). Experiences with Workflow Management: Issues for the Next Generation. In Furuta, R.; Neuwirth, C. (eds.). *Proceedings of the Conference on Computer-Supported Cooperative Work.* ACM, 22-26 October, Chapel Hill, North Carolina: 113-120

ACM (1988). Special issue on the language/action perspective. *Transactions on Office Information Systems,* 6-4

ACM (1992). Special issue on information filtering. *Communications of the ACM,* 35-12: 26-81

Agostini, A.; De Michelis, G.; Grasso, M.A.; Patriarca, S. (1993). *Reengineering a Business Process with an Innovative Workflow Management Systems: A Case Study.* In Kaplan, S. (ed.). *Conference on Organizational Computing Systems.* ACM, New York: 154-165

Agostini, A.; De Michelis, G.; Patriarca, S.; Tinini, R. (1994). A Prototype of an Integrated Coordination Support System. *Computer Supported Cooperative Work (CSCW): An International Journal.* Kluwer Academic Press, Dordrecht, 2-94: 209-238

Albrecht, E. (1982) (ed.). *Zyklus Wissenschaft-Technik-Produktion: Wissenschaftstheoretische Studie zur Wechselwirkung von wissenschaftlicher und technischer Revolution im 20. Jahrhundert.* Deutscher Verlag, Berlin

APPLICA (1993). *Proceedings of the First International Conference on Technologies and Theories for Human Cooperation, Collaboration and Coordination.* Lille, France, 23-25 March

Argyris, C.; Schön, D.A. (1978). *Organizational Learning: A Theory of Action Perspective.* Addison-Wesley, Reading, Massachusetts

ATI (1987). *The Coordinator Workbook & Tutorial Guide.* Action Technologies Inc., Emeryville, California

ATI (1988). *The Coordinator Version II: User's Guide.* Action Technologies Inc., Emeryville, California

ATI (1988b). *Message Handling Service: Installation and Operation Guide.* Action Technologies Inc., Emeryville, California

ATI (1988c). *What is the Coordinator system? A Product Overview.* Action Technologies Inc., Emeryville, California

ATI (1990). *Essentials of Workflow Management Technology.* Action Technologies Inc., Emeryville, California

ATI (1993). *What is ActionWorkflow?* Action Technologies Inc., Emeryville, California

Austin, J.L. (1962). *How to do things with words.* Harvard University Press, Cambridge, Massachusetts

AWK (1990). Organisationskonzepte für die Produktion von morgen. In Eversheim, W. *et al.* (eds.). *Produktionstechnik – Auf dem Weg zu integrierten Systemen.* VDI-Verlag, Düsseldorf: 1-42

Bagnara, S.; Rizzo, A; Stablum, F. (1991). Partners' Credibility Development and Assessment in Distributed Decision Making. *Journal of Human Factors in Manufacturing*, vol. 2, April: 109-119

Bair, J.H.; Gale, S. (1988). *An Investigation of The Coordinator as an Example of Computer Supported Cooperative Work*. Submitted paper to the panel session on Communication, Coordination and Group Performance at the Second Conference on Computer Supported Cooperative Work, Portland, Oregon, 26-28 September

Baker, D.; Ould, M. (1993). The Case for Business Process Modelling. *Workflow World*. Sodan, Uxbridge, UK, 1-1: 11-12

Bannon, L.J.; Robinson, M.; Schmidt, K. (1991). Editors' notes. In Bannon, L.; Robinson, M.; Schmidt, K. (eds.). *Proceedings of the Second European Conference on Computer-Supported Cooperative Work*. Kluwer Academic Publishers, Dordrecht: rear cover page

Bannon, L.J.; Schmidt, K. (1989). *CSCW: Four Characters in Search of a Context*. In Proceedings of the First European Conference on Computer Supported Cooperative Work. Gatwick, London, 13-15 September: 358-372 (reprinted in Bowers, J.M.; Benford, S.D. (eds.) (1991). *Studies in Computer Supported Cooperative Work. Theory, Practice and Design*. North-Holland, Amsterdam: 3-16)

Barber, G.R.; de Joung, P.; Hewitt, C. (1983). Semantic Support for Work in Organizations. In Mason, R.E.A. (ed.). *Proceedings of the IFIP 9th World Computer Congress*. Paris, 19-23 September, North-Holland, Amsterdam: 561-566

Beckhard, R.; Harris, R.T. (1987). *Organizational Transition: Managing Complex Change*. Addison-Wesley, Reading, Massachusetts

Begeman, M.; Cook, P.; Ellis, C.E.; Graf, M.; Rein, G.; Smith, T. (1986). *Project NICK: Meetings Augmentation and Analysis*. In Proceedings of the First Conference on CSCW. ACM, Austin, Texas, 3-5 December: 1-6

Belussi, F.; Ciconte, A.; Schäl, T. (1991). *Innovation through Network Economy: The Emergence of Network Companies and the Benetton Case in the Veneto Region of Italy*. Proceedings of the 3. Bremer Symposium Arbeit und Technik. Bremen, 17-18 June

Bicard-Mandel, J.; Ader, M.; Monguio, J. (1993). *COP: a Petri Net based coordination mechanism for scheduling production workflows*. In Proceedings of the workshop on 'Computer-Supported Cooperative Work, Petri Nets and Related Formalism'. Petri Nets 1993, Chicago, 22 June: 42-55

Bignoli, C.; De Michelis, G.; Tinini, R. (1991). UTUCS: A Support for Synchronous and Asynchronous Communication. In Gorling K.; Sattler C. (eds.). *International Workshop on CSCW*. Informatik: Informationen - Reporte, No 4/91, Institut für Informatik und Rechentechnik, 9-11 April, Berlin: 74-84

Bowers, J.M.; Churcher, J. (1988). *Local and Global Structuring of Computer Mediated Communication: Developing Linguistic Perspectives on CSCW in COSMOS*. Proceedings of the 2nd Conference on CSCW, Portland, Oregon, 26-28 September: 125-139

Bowers, J.M.; Churcher, J.; Roberts, T. (1988). Structuring Computer-Mediated Communication in COSMOS. In Speth, R. (ed.). *European Teleinformatics Conference on Research into Networks and Distributed Applications EUTECO'88*. North-Holland, Brussels: 195-209

Bowers, J.M.; Benford, S.D. (eds.) (1991). *Studies in Computer Supported Cooperative Work: Theory, Practice and Design*. North-Holland, Amsterdam

Braverman, H. (1974). *Labour and Monopoly Capital - The Degradation of Work in the Twentieth Century*. Monthly Review Press, New York

Brödner, P. (1985). *Fabrik 2000 - Alternative Entwicklungspfade in die Zukunft der Fabrik*. Edition Sigma, Berlin

Brödner, P.; Prekuhl, U. (1991). *Die Rückkehr der Arbeit in die Fabrik – Wettbewerbsfähigkeit durch menschzentrierte Erneuerung kundenorientierter Produktion.* IAT, Gelsenkirchen

Bullen, C.V.; Bennett, J.L. (1990). *Groupware in Practice: An Interpretation of Work Experiences.* CISR Working Paper # 205, MIT, Cambridge, Massachusetts

Bullen, C.V.; Bennett, J.L. (1990b). *Learning from User Experience with Groupware.* In Proceedings of the 3rd Conference on Computer Supported Cooperative Work. Los Angeles, 7-10 October: 291-302

Bullinger, H.J.; Ganz, W. (1990). Ohne Human Integrated Manufacturing kein CIM. *Management Zeitschrift,* 59-6: 48-52

Burt, R.S. (1982). *Toward a Structural Theory of Action.* Academic Press, New York

Burt, R.S.; Minor, M.J. (1983). *Applied Network Analysis.* Sage Publications, Beverly Hills, California

Bush, V. (1945). As we may think. *The Atlantic Monthly,* 176(1), June: 101-108

Business Week (1991). *Is it time to junk the way you use computers? Re-engineering might cut costs to businesses by as much as 80%.* July 22: 38-39

Butera, F. (1987). *Dalle occupazioni industriali alle nuove professioni: tendenze, paradigmi e metodi per l'analisi e la progettazione di aree professionali emergenti.* Franco Angeli, Milano

Butera, F. (1990). Options for the Future of Work. In Butera, F.; Di Matino, V.; Köhler, E. (eds.). *Technological Development and the Improvement of Living and Working Conditions: Options for the Future.* Kogan Page, London: 17-93

Butera, F. (1991). *Il castello e la rete.* Franco Angeli, Milano

Butera, F. (1995) Quality of Working Life and Empowerment in Re-Engineering and Continuous Improvements of Network Organizations Supported by Information Technologies. Working paper 2/1995, Istituto RSO, Milano

Carasik, R.P.; Grantham, C.E. (1988). *A Case Study of CSCW in a Dispersed Organization.* Proceedings of SIGCHI '88, ACM, New York: 61-66

Caron, J.R.; Jarvenpaa, S.L.; Stoddard, D.B. (1994). Business Reengineering at CIGNA Corporation: Experiences and Lessons Learned From the First Five Years. *Management Information Systems Quarterly,* 18(3)

Casonato, R. (1993). *Business-process Re-engineering for Competitiveness.* Gartner Group, Office Information Systems, Research Note, Event E-260-1104, 22 February

Cavedoni P. (1991). Workflow Automation Boots Office Productivity. *OSA – Open System Architecture: A Pathway to the Future.* Olivetti, Ivrea, Italy, June

Champy, J. (1995). *Reengineering Management – The New Mandate for New Leadership.* Harper Business, New York

Chiopris, C. (1992). The SECReTS Banking Expert System from Phase 1 to Phase 2. In Proceedings of the 2nd International Logics Programming Summer School on 'Logic Programming in Action'. Zürich (reprinted in *Lector Notes in Artificial Intelligence,* Springer Verlag, n° 636: 91-99)

Chiopris, C. (1993). The SECReTS banking expert system moves into new phase: integration IBIsys environment. *Systems&Networks,* Olivetti, Ivrea, 93-12: 18-21

Ciborra, C.U. (1987). Reframing the Role of Computers in Organisations: The Transaction Costs Approach. *Office, Technology and People,* 3

Ciborra, C.U. (1993). *Teams, Markets and Strategies – Business Innovation and Information Technology.* Cambridge University Press, New York

Ciborra, C.U.; Olson, M.H. (1988). *Encountering Electronic Work Groups: A Transaction Costs Perspective.* In Proceedings of the Second Conference on CSCW, ACM, Portland, Oregon, 26-28 September: 94-101

Colazzo, L.; Mich, L.; Malinverni Silvestri, D.; Schäl, T. (1991). An experiment on Computer Mediated Communication Supported by The Coordinator Using a Pragmatic Model. In Gorling K.; Sattler C. (eds.). *International Workshop on CSCW*. Informatik: Informationen – Reporte, No 4/91, Institut für Informatik und Rechentechnik, 9-11 April, Berlin: 34-58

Colazzo, L.; Mich, L.; Malinverni Silvestri, D.; Schäl, T. (1991b). Interpretation of Human Relations in Computer Supported Communication: A Test with a Pragmatic Model. In Stamper, R.; Kerola, P.; Lee, R.; Lyytinen, K. (eds.). *Collaborative Work, Social Communication and Information Systems*. North Holland, Amsterdam: 77-92

Coulson-Thomas, C. (1994). *Business Process Re-engineering – Myth & Reality*. Kogan Page, London

Conklin, J. (1987). Hypertext: An Introduction and Survey. *IEEE Computer*, September: 17–41

Conklin, J.; Begeman, M.L. (1988). gIBIS: A Hypertext Tool for Exploratory Policy Discussion. *ACM Transactions on Office Information Systems*, 6-4: 303-331

COOCS (1991). Conference on Organizational Computing Systems. In De Joung, P. (ed.). *Proceedings of the Conference on Organizational Computing Systems*. ACM, New York

COOCS (1993). Conference on Organizational Computing Systems. In Kaplan, S. (ed.). *Conference on Organizational Computing Systems*. ACM, New York

COOCS (1995). Conference on Organizational Computing Systems. In Kaplan, S. et al. (ed.). *Conference on Organizational Computing Systems*. ACM, New York

Cooley, M. (1987). *Architect or Bee: The Human Price of Technology*. The Hogarth Press, London

COSCIS (1991). Conference on Collaborative Work, Social Communication and Information Systems. In Stamper, R.; Kerola, P.; Lee, R.; Lyytinen, K. (eds.). *Collaborative Work, Social Communication and Information Systems*. North Holland, Amsterdam

CSCW (1986). *Proceedings of the First Conference on Computer Supported Cooperative Work*. ACM, Austin, Texas, 3-5 December

CSCW (1988). *Proceedings of the Second Conference on CSCW*. ACM, Portland, Oregon, 26-28 September

CSCW (1990). *Proceedings of the Third Conference on CSCW*. ACM, Los Angeles, California, 7-10 October

CSCW (1992). ACM 1992 Conference on Computer-Supported Cooperative Work - Sharing Perspectives. In Turner, J.; Kraut, R. (eds.). *Proceedings of the 4th Conference on Computer-Supported Cooperative Work*. ACM, 31 October – 4 November, Toronto, Canada

CSCW (1994). ACM 1994 Conference on Computer-Supported Cooperative Work - Transcending Boundaries. In Furuta, R.; Neuwirth, C. (eds.). *Proceedings of the Conference on Computer-Supported Cooperative Work*. ACM, 22-26 October, Chapel Hill, North Carolina

Curtis, B.; Kellner, M.I.; Over, J. (1992). Process Modelling. *Communications of the ACM*, September, 35-9: 75-90

Dahrendorf, R. (1959). *Sozialstruktur des Betriebes*. Gabler, Wiesbaden

Danielsen, T.; Pankoke-Babatz, U. (1988). The AMIGO Activity Model. In Speth, R. (ed.). Research into Networks and Distributed Applications. North Holland, Amsterdam: 227-241

Danielsen, T.; Pankoke-Babatz, U.; Prinz, W.; Patel, A.; Pays, P.A.; Smaaland, K.; Speth, R. (1986). *The AMIGO Project: Advanced Group Communication Model for Computer-Based Communication Environment*. In Proceedings of the First Conference on Computer Supported Cooperative Work. ACM, Austin, Texas, 3-5 December: 115-142

Davenport, T.H. (1993). *Process Innovation - Reengineering Work through Information Technology*. Harvard Business School Press, Boston, Massachusetts
Davenport, T.H. (1993b). Book Review of Hammer & Champy 'Reengineering the Corporation'. *Sloan Management Review*, Fall 1993
Davenport, T.H.; Short, J.E. (1990). The New Industrial Engineering: Technology and Business Process Redesign. *Sloan Management Review*, 31-4: 11-27
Davenport, T.H.; Stoddard, D.B. (1994). Reengineering: Business Change of Mythic Proportions. *Management Information Systems Quarterly*, 18-2: 121-128
Davis, D.B. (1991). Software That Makes Your Work Flow. *Datamation*, 37: 58-75
De Cindio, F.; De Michelis, G.; Simone, C. (1987). The Communication Disciplines of CHAOS. In Voss, K.; Genrich, H.J.; Rozenberg, G. (eds.). *Concurrency and Nets: Advances in Petri Nets*. Springer, Berlin: 115-138
De Cindio, F.; De Michelis, G.; Simone, C. (1988). Computer-Based Tools in the Language-Action Perspective. In Speth, R. (ed.). *EUTECO 88: Research in Networks and Distributed Applications*. North Holland, Amsterdam: 243-258
De Michelis, G. (1990). *Computer Support for Cooperative Work*. Position Paper, October 1990, Butler Cox Foundation, London
De Michelis, G. (1996). Computer Support for Cooperative Work: Computers between Users and Social Complexity. In Bagnara, S.; Zucchermaglio, C.; Stucky, S. (eds.). *Organizational Learning and Technological Change*. Springer, Berlin: forthcoming
De Michelis, G.; Donzelli, P.; Schäl, T.; Zeller, B. (1992). Computer Support for Cooperative Work in Space Science Activities. In Van der Veer, G.; Tauber, M.J.; Bagnara, S.; Antalovits, M. (eds.). *Human Computer Interaction: Tasks and Organization – Proceedings of the Sixth European Conference on Cognitive Ergonomics*. CUD, Rome: 71-85
De Michelis, G.; Grasso, M.A. (1993). Routines and Conversations. *Structured Programming*, 14-93: 110-118
De Michelis, G.; Grasso, M.A. (1994). Situating Conversations within the Language/Action Perspective: The Milan Conversation Model. In Furuta, R.; Neuwirth, C. (eds.). *Proceedings of the Conference on Computer-Supported Cooperative Work*. ACM, 22-26 October, Chapel Hill, North Carolina: 89-100
Denning; P.J. (1992). Work Is a Closed-Loop Process. *American Scientist*, 80, July/August: 314-317
Denning, P.J.; Medina-Mora, R. (1994). Case Study: George Mason University. In White, T.E.; Fischer, L. (eds.). *New Tools for New Times: The Workflow Paradigm*. Future Strategies Inc., Alameda, California: 235-251
Di Stefano, F.; Schäl, T.; Viviani, D.; Zeller, B. (1995). *Business process reengineering nelle aziende di servizi – alcuni casi italiani*. National conference on 'Lavoro e Organizzazione nel Mondo dei Cambiamenti', AISL – Associazione Italiana di Studio del Lavoro, Bologna, 15-16 June
Drucker, P.F. (1988). The Coming of the New Organization. *Harvard Business Review*, 66-1: 45-53
Drucker, P.F. (1989). *The New Realities*. Harper & Row, New York
Dunham, R. (1991). Business Design Technology: Software Development for Customer Satisfaction. In Proceedings of the 24th Annual Hawaii International Conference on Systems Sciences, IEEE: 792-798
Dyson, E. (1990). Why Groupware is gaining Ground. *Datamation*, March 1st: 52-56
Dyson, E. (1990b). Workflow: Software that automates routine tasks. *Forbes*, 11-92: 192
Earl, M.J. (1994). Viewpoint: The New and Old of Business Process Redesign. *Journal of Strategic Information Systems*, 3-1: 5-22
ECSCW (1989). Proceedings of the First European Conference on Computer Supported Cooperative Work. 13-15 September, Gatwick, London

ECSCW (1991). Proceedings of the Second European Conference on Computer Supported Cooperative Work. In Bannon, L.J.; Robinson, M.; Schmidt, K. (eds.). *Proceedings of the Second European Conference on Computer-Supported Cooperative Work*. Kluwer Academic Publishers, Dordrecht

ECSCW (1993). Proceedings of the Third European Conference on Computer Supported Cooperative Work. In De Michelis, G.; Simone, C.; Schmidt, K. (eds.). *Proceedings of the Third European Conference on Computer-Supported Cooperative Work*. Kluwer Academic Publishers, Dordrecht

Ellis, C.A. (1979). Information Control Nets: A Mathematical Model of Office Information Flow. In *Proceedings of the Conference on Simulation, Measurement and Modelling of Computer Systems*. ACM, New York: 225-239

Ellis, C.A.; Bernal, M. (1982). *Officetalk-D: An experimental office information system*. Proceedings ACM-SIGOA Conference on Office Information Systems. ACM, New York: 131-140

Ellis, C.A.; Gibbons, R.; Morris, P. (1979). Office Streamlining. In Naffah, N. (ed.). *Integrated Office Systems - Burotics*. North-Holland, Amsterdam

Ellis, C.A.; Gibbs, S.J.; Rein, G.L. (1991). Groupware: Some Issues and Experiences. *Communications of the ACM*, 34-1: 39-58

Ellis, C.A.; Naffah, N. (1987). *Design of Office Information Systems*. Springer, Berlin

Ellis, C.A.; Nutt, G.J. (1988). Office Information Systems and Computer Science. In Greif, I. (ed.). *Computer-Supported Cooperative Work: A Book of Readings*. Morgan Kaufmann, San Mateo, California

Ellis, C.A.; Nutt, G.J. (1993). Modelling and Enactment of Workflow Systems. In Marsan, M.A. (ed.). *Application and Theory of Petri Nets 1993*. Springer, New York: 1-16

Ellis, C.A.; Wainer J. (1994). Goal-based models of collaboration. *Collaborative Computing*, Chapman & Hall, March, 1-1: 61-86

Ellis, C.A.; Wainer J. (1994b). A Conceptual Model of Groupware. In Furuta, R.; Neuwirth, C. (eds.). *Proceedings of the Conference on Computer-Supported Cooperative Work*. ACM, 22-26 October, Chapel Hill, North Carolina: 79-88

Emery, F.E.; Trist, E.L. (1969). Sociotechnical Systems. Emery, F.E. (ed.). *Systems Thinking*. Penguin, Harmonsworth

Engelbart, D.C. (1982). *Toward High-Performance Knowledge Workers*. In Office Automation Conference '82 Digest, San Francisco: 279-290

Engelbart, D.C. (1984). *Collaboration Support Provisions in AUGMENT*. In Office Automation Conference '84 Digest, Los Angeles

Engelbart, D.C.; Watson, R.W.; Norton, J.C. (1973). *The augmented knowledge workshop*. In Proceedings of the AFIPS Conference, New York, June, volume 42

Flores, C.F. (1982). *Management and communication in the office of the future*. PhD Thesis, University of California at Berkeley

Flores, C.F.; Ludlow, J. (1981). Doing and Speaking in the Office. In Flick, G.; Sprague, R. (eds.). *DSS: Issues and Challenges*. Pergamon Press, London: 95-118

Flores, C.F.; Graves, M.; Hartfield, B.; Winograd, T. (1988). Computer Systems and the Design of Organizational Interaction. In *ACM Transactions on Office Information Systems*, 6-2: 153-172

Fricke, W.; Krahn, K.; Peter, G. (1985). *Arbeit und Technik als politische Gestaltungsaufgabe - Ein Gutachten aus sozialwissenschaftlicher Sicht*. Verlag Neue Gesellschaft, Bonn

Furuta, R.; Neuwirth, C. (eds.) (1994). *Proceedings of the Conference on Computer-Supported Cooperative Work*. ACM, 22-26 October, Chapel Hill, North Carolina

Gable, J. (1992). Workflow Processing Software. *Workgroup Computing Series: Strategies & LAN Services*. DATAPRO, Information Services Group, Delran, New Jersey, July 1992: 1-11

Gadamer, H.G. (1975). *Truth and Method*. Seabury Press, New York

Gadamer, H.G. (1976). *Philosophical Hermeneutics*. University of California Press, Berkeley, California
Gale, S. (1989). *Adding Audio and Video to an Office Environment,*. In Proceedings of the First European Conference on Computer Supported Cooperative Work, Gatwick, London, 13-15 September: 121-130
Galegher, J.; Kraut, R.; Egido, C. (1990). *Intellectual Teamwork: Social and Technological Foundations of Cooperative Work*. Lawrence Erlbaum Associates, Hillsdale, New Jersey
Gerson, E.M.; Star, S.L. (1986). Analyzing Due Processes in the Workplace. *ACM Transactions on Office Information Systems*, 4-3: 257-270
Gibbs, S.; Verrijn-Stuart, A.A. (1990). *Multi-User Interfaces and Applications*. North-Holland, Amsterdam
Goldratt, E.M.; Cox, J. (1986). *The Goal – Beating the Competition*. McGraw-Hill, New York
Greenberg, S. (ed.) (1991). *Computer Supported Cooperative Work and Groupware*. Academic Press, London
Greif, I. (ed.) (1988). *Computer-Supported Cooperative Work: A Book of Readings*. Morgan Kaufmann Publishers, San Mateo, California
Greif, I. (1988b). Introduction to Computer-Supported Cooperative Work: A Book of Readings. In Greif, I. (ed.). *Computer-Supported Cooperative Work: A Book of Readings*. Morgan Kaufmann Publishers, San Mateo, California
Greif, I.; Sarin, S.K. (1986). Data Sharing in Group Work. In Proceedings of the First Conference on CSCW, ACM, Austin, Texas, 3-5 December: 175-183
Grinda, S.; Pieper, A.; Strina, G.; Strötgen, J.; Süthoff, M. (1993). *Vom Mitarbeiter zum Mitdenker – Gestaltungsbausteine für die dezentrale Organisation*. VDI/DWI, Köln
GROUPWARE (1992). *Proceedings of the GroupWare'92 Conference*. Morgan Kaufmann Publishers, San Mateo, California
GROUPWARE (1993). *Proceedings of the GroupWare'93 Conference*. August 9-13, San Jose, California
GROUPWARE (1994). *Proceedings of the GroupWare'94 Conference*. London, UK
Grudin, J. (1988). *Why CSCW Applications Fail: Problems in the Design and Evaluation of Organizational Interfaces*. In Proceedings of the Second Conference on CSCW, ACM, Portland, Oregon, 26-28 September: 85-92
Grudin, J. (1989). Why Groupware Applications Fail: Problems in Design and Evaluation. *Office: Technology and People*. 4-3: 245-264
Grudin, J. (1991). *CSCW: The Convergence of Two Development Contexts*. Proceedings of the CHI'91 Conference on 'Reaching Through Technology', New Orleans, Louisiana, 27 April-2 May, ACM, New York: 91-97
Grudin, J. (1991b). CSCW. *Communications of the ACM*, 34-12: 30-34
Grudin, J. (1994). Groupware and social dynamics: Eight challenges for developers. *Communications of the ACM*, 37-1: 92-105
Gunn, T.G. (1987). *Manufacturing for Competitive Advantage: Becoming a World Class Manufacturer*. Ballinger, Cambridge, Massachusetts
Habermas, J. (1973). Wahrheitstheorien. In Fahrenbach, H. (ed.). *Wirklichkeit und Reflexion*. Neske, Pfullingen: 211-265
Hales, K.; Lavery, M. (1991). *Workflow Management Software: The Business Opportunity*. Ovum Ltd., London
Hall, G.; Rosenthal, J.; Wade, J. (1993). How to Make Reengineering Really Work. *Harvard Business Review*, November-December: 119-131
Hammer, M. (1984). The OA Mirage. *Datamation*, 30-2: 36-46
Hammer, M. (1990). Reengineering Work: Don't Automate, Obliterate. *Harvard Business Review*, July/August: 104-111

Hammer, M.; Champy, J. (1993). *Reengineering the Corporation: A Manifesto for Business Revolution.* Harper, New York

Harendt, B.O.L. (1991). Ein kybernetischer Ansatz zur Lösung komplexer technischer Qualitätsprobleme in einem internationalen Konzern der Konsumgüterindustrie. *Fortschrittsberichte des VDI*, Reihe 2: Fertigungstechnik, Nr. 222, VDI-Verlag, Düsseldorf (Diss. RWTH Aachen)

Hartfield, B.; Graves, M. (1991). Issue-Centred Design for Collaborative Work. In Stamper, R.; Kerola, P.; Lee, R.; Lyytinen, K. (eds.). *Collaborative Work, Social Communication and Information Systems.* North-Holland, Amsterdam: 295-310

Heidegger M. (1927). *Sein und Zeit.* Niemeyer, Tübingen, 1960 (original edition in Husserl E. (ed.). *Jahrbuch für Philosophie und phänomenologische Forschung.* Band VIII, 1927)

Henning, K. (1993). *Spuren im Chaos – Christliche Orientierungspunkte in einer komplexen Welt.* Olzog Verlag, München

Henning, K. (1993b). *Kybernetische Verfahren der Ingenieurwissenschaften.* Vorlesungsmanuskript, 4. Auflage, HDZ/IMA, RWTH Aachen, Augustinus Buchhandlung, Aachen

Henning, K.; Ochterbeck, B. (1988). Anwendung eines Dualen Entwurfsverfahrens am Beispiel eines Betriebsführungssystems. In Fahrion, R. (ed.). *Kybernetische Aspekte moderner Kommunikationstechnik.* Duncker & Humblot, Berlin

Henning, K.; Ochterbeck, B. (1988b). Dualer Entwurf von Mensch-Maschine-Systemen. Meyer-Dohm, P. (ed.). *Der Mensch im Unternehmen.* Bern, Stuttgart: 225-245

Henning, K; Kutscha, S. (1994). *Informatik im Maschinenbau.* Springer, Berlin

Henning, K.; Strina, G.; Wollenweber, D. (1994). Die selbstähnliche Fabrik – eine Sichtweise zu technischen und menschlichen Fragen unserer Zeit. In Scheel, J.; Hacker, W.; Henning, K. (eds.). *Fabrikorganisation neu beGreifen.* TÜV Rheinland, Köln: 11-4

Hewitt, C. (1986). Offices are open systems. *ACM Transactions on Office Information Systems*, 4-3: 271-287

Hinterhuber, H.H. (1984). *Strategische Unternehmensführung.* De Gruyter, Berlin

Holt, A.W. (1986). Coordination Technology and Petri Nets. In Rozemberg, G. (ed.). *Advances in Petri Nets.*

Holt, A.W. (1988). Diplans: A new language for the study and implementation of coordination. *ACM Transactions on Office Information Systems*, 6-2: 109-125

Holt, A.W.; Ramsey, H.R.; Grimes, J. (1983). System technology as a basis for a programming environment. *ITT Electrical Communication.* 57-4: 307-314

Hsu, M.; Howard, M. (1994). Work-Flow and Legacy Systems: Adding work-flow support will become critical to legacy transaction-processing applications. *Byte*, July: 109-116

Huber, G.P. (1991). Organizational Learning: The Contributing Processes and the Literature. *Organizational Science*, 2-91: 88-115

Hughes, J.; Randall, D.; Shapiro, D. (1991). CSCW: Discipline or Paradigm? A Sociological Perspective. In Bannon, L.J.; Robinson, M.; Schmidt, K. (eds.). *Proceedings of the Second European Conference on Computer-Supported Cooperative Work.* Kluwer Academic Publishers, Dordrecht: 309-323

IAO (1995). *Business Reengineering – Aktuelle Managementkonzepte in Deutschland: Zukunftsperspektiven und Stand der Umsetzung.* FhG-IAO, Stuttgart

IFIP8.4 (1990). *Conference on multi-user interfaces and applications.* Heraklion, Crete, 24-26 September

IFIP8.5 (1992). *Working Conference on Computer Supported Cooperative Work and Public Administration.* Linz, Austria, 25-27 February

Isenhardt, I. (1994). *Komplexitätsorientierte Gestaltungskriterien für Organisationen, dargestellt am Beispiel eines Großkrankenhauses.* Augustinus, Aachen

Jensen, K. (1992). *Coloured Petri Nets.* Springer, Berlin

Johansen, R. (1988). *Groupware: Computer Support for business teams*. The Free Press, New York

Johansen, R.; Sibbet, D.; Benson, S.; Martin, A.; Mittman, R.; Saffo, P. (1991). *Leading Business Teams: How Teams Can Use Technology and Group Process Tools to Enhance Performance*. Addison-Wesley, Reading, Massachusetts

Johnson, B.; Weaver, G.; Olson, M.H.; Dunham, R. (1986). *Using a Computer-Based Tool to Support Collaboration: A Field Experiment*. In Proceedings of the First Conference on CSCW, ACM, Austin, Texas, 3-5 December: 343-352

Kaplan, S.M.; Carroll, A.M.; MacGregor, K.J. (1991). Supporting collaborative processes with ConversationBuilder. In De Jong, P. (ed.). *Proceedings ACM Conference on Organizational Computer Systems (COCS)*. ACM, New York: 69-79

Keen, P.G.W. (1991). *Shaping the Future: Business Design through Information Technology*. Harvard Business School Press, Boston, Massachusetts

Keen, P.G.W.; Scott-Morton, M.S. (1978). *Decision-Support Systems: An Organizational Perspective*. Addison-Wesley, Reading, Massachusetts

Kensing, F.; Winograd, T. (1991). The Language/Action Approach to Design of Computer-Support for Cooperative Work: A Preliminary Study in Work Mapping. In Stamper, R.; Kerola, P.; Lee, R.; Lyytinen, K. (eds.). *Collaborative Work, Social Communication and Information Systems*. North-Holland, Amsterdam: 311-331

Kern H.; Schumann, M. (1970). *Industriearbeit und Arbeiterbewußtsein – Eine empirische Untersuchung über den Einfluß der aktuellen technischen Entwicklung auf die industrielle Arbeit und das Arbeiterbewußtsein*. Europäische Verlagsanstalt, Frankfurt am Main

Kern H.; Schumann, M. (1984). *Das Ende der Arbeitsteilung? Rationalisierung in der industriellen Produktion: Bestandsaufnahme, Trendbestimmung*. C.H. Beck, München

Kling, R. (1991). Cooperation, Coordination and Control in Computer Supported Work. *Communications of the ACM*, 34-12: 83-88

Knoke, D.; Kuklinski, J.H. (1982). *Network Analysis*. Sage Publications, Beverly Hills, California

Kraut, R.; Egido, C.; Galegher, J.(1988). *Patterns of Contact and Communication in Scientific Research Collaboration*. In Proceedings of the Second Conference on CSCW, ACM, Portland, Oregon, 26-28 September: 1-24

Kreifelts, T.; Hinrichs, E.; Klein, K.H.; Seuffert, P.; Woetzel, G. (1991). Experiences with the DOMINO Office Procedure System. In Bannon, L.; Robinson, M.; Schmidt, K. (eds.). *Proceedings of the Second European Conference on Computer-Supported Cooperative Work*. Kluwer Academic Publishers, Dordrecht: 117-130

Kreifelts, T.; Licht, U.; Woetzel, G. (1984). DOMINO: A System for the Specification and Automation of Cooperative Office Processes. In Myrhaug, B.; Wilson, D.R. (eds.). *Proceedings EUROMICRO'84*, North-Holland, Amsterdam: 33-41

Kreifelts, T.; Woetzel, G. (1987). Distribution and Error Handling in an Office Procedure System. In Bracchi, G.; Tsichritzis, D. (eds.). *Office Systems: Methods and Tools*. North-Holland, Amsterdam: 197-208

Kutscha, S. (1995). Business Process Reengineering – revolutionäres Konzept oder Modeerscheinung? In Henning, K.; Staufenbiel, J.E. (eds.). *Berufsplanung für Ingenieure*. Institut für Ausbildungsplanung, Düsseldorf, 10. Auflage: 265-270

Lai, K.Y.; Malone, T.W. (1988). *Object Lens: A "Spreadsheet" for Cooperative Work*. In Proceedings of the Second Conference on CSCW. ACM, Portland, Oregon, 26-28 September: 115-124

Lundrigan, R. (1986). What is this thing called OPT? *Production and Inventory Management*, volume II: 2-12

Mackay, W.E. (1988). *More than just a Communication System: Diversity in the Use of Electronic Mail*. In Proceedings of the Second Conference on CSCW, ACM, Portland, Oregon, 26-28 September: 344-353

Mackay, W.E.; Malone, T.W.; Crowston, K.; Rao, R.; Rosenblitt, D.; Card, S.K. (1989). *How do experienced Information Lens Users use rules*. In Proceedings CHI'89 Conference on Human Factors in Computing Systems, ACM, Austin, 30 April – 4 May: 211-217

Madnick, S.E. (1991). The Information Technology Platform. In Scott Morton, M.S. (ed.). *The Corporation of the 1990s – Information Technology and Organizational Transformation*. Oxford University Press, New York/Oxford: 27-60

Malone, T.W.; Grant, K.R.; Lai, K.Y.; Rao, R.; Rosenblitt, D. (1986). *Semi-Structured Messages are Surprisingly Useful for Computer-Supported Coordination*. In Proceedings of the First Conference on CSCW, ACM, Austin, Texas, 3-5 December: 102-114

Malone, T.W.; Grant, K.R.; Turbak, F.A. (1986b). *The Information Lens: An intelligent system for information sharing in organisations*. In Proceedings of the CHI '86 Conference on Human Factors in Computing Systems, ACM, Boston, Massachusetts, 13-17 April: 1-8

Malone, T.W.; Grant, K.R.; Turbak, F.A.; Brobst, F.A.; Cohen, M.D. (1987). Intelligent information-sharing systems. In *Communications of the ACM*, 30-5: 390-402

Malone, T.W.; Benjamin, R.I.; Yates, J. (1987b). Electronic Markets and Electronic Hierarchies. *Communications of the ACM*, 30-6: 484-497

Malone, T.W.; Crowston, K. (1990). *What is Coordination Theory and How Can It Help Design Cooperative Work Systems?* In Proceedings of the Third Conference on CSCW, ACM, Los Angeles, California, 7-10 October: 357-370

Malone, T.W.; Crowston, K. (1991). *Toward an Interdisciplinary Theory of Coordination*. CCR Technical Report #120, MIT, Massachusetts

Malone, T.W.; Lai, K.Y.; Fry, C. (1992). Experiments with Oval: A Radically Tailorable Tool for Cooperative Work. In Turner, J.; Kraut, R. (eds.). *Proceedings of the 4th Conference on Computer-Supported Cooperative Work*. ACM, 31 October-4 November, Toronto, Canada: 289-297

Malone, T.W.; Crowston, K.; Lee, J.; Pentland, B. (1993). *Tools for inventing organizations: Toward a handbook of organizational processes*. In Proceedings of the Second IEEE Workshop on Enabling Technologies Infrastructure for Collaborative Enterprises, IEEE, Morgantown, WV, 20-22 April; CCS Technical Report #141, MIT, Massachusetts

Marca, D.A. (1989). *Requirements, Paradigms and Design Guidance For Developing Coordinator Programs*. In Proceedings 11th International Conference on Software Engineering, IEEE, 15-18 May, Pittsburg, Pennsylvania

Marca, D.A. (1991). *Augmenting SADT™ to Develop Computer Support for Cooperative Work*. In Proceedings 11th International Conference on Software Engineering, IEEE, Los Alamitos, California (reprinted in Marca, D.A.; Bock, G. (1992). *Groupware: Software for Computer-Supported Cooperative Work*. IEEE Computer Society Press, Los Alamitos, California: 162-171)

Marca, D.A.; Bock, G. (1992). *Groupware: Software for Computer-Supported Cooperative Work*. IEEE Computer Society Press, Los Alamitos, California

Marca, D.A.; McGowan, C.L. (1988). *SADT: Structured Analysis and Design Technique*. McGraw-Hill, New York

Marks, S. (1991). Gemeinsame Gestaltung von Technik und Organisation in soziotechnischen kybernetischen Systemen. *Fortschrittsberichte des VDI*, Reihe 16: Technik und Wirtschaft, Nr. 60, VDI-Verlag, Düsseldorf (Diss. RWTH Aachen)

Marshak, R.T. (1992). And Then a Miracle Happens. *Workgroup Computing Report*. Patricia Seybold Group, Boston, Massachusetts, 15-1: 2

Marshak, R.T. (1992b). Requirements for Workflow. *Workgroup Computing Report*. Patricia Seybold Group, Boston, Massachusetts, 15-3: 3-8

Marshak, R.T. (1993). Young & Rubicam improves productivity with workflow. *Workgroup Computing Report.* Patricia Seybold Group, Boston, Massachusetts, 16-5: 12-20

Marshak, R.T. (1994). Perspectives on Workflow. In White, T.E.; Fischer, L. (eds.). *New Tools for New Times: The Workflow Paradigm.* Future Strategies Inc., Alameda, California: 165-176

Martin, T.; Ulich, E.; Warnecke, H.J. (1988). Angemessene Automation für flexible Fertigung. *Werkstattstechnik,* Nr. 78: 17-23 and 119-122

Maturana, H.R.; Varela, F. (1980). *Autopoiesis and Cognition: the realization of the living.* Reidel, Dordrecht

McCarthy, J.C.; Monk, A.F. (1994). Channels, conversation, co-operation and relevance: All you wanted to know about communication but were afraid to ask. *Collaborative Computing,* Chapman & Hall, March, 1-1: 35-60

Medina-Mora, R.; Winograd, T.; Flores, R.; Flores, C.F. (1992). The Action Workflow Approach to Workflow Management Technology. In Turner, J.; Kraut, R. (eds.). *Proceedings of the 4th Conference on Computer-Supported Cooperative Work.* ACM, 31 October-4 November, Toronto, Canada: 281-288

Mintzberg, H. (1973). *The Nature of Managerial Work.* Harper & Row, New York

Mintzberg, H. (1979). *The Structuring of Organizations.* Prentice-Hall, Englewood Cliffs, New Jersey

Moran, T.P. (1981). The Command Language Grammar: a representation for the user interface of interactive computer systems. *International Journal of Man-Machine Studies,* 15: 3-50

Morawetz, A.; Schäl, T.; Viviani, D.: Zeller, B. (1991). *Distributed Business Processes: case study of a chemical company.* RSO, Internal Working paper prepared for Esprit Project ITHACA, Milano

Morris, D.C.; Branson, J. (1993). *Reengineering your business.* McGraw-Hill, New York

Nonaka, I. (1993). *On a knowledge creating organization.* Paper presented at the National Congress of the Associazione Italiana Formatori, AIF, Parma, October 17-30

Nonaka, I.; Takeuchi, H. (1995). *The knowledge creating company.* Oxford University Press, New York

Ochterbeck, B. (1989). Dualer Entwurf eines Betriebsführungssystems für Umschlagbahnhöfe des kombinierten Verkehrs. *Fortschrittsberichte des VDI,* Reihe 12: Verkehrstechnik/Fahrzeugtechnik, Nr. 123, VDI Verlag, Düsseldorf (Diss. RWTH Aachen)

Olson, M.H. (ed.) (1989). *Technological Support for Work Group Collaboration.* Lawrence Erlbaum Associates, Hillsdale, New Jersey

Orlikowski, W.J. (1992). Learning from Notes: Organisational Issues in Groupware Implementation. In Turner, J.; Kraut, R. (eds.) *Proceedings of the 4th Conference on Computer-Supported Cooperative Work.* 31 October-4 November, Toronto, Canada, ACM, New York: 362-369

Ouchi, W.G. (1980). Markets, Bureaucracies and Clans. *Administrative Science Quarterly,* 25-3: 129-141

Petri, C.A. (1977). Modelling as a Communication Discipline. In Beilner, H.; Gelenbe, E. (eds.). *Measuring, modelling and evaluating computer systems.* North-Holland, New York

Petri, C.A. (1977b). Communication Disciplines. In Shaw, B. (ed.). *Computing System Design.* Newcastle Upon Time

Petri, C.A. (1979). Kommunikationsdisziplinen. In Petri, C.A. (ed.). *Ansätze zur Organisationstheorie Rechnergestützter Informationssysteme.* Oldenburg

Pinci, V.; Shapiro, R.M. (1993). *Work Flow Analysis.* In Proceedings of the workshop on 'Computer-Supported Cooperative Work, Petri Nets and Related Formalism'. Petri Nets 1993, Chicago, 22 June: 18-32

Piore, M.J.; Sabel, C.F. (1984). *Das Ende der Massenproduktion: Studie über die Requalifizierung der Arbeit und die Rückkehr der Ökonomie in die Gesellschaft*. Fischer, Frankfurt am Main

Piore, M.J.; Sabel, C.F. (1989). *The second industrial divide: Possibilities for prosperity*. Basic Books, New York

Pollock, S. (1988). A rule-based message filtering system. *ACM Transactions on Office Information Systems*, 6-3: 232-254

Popitz, H.; Bahrdt, H.P.; Jüres, E.A.; Kesting, H. (1957). *Technik und Industriearbeit. Soziologische Untersuchungen in der Hüttenindustrie*. Mohr, Tübingen

Prinz, W.; Pennelli, P. (1989). *Relevance of the X.500 directory to CSCW applications*. In Proceedings of the First European Conference on Computer Supported Co-operative Work, Gatwick, London, 13-15 September: 289-302

Redenbaugh, R. (1994). The New Common Sense. In White, T.E.; Fischer, L. (eds.). *New Tools for New Times: The Workflow Paradigm*. Future Strategies Inc., Alameda, California: 13-24

Reder, S.; Schwab, R.G. (1988). *The Communicative Economy of the Workgroup: Multi-Channel Genres of Communication*. In Proceedings of the Second Conference on CSCW, ACM, Portland, Oregon, 26-28 September: 354-368

Reder, S.; Schwab, R.G. (1990). *The Temporal Structure of Cooperative Activity*. In Proceedings of the Third Conference on CSCW, ACM, Los Angeles, California, 7-10 October: 303-316

Release 1.0 (1986). The Living Office: The Coordinator. *Release 1.0*, September

Rice, R.; Richards, W. (1985). Network Analysis Methods. In Dervin, B.; Voigt, M.J. (eds.). *Progress in Communication Sciences*. Ablex Publishing, Norwood, New Jersey

Rieckmann, H.; Weissengruber, P.H. (1990). Managing the Unmanageble? - Oder: Lassen sich komplexe Systeme überhaupt noch steuern? - Offenes Systemmanagement mit dem OSTO-Systemansatz. Kraus, H.; Kailer, N.; Sandner, K. (eds.). *Management Development im Wandel*. Manz, Wien: 27-96

Robinson, M. (1991). Double-Level Languages and Co-operative Working. *AI & Society*, vol. 5: 34-60

Robinson, M. (1993). Design for unanticipated use..... In De Michelis, G.; Simone, C.; Schmidt, K. (eds.). *Proceedings of the Third European Conference on Computer-Supported Cooperative Work*. Kluwer Academic Publishers, Dordrecht: 187-202

Sarin, S.K.; Abbott, K.R.; McCarthy, D.R. (1991). A Process Model for Supporting Collaborative Work. In De Joung, P. (ed.). *Proceedings of the Conference on Organizational Computing Systems*. ACM, New York

Schäfer, H. (1993). Ein systemorientierter Problemlöseansatz zur Leistungssteigerung des Kombinierten Verkehrs mittels organisatorischer und technischer Maßnahmen. *Fortschrittsberichte des VDI*, Reihe 12: Verkehrstechnik/Fahrzeugtechnik, Nr. 188, VDI-Verlag, Düsseldorf (Diss. RWTH Aachen)

Schäl, T. (1988). *Case study Coordinator*. Unpublished manuscript in Italian, ISMES, Bergamo

Schäl, T. (1991). Menschenorientierte CIM-Konzepte für die Flexible Fertigung. *Werkstattberichte*, Nr. 100, Ministerium für Arbeit, Gesundheit und Soziales, Düsseldorf

Schäl, T. (1991b). The Coordinator, il supporto alla cooperazione nell'Enaip Lombardia. *Skill*, Milano, vol. 3/91: 123-129

Schäl, T. (1992). *Information Systems in Public Administration: From Transaction Processing to Computer Supported Cooperative Work*. Proceedings of the IFIP WG 8.5 Working Conference on 'Computer Supported Cooperative Work and Public Administration', Linz, Austria, February 25-27 (to appear in Shapiro, D.; Tauber, M.; Traunmüller, R. (eds.). *The Design of Computer Supported Cooperative Work and Groupware Systems*. Elsevier Science, Amsterdam)

Schäl, T. (1993). *System Design for Cooperative Work in the Language/Action Perspective*. Proceedings of the 12th International Workshop on 'Informatics and Psychology', 1-3 June, Schärding, Austria (to appear in Shapiro, D.; Tauber, M.; Traunmüller, R. (eds.). *The Design of Computer Supported Cooperative Work and Groupware Systems*. Elsesvier Science, Amsterdam)

Schäl, T. (1996). Supporting Cooperative Work With Workflow Management Technology. In Zucchermaglio, C.; Bagnara, S.; Stucky, S.U. (eds.). *Organizational Learning and Technological Change*. NATO ASI Series F, Vol 141. Springer, Berlin: 287-306

Schäl, T.; Shapiro, D. (1992). *What's wrong with tasks? Objections in the large and objections in the small*. Proceedings of the 11th International Workshop on 'Informatics and Psychology', 9-11 June, Schärding, Austria (to appear in Tauber, M.; Waern, Y. (eds.). Proceedings of the International Conference on Task Analysis. North Holland, Amsterdam)

Schäl, T.; Zeller, B. (1989). *Rapporto sul viaggio studio 1989 del Laboratorio per le tecnologie della cooperazione*. RSO, internal report prepared for the members of the Laboratory for Co-operation Technologies, Milano

Schäl, T.; Zeller, B. (1990). *A Methodological Approach to Computer Supported Cooperative Work*. Proceedings Fifth European Conference on Cognitive Ergonomics, European Association of Cognitive Ergonomics, Urbino, 3-6 September: 291-304

Schäl, T.; Zeller, B. (1991). Design Principles for Cooperative Office Support Systems in Distributed Process Management. In Verrijn-Stuart, A.; Sol, H.G; Hammersley, P. (eds.). *Support Functionality in the Office Environment*. North-Holland, Amsterdam: 85-101

Schäl, T.; Zeller, B. (1992). *Organizational, Technological and Methodological Issues to Design Cooperative Networks*. Proceedings of the 11th International Workshop on 'Informatics and Psychology', 9-11 June, Schärding, Austria (to appear in Tauber, M.; Waern, Y. (eds.). Proceedings of the International Conference on Task Analysis. North Holland, Amsterdam)

Schäl, T.; Zeller, B. (1992b). Olivetti workflow helps bank meet new market challenges. *Systems&Networks*, Olivetti, Ivrea, 1-8: 29-34

Schäl, T.; Zeller, B. (1993). Workflow Management Systems for Financial Services. In Kaplan, S. (ed.). *Conference on Organizational Computing Systems*. ACM, New York: 142-153

Schäl, T.; Zenié, A. (1994). *Bootstrapping the Action 4 Business Process of the MARS Project by Workflow Analysis and Redesign*. Joint Research Centre of the Commission of the European Communities, CEO Technical Report #53/1994, February

Schäl, T.; Zenié, A. (1995). Analyzing and Redesigning a Remote Sensing Business Process for Rapid Estimates of Agriculture in Europe. *Conference on Organizational Computing Systems*. ACM, New York: 116-128

Schäl, T.; Zenié, A. (1996). Analyzing and redesigning a remote sensing business process for rapid estimates of agriculture in Europe. *Information Technology & People*, Volume 9, Issue 1, MCB University Press: 19-41

Scheel, J. (1994). Grundlagen der Neuorientierung. In Scheel, J.; Hacker, W.; Henning, K. (eds.). *Fabrikorganisation neu beGreifen*. TÜV Rheinland, Köln: 25-57

Schmidt, K. (1990). *Analysis of Cooperative Work. A Conceptual Framework*. Risø-M-2890, Risø National Laboratory, Roskilde, Denmark

Schmidt, K. (1991b). Riding a Tiger, or Computer Supported Cooperative Work. In Bannon, L.J.; Robinson, M.; Schmidt, K. (eds.). *Proceedings of the Second European Conference on Computer-Supported Cooperative Work*. Kluwer Academic Publishers, Dordrecht: 1-16

Schmidt, K. (1994). The Organization of Cooperative Work: Beyond the "Leviathan" Conception of the Organization of Cooperative Work. In Furuta, R.; Neuwirth, C. (eds.). *Proceedings of the Conference on Computer-Supported Cooperative Work.* ACM, 22-26 October, Chapel Hill, North Carolina: 101-112

Schmidt, K.; Bannon, L.J. (1992). Taking CSCW Seriously: Supporting Articulation Work. *Computer Supported Cooperative Work (CSCW): An International Journal*, 1-1/2, Kluwer Academic Press, Dordrecht: 7-40

Schmidt, K.; Rodden, T. (1993). *Putting it all together: Requirements for a CSCW platform.* Proceedings of the 12th International Workshop on 'Informatics and Psychology', 1-3 June, Schärding, Austria

Schrage, M. (1990). *Shared Minds: The New Technologies of Collaboration.* Random House, New York

Schwartz, J. (1993). Here Today, Here Tomorrow. *Information Week*, May 10th: 35

Scott Morton, M.S. (1991). *The Cooperation of the 1990s, Information Technology and Organizational Transformation.* Oxford University Press, New York

Searle, J.R. (1969). *Speech Acts: an Essay in the Philosophy of Language.* Cambridge University Press, Cambridge

Searle, J.R. (1975). A Taxonomy of Illocutionary Acts. In Gunderson K. (ed.). *Language, Mind and Knowledge.* University of Minnesota, Minneapolis: 344-369

Searle, J.R. (1975b). Indirect Speech Acts. In Cole; Morgan (eds.). *Syntax and Semantics.* Vol. 3: Speech Acts, Academic Press, New York

Searle, J.R. (1979). *Expression and Meaning: Studies in the Theory of Speech Acts.* Cambridge University Press, Cambridge

Sébillotte, S. (1988). Hierarchical planning as a method for task analysis: the example of office task analysis. *Behaviour and Information Technology*, 7-3: 275-293.

Senge, P.M. (1990). *The Fifth Discipline: the Art and Practice of the Learning Organization.* Currency, New York

Seybold, P. (1987). Collective Force: Tools for Group Productivity. *Computerworld*, 2-12

Shannon, C.E.; Weaver, W. (1949). *The Mathematical Theory of Communication.* University of Illinois Press, Urbana

Shepherd, A.; Mayer, N.; Kuchinsky, A. (1990). *Strudel - An Extensible Electronic Conversation Toolkit.* In Proceedings of the Third Conference on CSCW, ACM, Los Angeles, California, 7-10 October: 93-104

Shrivastava, P. (1983). A Typology of Organizational Learning Systems. *Journal of Management Studies*, 20(1): 7-20

Simon, H.A. (1957). *Models of Man.* Wiley, New York

Simon, H.A. (1976). *The New Science of Management Decision*, Prentice Hall, Englewood Cliffs, New Jersey

Simon, H.A. (1991). Bounded Rationality and Organizational Learning. *Organization Science*, 2(91): 125-139

Soles, S. (1994). Work Reengineering and Workflows: Comparative Methods. In White, T.E.; Fischer, L. (eds.). *New Tools for New Times: The Workflow Paradigm.* Future Strategies Inc., Alameda, California: 235-251

Sperber, D.; Wilson, D. (1986). *Relevance: Communication and Cognition.* Blackwell, Oxford

Stamper, R.; Kerola, P.; Lee, R.; Lyytinen, K. (eds.) (1991). *Collaborative Work, Social Communication and Information Systems.* North-Holland, Amsterdam

Strassman, P. (1985). *Information Payoff: The transformation of Work in the Electronic Age.* Free Press, New York

Suchman, L. (1983). Office Procedures as Practical Action: Models of Work and Systems Design. *ACM Transactions on Office Information Systems*, 1-4: 320-328

Suchman, L. (1987). *Plans and Situated Actions. The Problem of Human-Machine Communication.* Cambridge University Press, Cambridge

Suchman, L. (1987b). Review of 'Understand computers and cognition' by Terry Winograd and Fernando Flores. *Artificial Intelligence*, 31: 227-232
Suchman, L. (1993). *Do Categories Have Politics? The language/action perspective reconsidered*. In De Michelis, G.; Simone, C.; Schmidt, K. (eds.). *Proceedings of the Third European Conference on Computer-Supported Cooperative Work*. Kluwer Academic Publishers, Dordrecht: 1-14
Suchman, L. (1994). Do Categories Have Politics? The language/action perspective reconsidered. *Computer Supported Cooperative Work (CSCW): An International Journal*, Kluwer Academic Press, Dordrecht, 3-94: 177-190
Suchman, L.; Wynn, E. (1984). Procedures and Problems in the Office. *Office: Technology and People*, 2: 133-154
Swenson, K.D. (1993). Visual Support for Reengineering Work Processes. In Kaplan, S. (ed.). *Conference on Organizational Computing Systems*. ACM, New York: 130-141
Swenson, K.D.; Maxwell, R.J.; Matsumoto, T.; Saghari, B.; Irwin, K. (1994). A business process environment supporting collaborative planning. *Collaborative Computing*, Chapman & Hall, March, 1-1: 15-34
Taylor, F.W. (1911). *The Principles of Scientific Management*. Harper & Bros, New York
Terry, D.B. (1993). A Tour Through Tapestry. In Kaplan, S. (ed.). *Conference on Organizational Computing Systems*. ACM, New York: 21-30
Trevor, J.; Rodden, T.; Blair, G. (1993). COLA: A Lightweight Platform for CSCW. In De Michelis, G.; Simone, C.; Schmidt, K. (eds.). *Proceedings of the Third European Conference on Computer-Supported Cooperative Work*. Kluwer Academic Publishers, Dordrecht: 15-30
Trigg, R.H.; Suchman, L.A.; Halasz, F.G. (1986). *Supporting Collaboration in NoteCards*. In Proceedings of the First Conference on CSCW, ACM, Austin, Texas, 3-5 December: 153-162
Tschiersch, I. (1994). Eignung des objektorientierten Programmentwurfs für Problemstellungen der Mehrkörperdynamik. *Fortschrittsberichte des VDI*, Reihe 10: Informatik/ Kommunikationstechnik, Nr. 316, VDI-Verlag, Düsseldorf (Diss. RWTH Aachen)
Vajna, S. (1987). Gruppentechnologie als Bindeglied zwischen CAD und CAM. *VDI-Z*, VDI-Verlag, Düsseldorf, 129-11: 44-51
Verity, J.W. (1993). Getting Work To Go With The Flow. *Business Week*, 21 June: 68-69
Victor, F.; Sommer, E. (1989). *Supporting the Design of Office Procedures in the DOMINO System*, in Proceedings of the First European Conference on Computer Supported Cooperative Work, Gatwick, London, U.K., September 13-15: 148-159
Vomberg, E. (1989). *Gestaltungsperspektiven für Mensch-Maschine-Interaktionen im Lichte der Struktureigenschaften sprachlicher Kommunikation*. Augustinus, Aachen (Diss. RWTH Aachen)
Warnecke, H.J. (1992). *Die fraktale Fabrik*. Springer, Berlin
Watzlawick, P.; Beavin, J.H.; Jackson, D.D. (1967). *Pragmatics of human communication*. W.W.Norton & Company, New York
White, T.E.; Fischer, L. (eds.) (1994). *New Tools for New Times: The Workflow Paradigm*. Future Strategies Inc., Alameda, California
Whiteside, J. (1994). *The Phoenix Agenda: Power to Transform Your Workplace*. Oliver Wight Publications, Essex Junction, Vermont
Whiteside, J.; Wixon, D. (1988). *Contextualism as a world view for the reformation of meetings*. In Proceedings of the Second Conference on CSCW, ACM, Portland, Oregon, 26-28 September: 369-376
Williamson, O.E. (1975). *Markets and Hierarchies: Analysis and antitrust implications. A study in the economics of internal organization*. The Free Press, New York
Williamson, O.E. (1981). The Economics of Organization: The Transaction Cost Approach. *American Journal of Sociology*, 87-3: 548-577

Williamson, O.E. (1985). *The economic institutions of capitalism: firms, markets, relational contracting*. The Free Press, New York

Williamson, O.E. (1988). *The network enterprise*. Proceedings of the conference on 'L'impresa rete: riconoscerla, progettarla, gestirla', Camogli, Italy, June 1988

Wilson, P. (1991). *Computer Supported Cooperative Work: An Introduction*. Intellect Books, Oxford

Winograd, T. (1972). *Understanding Natural Language*. Academic Press, New York

Winograd, T. (1984). Computer software for working with language. *Scientific American*, September

Winograd, T. (1986). *A Language Perspective on the Design of Cooperative Work*. In Proceedings of the First Conference on CSCW, ACM, Austin, Texas, 3-5 December: 203-220

Winograd, T. (1987). A Language/Action Perspective on the Design of Cooperative Work. *Human-Computer Interaction*, 3-1 (1987/88): 3-30

Winograd, T. (1988). Where the Action Is. *BYTE*, December: 256A-257

Winograd, T. (1994). Categories, Disciplines, and Social Coordination. *Computer Supported Cooperative Work (CSCW): An International Journal*, Kluwer Academic Press, Dordrecht, 3-94: 177-190

Winograd, T.; Flores, C.F. (1986). *Understanding computers and cognition - a new foundation for design*. Ablex Publishing Corporation, Norwood, New Jersey

Woetzel, G.; Kreifelts, T. (1987). *The Office Procedure Language CoPlan* (in German). WISDOM Research Report FB-GMD-87-34, Gesellschaft für Mathematik und Datenverarbeitung, Bonn St. Augustin, Germany, December

Woetzel, G.; Kreifelts, T. (1993). *The Use of Petri nets for Modelling Workflow with the Domino System*. In Proceedings of the workshop on 'Computer-Supported Cooperative Work, Petri Nets and Related Formalism'. Petri Nets 1993, Chicago, 22 June: 33-41

Zisman, M. (1977). *Representation, Specification and Automation of Office Procedures*. PhD Thesis, Department of Business Administration, Wharton School, University of Pennsylvania

Zisman, M. (1978). Office Automation: Evolution or Revolution. *Sloan Management Review*, 19: 1-16

Zuboff, S. (1988). *In the Age of the Smart Machine: The Future of Work and Power*. Basic Books, New York

Appendix I: Business process modelling goals

Table I-1: Process modelling goals in business processes
(elaborated from Curtis et al., 1992; Schäl, 1996)

Support business process re-engineering

- Identify business goals and strategies to be achieved by processes
- Identify customers, suppliers and conditions of satisfaction
- Identify all necessary components of processes
- Reuse well-defined and effective processes for future processes
- Compare alternative processes
- Estimate impacts of potential changes to a process without first putting them into actual practice
- Assist in the selection and incorporation of technology (tools) into a process
- Help people maintaining ownership of the process and its outcomes
- Facilitate organisational learning regarding effective processes and from failures
- Support managed evolution of processes
- Design processes for error prevention and not for error correction
- Maximise the performance of the entire organisation instead of a single process or part of it
- Do as many tasks as possible concurrently, rather than sequentially
- Reduce cycle times by eliminating delays, hand-offs, set-up times, transports, exceptions

---

(*continued on next page*)

Table I-1: Process modelling goals in business processes (*continued*)

Facilitate business processes

- Represent processes in a form understandable for humans
- Represent the purpose of processes and how it contributes to the achievement of business goals
- Represent the constraints which the organisation imposes on what people can do and how they should operate
- Enable communication about and agreement on processes
- Support commitment negotiation
- Allow for informal communication
- Formalise processes so that people can work together more effectively
- Provide sufficient information to allow an individual or team to perform the process
- Define the roles of individuals and the interactions between them which are required to get the job done
- Provide sufficient information about the resources which are available to carry out the process
- Provide escape hatches to handle exceptions and emergencies
- Provide heuristic plans for situated action
- Form a basis for training the intended process
- Create jobs with cross-trained, multiskilled and highly flexible employees
- Provide a minimum critical specification of jobs and roles
- Enhance the quality of working life

Appendix II: Evaluation of co-operative networks

The performance of co-operative networks is defined by 'communication disciplines' (Petri, 1977, 1977b; 1979). Petri's *communication disciplines* offer a theoretical framework for pragmatics in human communication, moving the observer (user) from outside to inside the system. This pragmatic approach overcomes the perception that criteria for a good performance are only quick and reliable networks at low cost.

The classical *communication theory* is based on the concept developed by Shannon & Weaver (1949). This mechanistic system reflects an outstanding user's view describing communication by information *source*, *message*, *transmitter*, *signal*, *noise*, *receiver* and *destination*. The *unit of information* in Shannon & Weaver's theory is the *bit*. This is the average uncertainty reduced when some signal allows the receiver to choose between two equally likely alternatives. From an engineering point of view, the most important idea to come out of this theory is the idea of a *channel capacity* and the *rate* at which information can be transmitted. Performance is defined by speed, robustness and efficiency.

In their analysis of shortcomings of Shannon & Weaver's theory, Sperber & Wilson (1986) characterise information theory as an *encoding model of communication*. Watzlawick *et al.* (1967) claim that human communication involves information exchange in context, and not only in a mathematical coding model. Modern approaches want to realise flexible communication systems which are able to adjust themselves to the organisation of the social system where they are implemented. Communication factors allow therefore a network to maintain itself adequately in the presence of complex relations among nodes. The communication disciplines – synchronisation, identification, addressing, naming, delegation, authorisation, reorganisation, valuation, copying, cancellation and composition – can be seen as a set of network performance evaluation criteria. These criteria represent different and complementary critical factors for co-operation. The disciplines are discussed here in relation to co-operative networks. Relevant criteria are given for each discipline in relation to the performance of co-operative networks. Petri's model was originally intended for computing networks. The communication disciplines are, for example, embodied in the CHAOS research project (De Cindio *et al.*, 1987; 1988).

Aspects of communication are evaluated from the user's point of view in order to evaluate the network's performance and its characteristics. The communication disciplines are grouped together concerning

- *execution* (synchronisation, identification, addressing, naming),

Appendix II

- *organisation* (delegation, authorisation, re-organisation) and
- *administration* (valuation, copying, cancellation, composition).

The evaluation starts from the users' judgements for the basic level and the relative weights for the importance of every level. Thus the performance of an existing network can be evaluated and the demand for the network's performance expressed. The result is a guide-line for design of co-operative networks. The basic assumption of this approach is that information technologies have to be justified by their contribution to improve the organisational performance. Under that perspective the author suggests to analyse the characteristics of co-operation technologies in terms of their capability to cope with a specific set of communication disciplines.

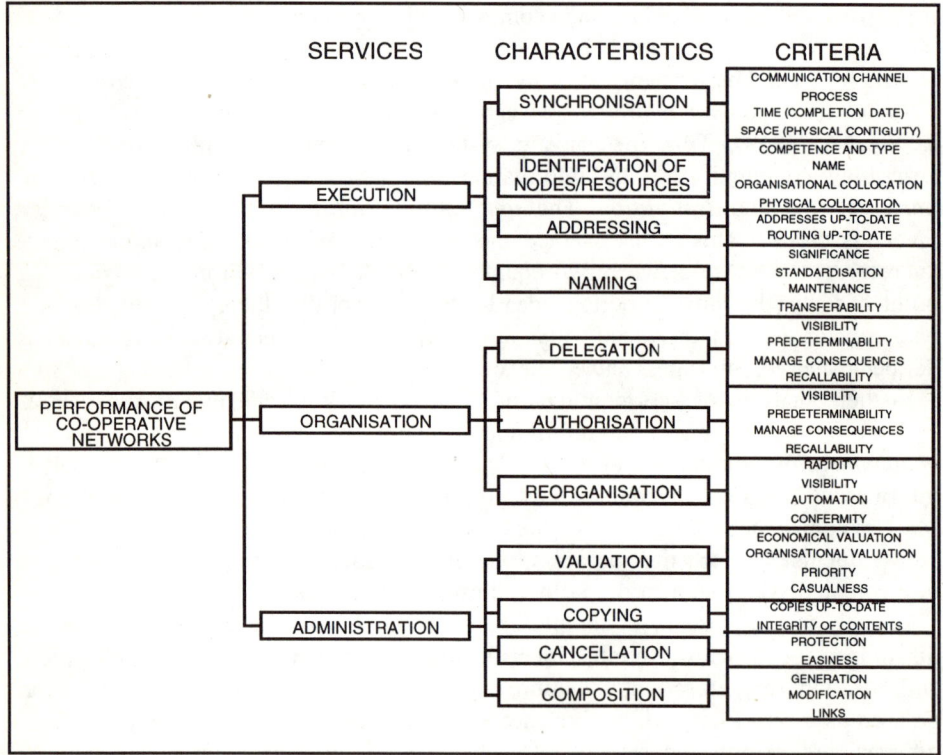

Figure II-1: Characteristics and criteria for co-operative network performance

Synchronisation

This discipline is concerned with getting proper timing restraints and it defines how different messages (e.g., speech acts) constituting a conversation and any other activity are synchronised among themselves. This could be referred to a measure of time (clock, agenda) or simply to the indication of temporal relations which link activities. In general, synchronisation should be based on a partial ordering in terms of causality as opposed to an ordering in time. Criteria for performance evaluation are the synchronisation of communication channels, process, time (e.g., completion dates for commitments) and space.

Identification of nodes and resources

This discipline defines the conditions which allow to recognise the source of messages which are exchanged on the network, and to establish the appropriateness of the message's receiver and destination. Criteria for a good network performance are the identification of nodes' competence and type, the identification of resources, its names, and its organisational and physical collocation.

Addressing

This discipline defines routes and system paths which allow to address a message on a co-operative network to an identified destination through a net of channels. Criteria for a good network performance are up-to-date addresses and routings.

Naming

This discipline is concerned with the modality how names are determined for various entities (persons and resources) on a network. This defines the bases for a common knowledge and to what extend its ambiguity could be avoided or resolved. Important criteria for naming are the significance of names, the standardisation of naming, the possibility to maintain names in time and to transfer them into other contexts.

Delegation

This discipline defines how and when a delegation can be made. This concerns both, the delegation of tasks and the delegation of responsibilities from one person to the other. Delegation has also to cope with some effects on synchronisation, addressing and other disciplines. Criteria for performance are the delegation's visibility on the co-operative network, its possible predetermination, its cancellation and the management of the delegation's consequences.

Authorisation

This discipline assigns and represents access rights to resources, priorities going along with these access rights, the rules and obligations for accessing resources and, if necessary, the rules for the supervision of all these activities. Criteria for performance are the authorisation's visibility on the co-operative network, its possible predetermination, its cancellation and the management of the authorisation's consequences. Both, delegation and authorisation, define the roles performed by persons on the co-operative network.

Reorganisation

This discipline defines the rules for up-dating the co-operative network with regard to changes and adoptions of the network caused by the impact of the other communication disciplines. Criteria for a good performance are the re-organisation on time, its visibility, its degree of automation and its capacity of a conformable adoption.

Valuation

This discipline has to resolve the problem of limited resources on the co-operative network. All the time algorithms and rules are defined to resolve conflicts among nodes who want to use, e.g., a communication channel. Nodes might get special rights on the use of resources or a node might be associated with a relative value on the co-operative network. The performance is examined by economical and organisational (hierarchical) criteria for valuation and rules for priority or casualness.

Copying

This discipline treats aspects of information handling which are related with copying documents. Furthermore it defines the necessary integrity and coherence of copied information. Copying is related to other disciplines, e.g., delegation and authorisation which define who has sufficient rights to copy certain information. The up-dating of existing copies and the integrity of contents after a partial or complete copying of information are criteria for a good network performance.

Cancellation

This discipline defines the possibilities to cancel information so that the main contents of documents and unique information cannot get lost. Protection and easiness are performance criteria.

Composition

This discipline defines the possibilities to compose a new document which can derive from existing documents or information. This is highly related to copying, but also to other disciplines like delegation and authorisation which define who has the right to compose what kind of information. Generation, modification and links of information are the performance criteria.

Appendix III: Functional requirements for workflow management technology

Traditional workflow systems (and office information systems) have been criticised because they prescribe inflexibly temporal task sequencing, and they dictate narrowly and restrict, rather than to broadly assist people in the roles they play. People are typically engaged in problem solving, informal communication and exception handling. In order *to get the job done* it might be necessary to circumvent standard office procedures creatively. These mechanisms to help people in their necessary problem solving and exception handling are typically still lacking in most today's workflow management systems (Ellis & Wainer, 1994).

This is only one point to improve the currently available systems. The actual state of the art is still far away from the vast number of needed functionality. This appendix gives an overview of functionality which might only be developed and/or integrated in the next generation of workflow systems (Hales & Lavery, 1991; Marshak, 1992; 1992b; 1994; Schäl, 1996; Swenson, 1993; Sarin *et al.*, 1991; Abbott & Sarin, 1994; Swenson *et al.*, 1994).

Process support requirements

Effective workflow systems must be customisable by end users and application programmers. This ensures that the people who know the business best can effect full-blown applications. Application developers can transcend individual application development efforts. This means that developers can build a baseline application which can then be leveraged by multiple user-driven application efforts. For end-users, however, the *authoring environment* has to be a *graphical environment* as a requirement for workflow definition. Successful products have to support the definition of workflow *steps* (actions), *sequences* (the order of actions), *routing* (who does the action) and *conditions* (rules for routing and doing actions). Experiences with non-programmers suggests the use of a *picture-oriented* approach describing a process (Swenson *et al.*, 1994).

In order to develop the workflow software script, the user organisation needs first to model the business process to be managed, and input this then to a workflow procedure set-up facility. Most workflow systems allow the programmer to display the process in a *flow diagram* form as the model for the process is built up. It is only now, that we enter into a stage of process automation which has *flexible workflow scripting languages*.

The graphical tool should include a *flow chart generator* that assists the user in visualising the flow. In the presence of a graphical process representation, the tool can already be used for the process analysis and re-engineering phases. The outcome of the newly designed process can directly be implemented in the software product without passing from paper or different software tools (e.g. graphical applications) to the workflow authoring environment. A more sophisticated tool will also write the script from the flow chart (actions, roles, rules, routing, etc.). A graphical language to support workflow models has been developed, e.g., in the *ActionWorkflow* Suite (Medina-Mora *et al.*, 1992; ATI, 1993) and in *Regatta* (Swenson, 1993; Swenson *et al.*, 1994).

Advanced authoring environments might also include *simulation functionality*, e.g., to see the consequences of a certain step for the entire flow. Simulations about processing bottlenecks and idle resources can be done using, e.g., *IDEF0/SADT* (Marca & McGowan, 1988; Marca, 1991), extended with behavioural details. Pinci & Shapiro (1993) have developed a program called *Work Flow Analyser* which automatically generates a coloured Petri Net (for CP-Net see, e.g., Jensen, 1992) complete with the logic for loading input files and printing reports containing the simulation results.

Workflow authoring tools should allow to re-use steps and rules from other workflows (library of primitives and already developed workflows). As real organisational processes are complex, the authoring environment should allow for *zooming* in the process. This helps the user to understand the granularity of the process and to identify the main steps. *Zooming* is important also during the process execution since every persons has a *different view on the process* representation. Higher level process participants and observers might prefer to use *generalisations* and *abstractions*, while operative participants would be more concerned with the *process decomposition* at a detailed level (Swenson, 1993; Swenson *et al.*, 1994).

Once a workflow has been developed, it should be able to be *copied or modified* directly by the user with sufficient permission rights. It would also be useful, if the user could modify the workflow within the already started process, rather than having to go back to the authoring environment. In other cases it might be important to let the user define parts of a process plan in order to get the process started; the missing part of the plan will be added as the process advances. *Partial definitions* are important for less recurrent and structured processes, for which it may not be possible to completely define them beforehand due to inconsistent strategies of how the process should be completed, or due to conflicts which cannot be resolved until after the process has been started (Hewitt, 1986).

The *modify functionality* could also be used to *re-open a blocking situation* in an already running workflow. A *simulation facility* would be very helpful for this kind of modifications (e.g., delete a step or change a rule and see what changes in the process).

Actions have to be accomplished by persons. Workflow products should allow to assign an action either to a specific person or to a role, such as a sales manager (addressing by name, title or role). Most products allow only for the one or the other, but not for a mixed assignment between *physical persons* and *alias roles*. When defining roles, the local name service should be invoked. E-mail names should be coupled to workflow roles and possibly stored in X.500 directories (Prinz & Pennelli, 1989).

When a step is routed to a role which corresponds to more than one person (e.g., salesman), there has to be some mechanism which notes that an individual has taken the action. The *assignment of actions* within a role to individuals could also be determined by rules, e.g., work-load balancing.

Each action should have a *deadline*. This deadline is usually expressed as a period for the task accomplishment. Deadlines might also be specified by specific or recurrent dates in the flow. Some workflow products support only the entire period for the process and do not break the flow down into single action deadlines. This makes it difficult to handle deadlines at the end of the process due to missing control for previous steps. Another point is that deadlines cannot always be established for each action by the initiator, but might be negotiated among the workflow users for every specific process. These negotiated deadlines constitute a network of commitments among the participants. The process of deadline negotiation is not supported for the time being by any of the existing products. In any case, the workflow system should support *variable calendar windows and time-scales*, because process duration and deadlines might vary from hours to months.

Users should also be *alerted if actions are overdue or pending* for a certain period. This might also activate automatically or by manual choice an alternative workflow path for time recovering.

The workflow application should *notify the user* that there is a step or action to do. These new actions to perform should be handled in a *mail in-box* (e.g., in a special folder or action items listed separately from other E-mail messages), but not isolated from the E-mail application. Most system currently handle a to-do list, but the integration with general purpose electronic mail is still missing (one has to quit the workflow application in order to read or to send an E-mail message, also if this is directly related to the action due).

The user should be able to view the personal *mailbox and/or to-do list* in a variety of manners: by date, deadline, process, type of step, sender, workflow initiator, etc. These *views should be tailorable* for the users. The user should also see the workload for the pending tasks and should have the possibility to delegate to others in several cases (absence, overload, etc.). The system should manage the delegation as a relation between the delegate and delegated person (accepting the delegation) and not as a one-way forward mechanism. Furthermore, the user might want to prioritise pending tasks in the mailbox and/or to-do list.

The *auditing functionality* serves for monitoring the status of objects, single flows or groups of flows for the same process. In addition to simple tracking reports (case status enquiry that flow 'Budget' is in step 'Approving' which is worked on by 'Mr. Smith' holding the role 'Project Manager'), systems should provide more sophisticated *management reports* (e.g., on productivity, quality, etc.).

In addition of being easy to programme, one purpose of the graphical representation is to visually *represent the current state of the process* to help the participants in the process understand what has happened, and what might happen next. Hence it 'allows every individual in a group to gain a better understanding of how their group or organisation works. It is not sufficient that a workflow tool acts as a black box process. It is furthermore not sufficient for the tool to assume that the present process is known, it must help in the discovery of the process.' (Swenson, 1993: 130)

Table III-1 summarises the functional requirements for workflow management systems to support process analysis, design and working. There is still a notable gap between the offered functionality of current systems and the desired level of functionality. Future workflow management systems have to be developed with this functionality to provide better support for process organisations.

Table III-1: Functional requirements for workflow analysis, design and use

Process support requirements
• customisable application development in a graphical end-user environment
• flowchart generator with object-oriented language to define steps, sequences, routing and conditions
• homogeneous business process analysis and design environment
• simulation facilities
• re-use of workflows (library of primitives and existing processes)
• process zooming in workflow maps (abstraction versus decomposition)
• partial definition of workflows before start
• dynamic workflow modification in use
• flexible assignment of actions to roles/individuals
• deadline negotiation and management
• process auditing

System integration requirements

Workflow applications must provide *electronic routing* of information, images, documents, files, etc., in a process to be supported. This routing can be simply *sequential* (predefined steps) or *rule-based* (dependent upon static and dynamic criteria). The rule-based routing can be *conditional* intended as being programmed or *exceptional* based on ad-hoc decisions. Furthermore, the flow might have a *ramification into parallel tracks* which converge again at a certain step. The rendezvous of parallel tasks has to be synchronised by the application.

The workflow systems available today seem to focus on tracking and managing the handling of tasks rather than facilitating and managing the tasks themselves (as well as the flow between them). What is missing is the work itself. A well-designed workflow application should do more than route the information associated with a task and keep track of progress. It should also facilitate the process itself. Therefore workflow applications support also the work done in a flow. The system provides users with the *proper tool(s)* to complete each action or step. This means that people need for the accomplishment of a task the right or preferred tool, like spreadsheets, form handlers, word processors, etc. New generation workflow applications can launch any application, like a spreadsheet or a procedure template, at a designed point in the routing of a workflow. These workflow applications allow also to *connect data from different sources* (database, file, template, etc.) to the actual application (e.g., paste data or text from different sources into the application file). This connection is insured by *running background applications* which are activated by scripts in the workflow application.

By designing a workflow application, one has to take into consideration also *individual preferences* for standard office tools. The foreseen use of a spreadsheet at a certain point could be supported by all existing spreadsheets if they fit into the task. Therefore the workflow designer should leave users their preferred office applications and concentrate on the connection of data to these applications (spreadsheets, word processors, graphical applications, etc.). The workflow system should have an *on-line help-system*. The flexible activation of applications and forms should also support *multi-lingual interfaces*, because processes might span different countries and ethnic groups with language preferences.

Certain steps will require creating forms for the workflow application. These forms must be *easy to create and to modify*, also by the workflow users.

However, not all data and information is generated or taken from company databases as the workflow progresses, but off-line paper documentation (e.g., from external sources at customers). The transcription of the information treated in these documents into workflow documents might be expensive or even impossible. Therefore workflow applications have to be able to *route a variety of data, documents, forms, mail messages*, as well as *scanned images* from external sources. The *image management* will be done in background by Document Management Systems and is not a functionality for workflow applications.

The same logic counts for non-electronic actions in a process. Not every step in a workflow might be computer-based, e.g., check references with a customer via phone. The workflow should allow the person assigned to indicate that the action was done, and to report on results of external events if necessary.

Workflows should also provide functionality to *link the workflow to other processes or sub-flows* which are recurrent in the organisation (e.g., administrative processes). Therefore workflows and workflow users should be able to launch other workflows or agents, as well as agents should be able to launch workflows. This counts especially for the possibility to define *ad-hoc workflows* and to link them to existing ones.

Table III-2 shows the necessary functional requirements to do system integration with workflow management technology.

Table III-2: Functional requirements for system integration with workflow management technology

---

System integration requirements

- provide proper tools for each action allowing for individual preferences
- connect data from different sources
- create and modify easily forms
- integrate workflow messages with general E-mail
- link the workflow to other processes

In order to allow this integration of different applications and data into a workflow application, it will be *developed jointly by the workflow users and information systems people*. The user (possibly aided by consultants) will prototype the application, determine the flow and define the forms and applications to be used. The computing specialists will write the back-end operations, e.g. sophisticated data-base access. Therefore workflow management systems have to supply an application programming interface (API). This is an advantage for both, users and information systems people: the user has direct control on the application definition and development; the developer concentrates on technical problems and is not in the old dilemma to try to understand what the users intend for the process application.

Abbreviations

ACM	Association for Computing Machinery
ADL	Activity Description Language
AMIGO	Advanced Messaging In Group Organisations
API	Application Programming Interface
ATI	Action Technologies, Inc.
AWK	Aachener Werkzeugmaschinen-Kolloquium
BPR	Business Process Re-engineering
CAD	Computer Aided Design
CAM	Computer Aided Manufacturing
CEFI	Central File
CEO	Chief Executie Officer
CHAOS	Commitments Handling Active Office System
CIM	Computer Integrated Manufacturing
COOCS	Conference on Orgnisational Computing Systems
COPLANS	Coordination Procedure Language
COSCIS	Collaborative Work, Social Communications and Information Systems
COSMOS	Configurable Structured Message System
CPM	Critical Path Method
CPT	Centre for Professional Training
CSC	Computer Science Company
CSCW	Computer Supported Cooperative Work
CUD	Consorzio per l'Università a Distanza
DB	Data Base
DBMS	Data Base Management System
DEC	Digital Equipment Corporation
DFD	Data Flow Diagram
DSI	Dipartimento Scienze dell'Informazione

DSS	Decision Support System
E-mail	Electronic Mail
ECSCW	European Conference on Computer Supported Cooperative Work
EDP	Electronic Data Processing
ESA	European Space Agency
ESPRIT	European Strategic Programme for Research and Development in Information Technology
GMD	Gesellschaft für Mathematik und Datenverarbeitung
GRE	Guardian Royal Exchange
HCI	Human-Computer Interaction
HDZ	Hochschuldidaktisches Zentrum der RWTH Aachen
ICN	Information Control Net
IFIP	International Federation for Information Processing
IMA	Institut für Informatik im Maschinenbau der RWTH Aachen
IS	Information Systems
ISO	International Standards Organisation
IT	Information Technology
LAN	Local Area Network
MHS	Message Handling Service
MIS	Management Information Systems
MIT	Massachusetts Institute of Technology
MS	Microsoft
OA	Office Automation
OIS	Office Information System
OPT	Optimised Production Technology
OSTO	Offene Sozio-Techno-Ökonomische Systeme
PC	Personal Computer
PERT	Programme Evaluation and Review Technique
PFMS	Personal Financial Management Services
PPIR	Product Performance Investigation Request
R&D	Research and Development
RDBMS	Relational Data Base Management System
RSO	Ricerca Intervento sui Sistemi Organizzativi
RWTH Aachen	Rheinisch-Westfälische Technische Hochschule Aachen
SADT	Structured Analysis and Design Technique

SIGCHI	Special Interest Group Computer and Human Interaction
SIGOA	Special Interest Group Office Automation
SIGOIS	Special Interest Group Office Information Systems
TP	Transaction Processing
UK	United Kingdom
USA	United States of America
UTUCS	User To User Communication Support
VDI	Verein Deutscher Ingenieure
WAN	Wide Area Network

Index

action 93
action management 102
Action Technologies, Inc. 100; 103
ActionWorkflow 100; 101
activity
   based costing 21
   model 26
   synchronisation 51
Activity Description Language 95
activity synchronisation 4; 77
adhocracy 8
Aetna Life & Casualty 103
AMIGO 26
Amnesty International 108
application processing 97
Application Programming Interface 98
archiviation 62
archivist 62
articulation 63
articulation of work 60; 61
assertive 29
AT&T 100
autopoiesis 29

back-office 14
Banca d'Italia 135; 148; 150
behaviour 60
Beyond 100
BeyondMail 100, 101
bounds 60; 61
breakdown 12; 40; 58; 73; 85; 96; 142
Bull 100
bureaucracy 8; 10
Business Design Language 36
business process 1; 2; 7; 24; 27; **28**; 113
   automation 101
   benefits 14
business process re-engineering 1; 15; 18
   complexity 23
   depth 23

   failure rate 20
   goals 21
   management 23
   problems 19
   responsibility 23
business process reengineering
   requirements 21

career 19
case study 43; 44; 66; 74; 104; 105; 106; 108; 113; 129
change management 22
CHAOS 35; 181
check point 13
CIGNA 20
clarification 81
CM1 100
co-authoring system 55
commissive 29
commitment 12; 29; 36; 53; 60; 61; **62**; 102; 106; 113; 118
   handler 126
Common User Access 103
communication 28; 55; 88
   direct 53
   filter 78
   management 62
   role 62
communication discipline 181
communication theory 181
competence 10
compiler language 88
complexity 2; 8; 23; 57
Computer Supported Cooperative Work 2; 54; **55**
conceptual scheme 52
condition of satisfaction 28; 41
conflict 85
connection 60
context 60
continuing education 8
Contract 105; 127

control 4; 7; 158
  function centralised 7
conversation 30; 78; 93; 102; 113; 117; 125
  for action 30; 31; 102; 103; 121
  for clarification 30
  for orientation 30
  for possibility 30; 34; 38; 81; 103
Conversation Manager 103; 109
conversation protocol 118; 121
co-operation 28; 51
  co-decision 4; 51; 60; **65**; 80
  collaboration 4; 51; 60; **64**; 74; 79
  co-ordination 4; 51; 60; **64**; 78
  dynamics 4
  effectiveness 77
  efficiency 77
  in the large 4; 51; 71; 72; 81
  in the small 4; 51; 71; 82
  interdependence of work 52
  mechanisms of interaction 52
  social interaction 53
  social organisation of work 52
  team science 74
co-operative network 3; 4; 13; 39; 51; 59; 60; **61**; 115
  articulation **63**
  establishment 72
co-operative work 4; 51; **53**
  taxonomy 51
co-ordination and control mechanism 22
co-ordination structure 40
CoPlanS 93; 109; 156
Corporate Memory Systems 100
COSMOS 26
cost
  direct 21
  indirect 21
  overhead 15; 52; 53
  reduction 8; 14; 21
credibility assessment 64; 80
credit granting 132
credit management 129; 138
critical factor
  analysis 41
customer 7; 12; 13; 28; 41; 61
  internal 14
  relation 10
  satisfaction 2; 3; 7; 10; 11; **12**; 13; 14; 28; 55; 61
cycle-time 28
  reduction 21

data control 97
data flow 88
  analysis 26
  diagram 7
database 97
DaVinci 100
decision 61
decision support system 157
declaration 30
delegation 8; 62
dequalification 7
design space 4; 77
Digital 100
Digital Equipment 105
directive 29
division of labour 7
document management systems 87
document routing 100
domain knowledge 53
domain service 82
DOMINO 93; 109; 155
drawing application 56

efficiency 4; 7
electronic data processing 56
electronic mail 57; 86; 121; 125
entity-relationship model 26
environment 8
European Space Agency 74; 75
exception handling 88; 93
execution 62
expert system 148; 157
expressive 30

factory automation 25
FCMC 98; 100
feed-back 13
FileNet 87; 98; 100
filter 102
flexibility 8; 14
FloWare 100
FlowMark 100
FlowPath 100; 101
Ford 16
foreman 4
form 93
front-office 14
Fujitsu 100
function 4; 10
functional manager 10
functional requirement
  workflow management technology 185

functional unit 10

George Mason University 43
gIBIS 100
GMD 93
group
  ad-hoc 71
  co-operative ensemble 53
  customer-focused business team 13
  members 13
  permanent 71
  project team 13
group technology 25
groupware 54; 56; 87; 113
  ad-hoc 101
Guardian Royal Exchange 105

health 7
hermeneutics 29
Hewlett-Packard 106
hierarchy 10
Human Computer Interaction 52
human resource 1
hypermedia 79
hypertext 79

IBIsys 100; 109; 131; 150
IBM 100; 101; 103; 151
ICL 100
ICON 131
illocutionary force 29
ImageFlow 100
InConcert 100
industrialisation 7
information 27; 55; 56; 63; 84; 88
  control net 87; 92
  flow model 26
  management 55; 79; 97
  process 26
  sharing 4; 51; 55; 77; 80; 93
  space 53
initiator 110
innovation 4; 8
input/output relation 93
interaction 60
Internet 82
invoiceless payment 18
ITHACA 95

JobMaker 100; 101
junk mail 106

kanban 52

key process 18
Keyfile 100
knowledge 64
knowledge worker 10

language/action perspective 2; 3; 7;
  28; 102; 113; 115; 117
lead-time 8
learning capacity 21
linguistic theory 29
LinkWorks 100
Local Area Network 102; 119
logistics 26
Lotus 100

mainframe 55; 151
management structure 10
material process 25
Mazda 16
MCC 100
message control 96
Message Handling Service 119
modelling
  communication 28
  co-operation 71
  co-operative network 65
  network 59
  procedure 10
  types of co-operation 64
  work 51
  workflow 12; 36
MS-DOS 103; 151
MS-Windows 151
multimedia 98

NCR 100
negotiation 36; 118
network analysis 59
network communication 26
network of help 73; 85
node 60; 62; **63**
Notes 100; 101

offer 31
Office Automation 54; 57; 83; 84
Office Information Systems 54; 87
office procedure systems 26
Officetalk 87
OfisProcedure 88; 100
Olivetti 100; 109; 131
on-line computing 55
open service 81
OPEN/workflow 100

optimised production technology   26
Oracle   150
organisation   7
   ad-hoc workgroup   1
   business   11
   customer-oriented   11
   flattening out   1
   functional   2; 7; 8; 10
   functional division   4
   hierarchical   4; 8; 11; 14
   interface with customers   10
   learning   9
   market-oriented   2
   networked   9
   process organisation   3; 7; 9; 14
   project team   2
   structure   1; 52
   Tayloristic   3; 7
organisational handbook   110
organisational role   41
orientation   81
overdraft   129

Pacific Bell   104
participation   53
partnership   21
performer   62
period batch control   26
personal computing   55; 56; 57
Petri-Net   88; 91; 92
phenomenology   29
place   58
plan   52; 84; 95
planning   7
Plexus   100
Powerflow   88; 100
pragmatics   29
problem solving   2
   business process re-engineering   3
   organisation-oriented   3
   technology-oriented   3
procedural model   26
procedure   8; 10; 52; 84; 88; 93
   automation   83
   definition language   91
   history   110
   input   10
   output   10
   status   110
process   61
   cost   21
   handbook   15
   information   7
   innovation   15; 16

   interfunctional   9
   management   9; 18; 88
   manager   10; 28
   market centred   12
   material   7
   owner   10; 28
   production centred   12
process automation   19
   technology   3
process modelling   24
ProcessIT   100; 101
product   61
   value added   8
productivity   1; 2; 19; 21; 77
   personal   56
professional computing   57
professional role   8; 22
professional training   113
profitability   1; 7; 21
Prolog   150
public administration   11

quality   4; 9; 11
   model   11
quality of working life   14

Reach Software   100
realisation   61
Recognition Equipment Inc.   100
referential component   29
Regatta   100
relation   60; **63**
   communicative   12
   conversational   2
   customer/supplier   2; 3; 12; 13; 14; 28; 115; 156
relationships   55
reporting system   129; 142
request   31
response time   9
responsibility   10; 28; 61
reverse engineering   15
Rhapsody   88; 100
risk centre   135
role   8; 28; 61; 71; 93; 110
   co-ordinative   62
   distinct   64
   equal   64
   informative   62
   operative   62
routine task   7
routing mechanism   88
RSO   130

Index

rule 8

schedule 52
Scientific Management 7; 8; 84
SCOOP 87
SECReTS 131; 150
semantics 29
service 4; 9; 11; 61
   domain 77
   open 77
   value added 8
shared group calendar 55
shared knowledge 64
sharing 61
Siemens-Nixdorf 100
situated action 84
skill 4
social network 60
socio-technical system 22
software engineering 66
speech act 29; 93; 102; 118
   declare 37
   promise 37
   propose 38
   report 37
   request 37
   suggest 38
speech act theory 29
   critique 35
spreadsheet 56
stable organisational unit 71
Staffware 88; 100; 101
state transition diagram 92
status 64
steps
   parallel 13
   sequential 13
storage management 97
store-and-forward mechanism 107
store-and-forward network 120
strategy 1
structure 63
supplier 28; 41
   internal 14
synchronisation 61; 64
syntax 29
system analysis 26

task 4; 8; 26; 53; 61
   analysis 40; 52
   management 18
   structure 40
Taylor 8

team
   flexible 8
TeamFlow 100
TeamLinks 100
teamwork 13
teleconferencing system 109
temporary project team 72
The Coordinator 100; 101
   version I 104; 106
   version II 105; 108; 113
time 58
time-to-market 21
training 104; 120; 124
transaction cost 78
transaction processing 25; 26; 43; 56; 83; 86
transformation 12
transparency 158

unemployment 20
Unisys 100
UNIX 152
user interface 96; 98; 103
utterance 29
UTUCS 35; 95

value 21; 28
value engineering 105
value-added service 21
Visual Basic 151
VSAM 151

Wang 100
Wide Area Network 102; 119
WooRKS 95
word processor 56
work study 8
work-analysis 15
workflow 7; 12; 14
   action workflow protocol 36
   ad-hoc 13
   basic 41
   case-based 13
   coalition 98
   co-operative 2
   execution component 90
   incomplete 42
   modelling component 90
   secondary 41
   specification language 92
WorkFlow Business System 100
Workflow for Co-operation 100

workflow management technology 1; 3; 4; 83
Workgroup Computing 55
Workhorse 88; 98; 100
WorkMAN 100; 101
WorkParty 100; 101

X.400 mail 150

}

Xerox 100
Xerox PARC 87
XSoft 100
X_Workflow 92; 100; 101; **109**; 129; 152

Young & Rubicam 43

Springer-Verlag and the Environment

We at Springer-Verlag firmly believe that an international science publisher has a special obligation to the environment, and our corporate policies consistently reflect this conviction.

We also expect our business partners – paper mills, printers, packaging manufacturers, etc. – to commit themselves to using environmentally friendly materials and production processes.

The paper in this book is made from low- or no-chlorine pulp and is acid free, in conformance with international standards for paper permanency.

Lecture Notes in Computer Science

For information about Vols. 1–1022

please contact your bookseller or Springer-Verlag

Vol. 1023: K. Kanchanasut, J.-J. Lévy (Eds.), Algorithms, Concurrency and Knowlwdge. Proceedings, 1995. X, 410 pages. 1995.

Vol. 1024: R.T. Chin, H.H.S. Ip, A.C. Naiman, T.-C. Pong (Eds.), Image Analysis Applications and Computer Graphics. Proceedings, 1995. XVI, 533 pages. 1995.

Vol. 1025: C. Boyd (Ed.), Cryptography and Coding. Proceedings, 1995. IX, 291 pages. 1995.

Vol. 1026: P.S. Thiagarajan (Ed.), Foundations of Software Technology and Theoretical Computer Science. Proceedings, 1995. XII, 515 pages. 1995.

Vol. 1027: F.J. Brandenburg (Ed.), Graph Drawing. Proceedings, 1995. XII, 526 pages. 1996.

Vol. 1028: N.R. Adam, Y. Yesha (Eds.), Electronic Commerce. X, 155 pages. 1996.

Vol. 1029: E. Dawson, J. Golić (Eds.), Cryptography: Policy and Algorithms. Proceedings, 1995. XI, 327 pages. 1996.

Vol. 1030: F. Pichler, R. Moreno-Díaz, R. Albrecht (Eds.), Computer Aided Systems Theory - EUROCAST '95. Proceedings, 1995. XII, 539 pages. 1996.

Vol.1031: M. Toussaint (Ed.), Ada in Europe. Proceedings, 1995. XI, 455 pages. 1996.

Vol. 1032: P. Godefroid, Partial-Order Methods for the Verification of Concurrent Systems. IV, 143 pages. 1996.

Vol. 1033: C.-H. Huang, P. Sadayappan, U. Banerjee, D. Gelernter, A. Nicolau, D. Padua (Eds.), Languages and Compilers for Parallel Computing. Proceedings, 1995. XIII, 597 pages. 1996.

Vol. 1034: G. Kuper, M. Wallace (Eds.), Constraint Databases and Applications. Proceedings, 1995. VII, 185 pages. 1996.

Vol. 1035: S.Z. Li, D.P. Mital, E.K. Teoh, H. Wang (Eds.), Recent Developments in Computer Vision. Proceedings, 1995. XI, 604 pages. 1996.

Vol. 1036: G. Adorni, M. Zock (Eds.), Trends in Natural Language Generation - An Artificial Intelligence Perspective. Proceedings, 1993. IX, 382 pages. 1996. (Subseries LNAI).

Vol. 1037: M. Wooldridge, J.P. Müller, M. Tambe (Eds.), Intelligent Agents II. Proceedings, 1995. XVI, 437 pages. 1996. (Subseries LNAI).

Vol. 1038: W: Van de Velde, J.W. Perram (Eds.), Agents Breaking Away. Proceedings, 1996. XIV, 232 pages. 1996. (Subseries LNAI).

Vol. 1039: D. Gollmann (Ed.), Fast Software Encryption. Proceedings, 1996. X, 219 pages. 1996.

Vol. 1040: S. Wermter, E. Riloff, G. Scheler (Eds.), Connectionist, Statistical, and Symbolic Approaches to Learning for Natural Language Processing. IX, 468 pages. 1996. (Subseries LNAI).

Vol. 1041: J. Dongarra, K. Madsen, J. Waśniewski (Eds.), Applied Parallel Computing. Proceedings, 1995. XII, 562 pages. 1996.

Vol. 1042: G. Weiß, S. Sen (Eds.), Adaption and Learning in Multi-Agent Systems. Proceedings, 1995. X, 238 pages. 1996. (Subseries LNAI).

Vol. 1043: F. Moller, G. Birtwistle (Eds.), Logics for Concurrency. XI, 266 pages. 1996.

Vol. 1044: B. Plattner (Ed.), Broadband Communications. Proceedings, 1996. XIV, 359 pages. 1996.

Vol. 1045: B. Butscher, E. Moeller, H. Pusch (Eds.), Interactive Distributed Multimedia Systems and Services. Proceedings, 1996. XI, 333 pages. 1996.

Vol. 1046: C. Puech, R. Reischuk (Eds.), STACS 96. Proceedings, 1996. XII, 690 pages. 1996.

Vol. 1047: E. Hajnicz, Time Structures. IX, 244 pages. 1996. (Subseries LNAI).

Vol. 1048: M. Proietti (Ed.), Logic Program Syynthesis and Transformation. Proceedings, 1995. X, 267 pages. 1996.

Vol. 1049: K. Futatsugi, S. Matsuoka (Eds.), Object Technologies for Advanced Software. Proceedings, 1996. X, 309 pages. 1996.

Vol. 1050: R. Dyckhoff, H. Herre, P. Schroeder-Heister (Eds.), Extensions of Logic Programming. Proceedings, 1996. VII, 318 pages. 1996. (Subseries LNAI).

Vol. 1051: M.-C. Gaudel, J. Woodcock (Eds.), FME'96: Industrial Benefit and Advances in Formal Methods. Proceedings, 1996. XII, 704 pages. 1996.

Vol. 1052: D. Hutchison, H. Christiansen, G. Coulson, A. Danthine (Eds.), Teleservices and Multimedia Communications. Proceedings, 1995. XII, 277 pages. 1996.

Vol. 1053: P. Graf, Term Indexing. XVI, 284 pages. 1996. (Subseries LNAI).

Vol. 1054: A. Ferreira, P. Pardalos (Eds.), Solving Combinatorial Optimization Problems in Parallel. VII, 274 pages. 1996.

Vol. 1055: T. Margaria, B. Steffen (Eds.), Tools and Algorithms for the Construction and Analysis of Systems. Proceedings, 1996. XI, 435 pages. 1996.

Vol. 1056: A. Haddadi, Communication and Cooperation in Agent Systems. XIII, 148 pages. 1996. (Subseries LNAI).

Vol. 1057: P. Apers, M. Bouzeghoub, G. Gardarin (Eds.), Advances in Database Technology — EDBT '96. Proceedings, 1996. XII, 636 pages. 1996.

Vol. 1058: H. R. Nielson (Ed.), Programming Languages and Systems – ESOP '96. Proceedings, 1996. X, 405 pages. 1996.

Vol. 1059: H. Kirchner (Ed.), Trees in Algebra and Programming – CAAP '96. Proceedings, 1996. VIII, 331 pages. 1996.

Vol. 1060: T. Gyimóthy (Ed.), Compiler Construction. Proceedings, 1996. X, 355 pages. 1996.

Vol. 1061: P. Ciancarini, C. Hankin (Eds.), Coordination Languages and Models. Proceedings, 1996. XI, 443 pages. 1996.

Vol. 1062: E. Sanchez, M. Tomassini (Eds.), Towards Evolvable Hardware. IX, 265 pages. 1996.

Vol. 1063: J.-M. Alliot, E. Lutton, E. Ronald, M. Schoenauer, D. Snyers (Eds.), Artificial Evolution. Proceedings, 1995. XIII, 396 pages. 1996.

Vol. 1064: B. Buxton, R. Cipolla (Eds.), Computer Vision – ECCV '96. Volume I. Proceedings, 1996. XXI, 725 pages. 1996.

Vol. 1065: B. Buxton, R. Cipolla (Eds.), Computer Vision – ECCV '96. Volume II. Proceedings, 1996. XXI, 723 pages. 1996.

Vol. 1066: R. Alur, T.A. Henzinger, E.D. Sontag (Eds.), Hybrid Systems III. IX, 618 pages. 1996.

Vol. 1067: H. Liddell, A. Colbrook, B. Hertzberger, P. Sloot (Eds.), High-Performance Computing and Networking. Proceedings, 1996. XXV, 1040 pages. 1996.

Vol. 1068: T. Ito, R.H. Halstead, Jr., C. Queinnec (Eds.), Parallel Symbolic Languages and Systems. Proceedings, 1995. X, 363 pages. 1996.

Vol. 1069: J.W. Perram, J.-P. Müller (Eds.), Distributed Software Agents and Applications. Proceedings, 1994. VIII, 219 pages. 1996. (Subseries LNAI).

Vol. 1070: U. Maurer (Ed.), Advances in Cryptology – EUROCRYPT '96. Proceedings, 1996. XII, 417 pages. 1996.

Vol. 1071: P. Miglioli, U. Moscato, D. Mundici, M. Ornaghi (Eds.), Theorem Proving with Analytic Tableaux and Related Methods. Proceedings, 1996. X, 330 pages. 1996. (Subseries LNAI).

Vol. 1072: R. Kasturi, K. Tombre (Eds.), Graphics Recognition. Proceedings, 1995. X, 308 pages. 1996.

Vol. 1073: J. Cuny, H. Ehrig, G. Engels, G. Rozenberg (Eds.), Graph Grammars and Their Application to Computer Science. Proceedings, 1994. X, 565 pages. 1996.

Vol. 1074: G. Dowek, J. Heering, K. Meinke, B. Möller (Eds.), Higher-Order Algebra, Logic, and Term Rewriting. Proceedings, 1995. VII, 287 pages. 1996.

Vol. 1075: D. Hirschberg, G. Myers (Eds.), Combinatorial Pattern Matching. Proceedings, 1996. VIII, 392 pages. 1996.

Vol. 1076: N. Shadbolt, K. O'Hara, G. Schreiber (Eds.), Advances in Knowledge Acquisition. Proceedings, 1996. XII, 371 pages. 1996. (Subseries LNAI).

Vol. 1077: P. Brusilovsky, P. Kommers, N. Streitz (Eds.), Mulimedia, Hypermedia, and Virtual Reality. Proceedings, 1994. IX, 311 pages. 1996.

Vol. 1078: D.A. Lamb (Ed.), Studies of Software Design. Proceedings, 1993. VI, 188 pages. 1996.

Vol. 1079: Z.W. Raś, M. Michalewicz (Eds.), Foundations of Intelligent Systems. Proceedings, 1996. XI, 664 pages. 1996. (Subseries LNAI).

Vol. 1080: P. Constantopoulos, J. Mylopoulos, Y. Vassiliou (Eds.), Advanced Information Systems Engineering. Proceedings, 1996. XI, 582 pages. 1996.

Vol. 1081: G. McCalla (Ed.), Advances in Artificial Intelligence. Proceedings, 1996. XII, 459 pages. 1996. (Subseries LNAI).

Vol. 1082: N.R. Adam, B.K. Bhargava, M. Halem, Y. Yesha (Eds.), Digital Libraries. Proceedings, 1995. Approx. 310 pages. 1996.

Vol. 1083: K. Sparck Jones, J.R. Galliers, Evaluating Natural Language Processing Systems. XV, 228 pages. 1996. (Subseries LNAI).

Vol. 1084: W.H. Cunningham, S.T. McCormick, M. Queyranne (Eds.), Integer Programming and Combinatorial Optimization. Proceedings, 1996. X, 505 pages. 1996.

Vol. 1085: D.M. Gabbay, H.J. Ohlbach (Eds.), Practical Reasoning. Proceedings, 1996. XV, 721 pages. 1996. (Subseries LNAI).

Vol. 1086: C. Frasson, G. Gauthier, A. Lesgold (Eds.), Intelligent Tutoring Systems. Proceedings, 1996. XVII, 688 pages. 1996.

Vol. 1087: C. Zhang, D. Lukose (Eds.), Distributed Artificial Intelliegence. Proceedings, 1995. VIII, 232 pages. 1996. (Subseries LNAI).

Vol. 1088: A. Strohmeier (Ed.), Reliable Software Technologies – Ada-Europe '96. Proceedings, 1996. XI, 513 pages. 1996.

Vol. 1089: G. Ramalingam, Bounded Incremental Computation. XI, 190 pages. 1996.

Vol. 1090: J.-Y. Cai, C.K. Wong (Eds.), Computing and Combinatorics. Proceedings, 1996. X, 421 pages. 1996.

Vol. 1091: J. Billington, W. Reisig (Eds.), Application and Theory of Petri Nets 1996. Proceedings, 1996. VIII, 549 pages. 1996.

Vol. 1092: H. Kleine Büning (Ed.), Computer Science Logic. Proceedings, 1995. VIII, 487 pages. 1996.

Vol. 1093: L. Dorts, M. van Lambalgen, F. Voorbraak (Eds.), Reasoning with Uncertainty in Robotics. Proceedings, 1995. VIII, 387 pages. 1996. (Subseries LNAI).

Vol. 1095: W. Mc Cune, R. Padmanabhan, Automated Deduction in Equational Logic and Cubic Curves. X, 231 pages. 1996. (Subseries LNAI).

Vol. 1096: T. Schäl, Workflow Management Systems for Process Organisations. XII, 200 pages. 1996.